For anyone seeking to do research involving peopl
should be required reading. It is both inspiring and u:
of some of the inventive qualitative methods that are b
by emerging scholars who bring a range of social ar
spectives. The book is also incredibly timely, showin;
of dementia studies negotiates the participatory turn, g..,pp....., ...
ally means to be doing research *with* people with dementia.

Alison Phinney, PhD, RN, *Professor, School of Nursing, Co-Director,*
Centre for Research on Personhood in Dementia, University of British
Columbia, Vancouver, Canada

The innovative methods of investigation, critical discussion and application
thereof, presented in this book enhance our understanding of the inner and social
lives of people with dementia and their care partners far more deeply than could
any randomised controlled trial. By entering their worlds and learning from
people diagnosed while supporting the dignity of everyone involved, the contributors take a wonderfully courageous but necessary step that improves the epistemology of dementia and the lives of those diagnosed.

Steven R. Sabat, PhD, *Professor Emeritus of Psychology,*
Georgetown University, Washington, D.C. 20057, U.S.A.

This book heralds a new era in social science research. The compiled papers
position people with dementia in their relational context from a range of
viewpoints. They also articulate new and innovative approaches to research that
challenge convention and drive a desire to better understand the authentic lived
experience of people with dementia in their own environments. It is a must read
for social scientists working in dementia research.

Andrew Robinson RN, MNS, PhD, *Professor of Aged Care Nursing,*
Co-Director, Wicking Dementia Research and Education Centre,
University of Tasmania, Australia

We have had to wait a long time for a new book about social research methods
involving people with dementia, but it has been worth the wait. This is a wonderfully rich textbook written by those actively engaged in cutting edge social
research. The book is current and packed full of creative ideas and approaches for
engaging with citizens with dementia and their families. I would recommend it to
anyone new to this area of research, as well as those looking to advance and
refresh their methodological techniques.

Ruth Bartlett PhD, FHEA, MA, BA, *Associate, Professor & Director,*
Doctoral Training Centre (Dementia Care), University of Southampton,
Southampton, UK

Social Research Methods in Dementia Studies

Traditionally, the most preferred social research methods in dementia studies have been interviews, focus groups and non-participant observations. Most of these methods have been used for a long time by researchers in other social research fields, but their application to the field of dementia studies is a relatively new phenomenon.

A ground-breaking book, *Social Research Methods in Dementia Studies*, shows researchers how to adapt their methods of data collection to address the individual needs of someone who is living with dementia. With an editorial team that includes Ann Johnson, a trained nurse and person living with dementia, this enlightening volume mainly draws its contents from two interdisciplinary social research teams in dementia, namely the Center for Dementia Research (CEDER) at Linköping University in Norrköping, Sweden and the Dementia and Ageing Research Team (DART) at The University of Manchester in Manchester, UK. Case examples are shared in each of the main chapters to help ground the social research method(s) in a real-life context and provide direction as to how learning can be applied to other settings. Chapters also contain key references and recommended reading.

This volume will appeal to undergraduate and postgraduate students, as well as postdoctoral researchers, interested in fields such as: Research Methods, Qualitative Methods and Dementia Studies.

John Keady is Professor of Older People's Mental Health Nursing, a joint appointment between The University of Manchester and the Greater Manchester Mental Health NHS Foundation Trust.

Lars-Christer Hydén is Professor of Social Psychology at Linköping University, Sweden and director of the Center for Dementia Research (CEDER).

Ann Johnson is a person living with a diagnosis of dementia in Greater Manchester, UK. She was a Nurse Tutor at The University of Manchester prior to taking early retirement in 2005.

Caroline Swarbrick is a Research Fellow in the Dementia and Ageing Research Team at The University of Manchester, UK.

Routledge Advances in Research Methods

www.routledge.com/Routledge-Advances-in-Research-Methods/book-series/RARM

Social Research Methods in Dementia Studies

Inclusion and Innovation

Edited by John Keady,
Lars-Christer Hydén, Ann Johnson
and Caroline Swarbrick

Routledge
Taylor & Francis Group

LONDON AND NEW YORK

First published 2018
by Routledge

2 Park Square, Milton Park, Abingdon, Oxfordshire OX14 4RN
52 Vanderbilt Avenue, New York, NY 10017

Routledge is an imprint of the Taylor & Francis Group, an informa business

First issued in paperback 2019

British Library Cataloguing in Publication Data
A catalogue record for this book is available from the British Library

Library of Congress Cataloging in Publication Data
A catalog record for this book has been requested

ISBN: 978-1-138-69920-5 (hbk)
ISBN: 978-0-367-87870-2 (pbk)

Typeset in Times New Roman
by Wearset Ltd, Boldon, Tyne and Wear

Contents

Contributors

Eleonor Antelius is a medical anthropologist currently holding a position as Senior Lecturer of Health and Society with a focus on communication and dementia, at the Division of Aging and Social Change and Centre for Dementia Research at the Department of Social and Welfare Studies at Linköping University. Her research primarily concerns communicative disorders in relation to meaning making processes and being able to maintain/uphold a sense of self. Social interaction, identity, embodiment, ethnicity and cross-cultural perceptions and experiences of illnesses and ageing are all central concepts in her research. She has initiated and coordinates the international research network *Different dementias* as well serving as president of *The Nordic Research Network on Ethnicity and Dementia*. She is co-editor of the book *Living with dementia: relations, responses and agency in everyday life* (Palgrave Macmillan) as well as leading guest editor of the special issue *Ethnocultural Contextualisation of Dementia Care: Cross-cultural Perceptions on the Notion of Self in Care Management Journals*.

Lucy Burke is Principal Lecturer in the Department of English at Manchester Metropolitan University. Her research explores the cultural dimensions of the current dementia crisis from two main perspectives: first, how dementia is represented across a range of literary, filmic, televisual and auto/biographical texts; and, second, the role of creativity and the arts and humanities in relation to the lived experiences of dementia and care. She is particularly interested in how we think about value in this context and what it means to try to measure and capture the value of the arts. She is also currently working with younger disabled people on a major AHRC Connected Communities project, D4D, which explores concepts of identity, community and exclusion through a range of arts based activities.

Sarah Campbell is a Research Associate and PhD candidate within the Dementia and Ageing Research Team in the School of Health Sciences at The University of Manchester. Sarah works on the ESRC/NIHR funded 'Neighbourhoods and Dementia: a mixed methods study' as part of work programme 4: 'Neighbourhoods: Our People, Our Places'. She is also working on a PhD in Dementia Studies exploring 'Atmospheres of Dementia Care' using an embodied and sensory narrative approach. This is supervised by Professor John Keady and Dr Richard Ward.

Anna Ekström is part of the research programme 'Life with dementia' at Linköping University. Her work focuses on interaction and collaboration in activities that involve people living with dementia. Using video documentation of how couples living together interact and collaborate around everyday household activities, questions related to agency, participation and distribution of knowledge and competences are investigated and discussed. She is also part of a European innovation project focusing on technical solution to support elderly people with cognitive impairment in their everyday activities. In this project, Anna is primarily working with digital communication support for people living with dementia.

Emma Ferguson-Coleman is a Deaf research associate based in the Social Research with Deaf People group at The University of Manchester. Emma completed her PhD in late 2016; her studies explored the everyday experiences of living with dementia from the perspectives of Deaf BSL users with dementia and their care partners, and also explored the Deaf community's knowledge and understanding of dementia, its symptoms and impact on everyday life. Emma has worked in the field of mental health and Deafness for over 20 years, both as an activist and as an advocate.

Lars-Christer Hydén received his PhD in Psychology from Stockholm University, Sweden. His current position is as full professor of Social Psychology at Linköping University, Sweden, and as director of the Centre for Dementia Research. His research primarily concerns how people with Alzheimer's disease and their significant others interact and use language – especially narrative – as a way to sustain and negotiate identity and a sense of self.

Ann Johnson was diagnosed with young onset Alzheimer's disease in 2005 at the age of 52. She was a Nurse Tutor at The University of Manchester prior to taking early retirement in 2005. Ann gives talks about her experiences of living with dementia. She has appeared on television, radio and is an invited member of numerous committees and groups. In 2013, Ann was awarded an MBE for services to healthcare.

John Keady is a professor in Older People's Mental Health Nursing at The University of Manchester and is lead of the inter-disciplinary Dementia and Ageing Research Team at the Division of Nursing, Midwifery and Social Work. John completed his PhD at Bangor University in 1999 and is founding and co-editor of the Sage journal 'Dementia: the international journal of social research and practice' (first edition 2002). John is currently a Senior Fellow at the NIHR School for Social Care Research and Chief Investigator of the NIHR/ESRC funded 'Neighbourhoods and Dementia: a mixed methods study' (2014–2019).

Jackie Kindell is a Speech and Language Therapist who has specialised in dementia care since 1992, working in a variety of health and social care settings. Jackie completed her PhD in 2015 and her main interest in both research and practice is communication in dementia, in particular how creative methods can be used to make and maintain meaningful interactions with people living with dementia in everyday life. Clinically, Jackie works in Pennine Care NHS Foundation Trust, in older people's mental health, working with people living with dementia from the earliest stages to those at end of life. Jackie is also an Honorary Lecturer at The University of Manchester.

Mahin Kiwi is a PhD student at Division of Ageing and Social Life at the Department of Social and Welfare Studies, Linköping University. Mahin has a background in sociology and is currently working on her doctoral dissertation concerning Iranian immigrants and ethnically profiled dementia care in Sweden. Her main research interest revolves around transnational family based caregiving and the transitions taking place when people migrate.

May Yeok Koo is the Assistant Director in the School of Health Sciences (Nursing) at Nanyang Polytechnic (Singapore). She is a member of the Sigma Theta Tau International (Honour Society of Nursing) and reviewer and board member of the Editorial Committee, Intensive and Critical Care Nursing Journal (United Kingdom). She received her qualifications in the Bachelor of Nursing, Lincoln School of Health Sciences, La Trobe University (Melbourne, Australia), MSc Advanced Practice (Critical Care), European Institute of Health and Medical Sciences, University of Surrey (Surrey, United Kingdom) and is a PhD student in the Division of Nursing, Midwifery and Social Work, The University of Manchester (United Kingdom).

Agneta Kullberg is a Registered Nurse and District Nurse, with work experiences in home care settings and her PhD in Public Health had focus on well-being and safety in different types of neighbourhoods in Sweden. Agneta works as a Senior Lecturer at Linköping University and the research focuses on the role of the neighbourhood and the lived experiences in everyday life for people living with dementia. She currently directs a research project on 'Dementia-friendly Community – the Norrköping model', involving people living with dementia as co-researchers using participatory methods.

Annika Taghizadeh Larsson is a Senior Lecturer in Ageing and Later Life and has a background in social work. Her research interests comprise questions and issues at the intersection of social gerontology and disability studies, including social policy and welfare for older people and people with disabilities. Her mainly qualitative research has been based on a variety of empirical materials such as interviews, observations, audio-recordings of meetings in institutional contexts, policy documents, forms and web pages.

Ali Reza Majlesi has a PhD in Language and Culture and has specialised in social interaction with people with various communicative and cognitive abilities. Ali Reza is a collaborator with the Center for Dementia Research at

Linköping University where he focuses on communication and joint activities with people living with dementia. His research draws on ethnomethodology and conversation analysis with social practice as an analytic object. His interests lie in the mobilisation of verbal as well as non-verbal resources in interaction. Ali Reza is currently affiliated with Stockholm University as a Senior Lecturer in the Department of Education.

Ann-Charlotte Nedlund is a Senior Lecturer of Politics and Policy Analysis in Ageing and Later Life at the Division of Ageing and Social Change and the Centre for Dementia Research, Department of Social and Welfare Studies at Linköping University, Sweden. She is also affiliated to the National Centre for Setting Priorities in Health Care and to Medical Education: Inter-professional Learning, both also at Linköping University. She has initiated and is the coordinator of the International research network on Citizenship and Dementia. Her research primarily concerns issues related to citizenship, legitimacy, democracy and the welfare system. Special interest comprises how the conditions for citizens with dementia to practice their citizenship is regarded and realised.

Elin Nilsson is a PhD student in social work with a background in social psychology. The focus for Elin's research is about how couples, in which one person is living with dementia, deal with everyday obstacles connected to life with dementia, aiming to provide useful knowledge for gerontological social work and dementia care. Drawing on conversation analysis, both verbal and non-verbal interaction in couples is analysed regarding, for instance, trouble with memory recollection and loss of common ground. Besides writing a dissertation, Elin works as a teacher in social work education at Linköping University since 2011.

Jonas Nordh is a political scientist and has a PhD in Health and Society. His PhD project, which was carried out at the Center for Dementia Research, was concerned with social citizenship and people living with dementia. The focus in his dissertation is how people living with dementia, as citizens, are constructed, in policy documents, as a social problem, its solutions and also on which rationalities and knowledge these constructions are based. Furthermore, it focuses on how public officials, such as care managers, enact policies concerning people living with dementia in their work.

Elzana Odzakovic is a District Nurse with clinical experience from neurological care. She is also a Junior Lecturer and PhD student in medical science at Linköping University as part of the multi-site ESRC/NIHR 'Neighbourhoods and Dementia: a mixed methods study'. The overall aim of the planned thesis is to explore the lived experience of the neighbourhood among people living with dementia. The thesis will also include a cross-sectional study on what type of housing form and home care services people with a dementia diagnosis are granted in Sweden. Elzana is also involved in the research project 'Dementia-friendly Community – the Norrköping model'.

The **Open Doors** service (based in Salford, UK) is a friendship and support network for people living with dementia, which provides post-diagnostic education and support. Founded in 2010, Open Doors is funded by Greater Manchester Mental Health NHS Foundation Trust and employs several people living with dementia to facilitate its activities, including numerous support groups, dementia cafés, a book club and dining group. Open Doors members have also been involved in consultations around service design and delivery, as well active involvement in dementia research. Managed by Cathy Riley, Open Doors are Co-Investigators and co-researchers on the NIHR/ESRC 'Neighbourhoods and Dementia: a mixed methods study'.

Johannes H. Österholm has a PhD in Health and Society and has been a registered occupational therapist since 2009. Johannes is currently working as a senior lecturer at the department of occupational therapy at Linköping University. His main research interest is in citizenship and dementia; in particular how professionals use of communication can affect the person's participation in decision-making in relation to health and social care services.

Helen Pusey is Senior Lecturer in the Division of Nursing, Midwifery and Social Work at The University of Manchester. Her background is in mental health nursing where she undertook her PhD and she developed the University's MSc in Dementia Care. Helen teaches across the undergraduate and postgraduate provision on dementia and the mental health of older people. She has a particular research interest in the arts and dementia, working most recently with the Manchester Camerata orchestra.

Lisa Strandroos is a PhD student at Center for Dementia Research and Division of Ageing and Social Change, Linköping University. She has a masters in social anthropology and has conducted an ethnographical fieldwork at a dementia care facility. Her research focuses on everyday life at the facility and takes a particular interest in interaction, meaning making and institutional practices.

Caroline Swarbrick is a Research Fellow and Deputy of the Dementia and Ageing Research Team at The University of Manchester. With a Social Science background, Caroline's research interests focus on co-production and co-research alongside people living with dementia. She is the Principal Investigator of work programme 1 of the ESRC/NIHR-funded 'Neighbourhoods and Dementia: a mixed methods study'. Using participatory research methodologies, Caroline is working alongside four UK-based groups of people living with dementia to support group members to design and undertake their own research projects. Current projects include producing three cultural heritage films, a campaign aimed at raising awareness of dementia in schools and developing dementia training materials.

Richard Ward is a Registered Social Worker with a background in older people's services where he specialised in working with people living with dementia. He is currently Course Director for the Masters in Dementia Studies at the University of Stirling and is the lead for the 'Neighbourhoods: our people, our places' five-year programme of work (2014–2019) as part of the NIHR/ESRC 'Neighbourhoods and Dementia: a mixed methods study'. The focus for Richard's research is upon participatory approaches to exploring the everyday experience of living with dementia and the implications for social care practice. He is a co-founder of the Memory Friendly Neighbourhoods programme: http://memoryfriendly.org.uk/

Ray Wilkinson is Professor of Human Communication in the Department of Human Communication Sciences at the University of Sheffield. His research draws primarily on Conversation Analysis to investigate spontaneously-occurring conversations and other forms of social interaction and to plan, implement and evaluate intervention programmes to improve the ability of participants to engage in social interaction. Much of his work focuses on participation in conversation by people with a range of acquired communication impairments, including people living with dementia.

Alys Young is a hearing BSL user who has worked alongside Deaf colleagues for nearly 25 years. She is Professor of Social Work and convenes the Social Research with Deaf People group at The University of Manchester. She is also distinguished visiting professor at the Centre for Deaf Studies at the University of the Witwatersrand, South Africa. In 2015 she was conferred FAcSS (Fellow of the Academy of Social Sciences) for her thought leadership and contribution to both social work and to Deaf studies and in 2016 won the Times Higher Education Outstanding Research Supervisor of the Year Award for her work in social research with Deaf people and in social work.

Hannah Zeilig is a Senior Research Fellow at the University of the Arts, London and an Honorary Research Fellow at the University of East Anglia. Her work explores the intersections between literature, culture and ageing and she seeks to combine the theoretical with the practical. She was the principal researcher for Mark Making (2014–2015) an AHRC funded UK based project that explored the role and value of the arts for people living with dementia. Hannah is currently a collaborator on the Wellcome Hub 'Created out of Mind' project (2016–2018) exploring dementia and the arts as part of an interdisciplinary network that will examine and challenge perceptions of dementia through scientific and creative experimentation.

Foreword

I was working as a Nurse Tutor at The University of Manchester, UK prior to taking early retirement in 2005 following a diagnosis with young onset Alzheimer's disease when I was 52. I am now 63. In my opinion, research should be directed towards what it is like to live with dementia, to help and support us to remain independent for as long as possible. It should look at ways in which people handle their dementia as part of their everyday lives, the difficulties they face and their ways of coping. People living with dementia do not know what the future holds. Each person living with dementia is unique and it is important that research *and* researchers must acknowledge and be open to this.

I have been involved in research as a participant, co-researcher and advisor for many years. I also give talks about what it is like for me as a person living with dementia. I do what I can to help. It is so important that people living with dementia are given the opportunity to be involved in research as co-researchers and advisors because they need to feel part of the process and retain some control. This is only right given we are the ones with the lived experience.

This book highlights the importance of the social and creative aspects involved in dementia research, seeing those living with dementia as individuals. I trust this book will set a guideline for future research in dementia which will be practical and useful.

'I believe the biggest thing anyone can do for me is love me and be with me.'

Dr Ann Johnson MBE, April 2017

Acknowledgements

I would like to thank all the contributors to this book as I find all the contents inspiring and an honest, reflective account about where we are and where we need to go. I would especially like to thank my past and present PhD students (some in this volume, others not) who have always risen to the challenge that is set by working alongside people living with dementia. This book is a testimony and legacy to our times together. I would also like to thank my fellow co-Editors for their friendship and peer working and also to our publishers at Routledge for their support of this work. Thank you also to members of my family. Last, but certainly not least, I would like to thank Linda Welch who worked so hard on the book and has been a truly fabulous research secretary since joining the Dementia and Ageing Research Team in 2014.

John Keady, The University of Manchester, UK, April 2017

I would also like to thank all the contributors to this book for their innovative thinking, their engagement and deep interest in all ways a human life can be lived. I have learnt a lot by working with you. Thank you to my co-Editors and to Linda Welch for all their dedicated work.

Lars-Christer Hydén, Linköping University, Sweden, April 2017

I would like to thank Christine Redfern.

Ann Johnson MBE, Greater Manchester, UK, April 2017

I would like to thank the Open Doors Network, Cathy Riley and all of the co-researchers that I have been privileged and blessed to work alongside over the years. For your inspiration, wisdom and humour which continues to influence and shape my own way of thinking. To Greg and William, who are the centre of my world. And finally, thanks to a special friend and role model who has never stopped believing in me and has guided, encouraged and supported me unconditionally, and who has never lost sight of what really matters most.

Caroline Swarbrick, The University of Manchester, UK, April 2017

Introduction

*John Keady, Lars-Christer Hydén, Ann Johnson and
Caroline Swarbrick*

> *'Dementia is not an identity, it is a label ... I have dementia: I also have a life.'*
> (Ann Johnson quoted in Sabat *et al.*, 2011)

For around 20 years now it has been accepted that the weight of psychosocial research, practice and social policy should be framed around the person living with dementia and their relational context (Kitwood, 1997). Recently, this understanding has seen the field of dementia studies move forward to embed person-centred values within a framework of citizenship (Bartlett and O'Connor, 2010) and position creative arts and the body as legitimate outlets for social research enquiry (Kontos, 2014; Zeilig *et al.*, 2014; Ward *et al.*, 2016). These important advancements have also been mirrored, to a certain extent, in policy and practice architecture. In the United Kingdom, the first Prime Minister's Challenge on Dementia (Department of Health, 2012) set out three key areas for attention: (i) Driving improvements in health and care; (ii) Creating dementia friendly communities that understand how to help; and (iii) Better research. Interestingly, 'Better research' mapped out the importance of involving people living with dementia in the conduct of research, whilst 'Creating dementia friendly communities' challenged society and civic amenities to change and be inclusive of people living with dementia. In other words, dementia was to be seen as everyone's business and responsibility, from architects to town planners, public transport providers to shop owners, next-door neighbours on the street where the person living with dementia lives – the list is seemingly endless. As the field of dementia studies opens up, so too does the need for more varied naturalistic research methods to study everyday life.

This contextual shift in the landscape of dementia studies is on an international scale. For example, in Sweden and the other Nordic countries, there is an emerging interest in books and materials that go beyond a strict caring perspective. There is, in particular, a growing interest in the everyday life of people living with dementia in different residential settings – such as the family home, care homes and group living homes – and how these environments intersect with other important domains – such as ethnicity, gender and identity as a citizen. This new understanding of dementia implies a need to find approaches that both place, and understand, people living with dementia in their own local environment. Helping interested parties explore how this could be achieved is a key aim of the book together with opening up some of the new directions in social research, such as the use of video to capture embodied practices and meanings.

By tradition, the most preferred social research methods in dementia studies have been interviews, focus groups and non-participant observations. As the field of dementia studies has grown over recent years, a number of new methods have started to be used for understanding and reporting the experience of people living with dementia and their family carer(s) and in finding innovative ways to engage participants in the research process. Most of these methods have been used for a long time by researchers in other social research fields, for example 'walking interviews' in human geography instead of conventional sit down interviews, but their application to the field of dementia studies is a relatively new phenomenon. This is because most methods used in other social research fields cannot easily be transposed into dementia studies due to the difficulties arising from undertaking research alongside a person who will (in most instances) have difficulties with linguistic, behavioural and cognitive functioning. Researchers, therefore, need to be creative and adapt their methods of data collection in order to address the individual needs of someone who is living with dementia. It is at this intersection where the book is situated and where the vision and values of the Editors in support of the text are positioned.

Vision and values

This book is a culmination of several years of thought, debate and partnership working/friendship between all four Editors. As an Editorial team/exercise, the book is largely (but not exclusively) an amalgamation of two social research and dementia teams and their respective PhD students/networks, namely the Center for Dementia Research (CEDER) at Linköping University in Norrköping, Sweden and the Dementia and Ageing Research Team (DART) at The University of Manchester in Manchester, UK. Three of the Editors – John Keady, Caroline Swarbrick and Lars-Christer Hydén – are employed through either DART or CEDER and have had a relatively long exposure to dementia studies in a variety of fields and directions, including direct clinical practice (John Keady as a mental health nurse, Lars-Christer Hydén as a psychologist and Caroline Swarbrick as a social care volunteer). The Editorial team, however, is held together by Ann Johnson, a trained nurse and person living with dementia. As shared in the Foreword to this book, Ann was a Nurse Tutor at The University of Manchester, UK prior to taking early retirement in 2005 following a diagnosis of young onset Alzheimer's disease at the age of 52. Ann has achieved so much since receiving her diagnosis and our admiration for her as a person, as a friend and as an Editor, simply grows day-by-day. Moreover, Ann's words at the start of this Introduction are a salient reminder about what truly matters most.

Whilst the book may have had a fairly long gestation period, it is driven by four personal and academic values which we will now share:

- As Editors we recognise the transcendent importance of the person living with dementia with this lived experience set within the person's relational, biographical and everyday context. There can be no research without the person living with dementia and thereby their perspectives, participation and knowledge are instrumental to turning any key of understanding.
- As Editors we view dementia as a 'whole system process' whereby cognition, the body and the five senses (sight; hearing; taste; smell; touch) mutually co-exist and continually intersect to enable the person to interact with the outside world. Any failure to understand the meaning(s) of such interaction is not a failure of the person living with dementia and is not an experience to be negatively positioned through figurative language, or otherwise.
- As Editors we have compiled and presented a book that holds social research methods and their workings at its centre. We view social research methods as the glue that holds (all) the applied social science research methodologies together whatever their epistemology and ontology, such as ethnography, grounded theory and phenomenology.
- As Editors we recognise that the use of social research method(s) can stimulate memories, awareness and growth for all those involved in the encounter, including the person living with dementia him or herself. Accounting for, and representing, such experiences is a crucial part of reporting and of method development. Indeed, we would suggest that such insights are predicated on the notion of shared values, meanings and enterprise.

This book is not, by any stretch of the imagination, a 'how-to-do-it' guide, although as Editors we have been careful to ask authors in each chapter to: present insights into the chosen social research method(s), together with applied example(s); outline key references/guidance about their chosen social research method(s); and describe ethical issues that arose in the conduct of the study. As highlighted earlier, it is also not a book that 'picks over' and debates the philosophical domains and underpinnings of the social science research methodologies. That much more comprehensive 'how-to-do-it-and-why' textbook will have to wait for another day and it will be a much more extensive and weightier tone when it appears than the one you are currently holding. No, rather, what we have done in approaching this book is to begin to fill a gap in the literature where, as a qualitative researcher in dementia studies and/or as someone setting out on the social research trail, until now it has simply not been possible to consult a book on social research methods in dementia studies and how they have been applied, creatively or otherwise, to inform the research question. This book, therefore, allows readers to inspect some – and we stress *some* – of these issues and to discover how other students and experienced researchers have attempted to frame and conduct their social research inquiry.

Book structure

The social research methods in each of the chapters have been carefully chosen and sequenced. After Chapter 1, which outlines a framework of person living with dementia's involvement in research, the book is divided into two parts. Part I will look at social research methods that develop participatory and visual media whilst Part II will look at the application and innovation of social research methods in dementia studies. We have equally balanced the number of chapters in Parts I and II and each chapter is based on empirical evidence and experience. A concluding chapter written by the Editors pulls together the key messages in the book. In the book we have been particularly keen to explore the use of film and video as a social research method as it is based on capturing a sensory reality of the world as it is lived by people with dementia. Each chapter starts with a brief chapter outline and has Highlighted learning points from the method; Key references; and Recommended future reading. Outside of the Introduction, Chapter 1 and Chapter 12, people living with dementia are not included as co-authors in the chapters. This is not because we do not want them to be. Rather, it is because the majority of the chapters are written by PhD, or post-doctoral, research students working in dementia studies and the present way of organising such work is via a singular academic activity, with supervisory support. It is where we are in 2017 and hopefully in another 20 years or so such actions will be looked back upon as a curiosity, rather than as the mainstream, as co-production and participatory designs gain the upper hand in representing authentic lived experience.

With these thoughts as a context, the book commences with Caroline Swarbrick and Open Doors outlining the development of the 'CO-researcher INvolvement and Engagement in Dementia' model, or COINED for short. This chapter stands alone at the start of the book as it is co-authored by people living with dementia and outlines both methodological and methods development through the use of co-operative inquiry, an approach that has so far received little attention in the literature on dementia studies. The power of the COINED model is in the representation by people living with dementia about the wide range of research activities that they wish to be engaged in/with/lead. The set challenge is to come together to figure out ways to facilitate such engagement and to democratise the research space. It is an agenda that travels far beyond this book but one which, we hope, sets a new horizon for action. Following this opening contribution, the book divides into two sections. As stated earlier, Part I looks at 'Social Research Methods that Develop Participatory and Visual Media' and is comprised of five chapters. This section commences with chapter (Chapter 2) written by Agneta Kullberg and Elzana Odzakovic and addresses walking interviews as a research method with people living with dementia in their local community. The chapter draws upon an existing study to provide an overview of the benefits of the walking interview, as opposed to the traditional sit-down interview, and the opening up of sensory experiences. As the authors argue in their chapter, walking interviews also enable people living with dementia to be active participants and situated agents in their everyday life. The next chapter (Chapter 3) by Johannes Österholm and Annika Taghizadeh Larsson explores the use of naturally occurring data during interactions between social workers and people living with dementia when the focus is on assessment and decision-making. Audio material is the main method of data collection shared in this chapter filtered through the lens of discourse analysis. The next three chapters then look directly at the use of video as a social research method and how it has been applied in different settings, situations and contexts involving people living with dementia and their families. Chapter 4 is written by Ali Reza Majlesi, Elin Nilsson and Anna Ekström and explores video data as a method to understand non-verbal communication in couples where one person is living with dementia. Storytelling is an important feature of the couple-relationship and as shared in the chapter, the audio-visual recordings capture both the vocal and the embodied to study interactive organisation of social activities. Conversational analysis helps facilitate such verbal and embodied narratives a theme that is continued in the next chapter (Chapter 5) written by Jackie Kindell and Ray Wilkinson. This chapter is based on Jackie's PhD work and presents a combination of conversation analysis and narrative analysis to explore everyday interaction at home where one person lives with a semantic dementia. The outcomes were then used to plan an individualised intervention for the participants. As Jackie and Ray share, the use of video became an important medium for conducting the work 'in-the-moment' and in co-producing meaningful products for those concerned. The final chapter in Part I of the book is written by Sarah Campbell and Richard Ward and it continues the theme on the use of video/videography in the conduct of research. Here, Sarah and Richard skilfully weave a story of video, observation, interviews and embodied narratives to describe the importance of appearance in the lives of people living with dementia. This is communicated through a setting of care-based hairdressing services and draws on data collected for the ESRC funded 'Hair and Care' study. A significant point raised in this chapter is that the mix of methods used in their research enabled the depiction of experiences that were multi-sensory and where the practices were shown rather than told. Part II of the book, 'Social Research Methods-Application and Innovation', comprises five chapters and provides a more rounded and discursive account of methods use in dementia studies. It starts with Chapter 7, written by Eleonor Antelius, Mahin Kiwi and Lisa Strandroos, and outlines the value, and practical application, of a range of methods such as participant observation, field note writing, video-ethnography and in-depth interviews. A particular focus of this chapter is on how such methods are used within a cultural context and the reflexivity of the researcher in such situations. The development of methods is continued in Chapter 8 by May Yeok Koo and Helen Pusey when the use of family interviews, photographs, drawings, walking interviews and co-created genograms and ecomaps were used in the development of in-depth case study work with intergenerational families where one member was living with dementia. Conducted in Singapore with Singapore-Chinese families who live together 'under one roof', these methods demonstrate the importance of relationship building, a longitudinal design and repeated interviewing to develop trust and an 'insider perspective' through cultural connections. Continuing the theme of 'cultural insider', Chapter 9 is written by Emma Ferguson-Coleman and Alys Young and provides an in-depth outline about Deaf British Sign Language users who are living with dementia and how their signed stories were shared with a wider hearing audience using an approach to re-presentation of data based around cultural brokering. This important study shares the visual methods used through storytelling and shares an approach where video and visual recording is an integral part/record of everyday communication rather than as an extension of method development. Next, Chapter 10, written by Ann-Charlotte Nedlund and Jonas Nordh, changes gears a little and illustrates how a critical and interpretive approach on policy processes can be used to develop an understanding about dementia policies including its practices. Here, narrative methods and approaches are used to shine a spotlight on power relations and how they are involved in the formation and shaping of policies that affect the everyday lives/citizenship of people living with dementia and their families. As this chapter reminds us, stories are found and framed in all sorts of ways and narrative methods can be used to tease out such connections. This use of story and storied narrative is continued in the final chapter of Part II of the book. Written by Hannah Zeilig and Lucy Burke, the authors eloquently outline how theatrical techniques may be used with people living with dementia in both care home and community settings. Hannah and Lucy draw on real-life case studies to identify the methods necessary to tap directly into the creativity of people living with dementia and to see the value in aesthetic, rather than instrumental, outcomes for such work. The book ends with Chapter 12 and a series of short paragraphs compiled by the Editors and led by Lars-Christer Hydén. The structure of this final chapter is more of a set of reflective thought processes rather than being a studious account of 'where next'. However, this formation of the final chapter is deliberate as we see the book as a beginning and not as an end point in itself.

Whilst recognising its foundation is in social research methods, we have also constructed a book that gently challenges the traditional knowledge hierarchy (usually depicted as a pyramid) where systematic reviews and randomised controlled trials are positioned at, or towards, its apex and the case study (with the social research methods that underpin such an approach) firmly located at its base and routinely excluded from the community of scientific studies. This is a puzzle as without knowledge of the individual there can be no individual knowledge, however that is subsequently framed and presented. In this book, authentic representation of the one is as important as a summary representation of the many.

Lastly, by writing the words Inclusion and Innovation in the suffix of the book's title we were stating our ambition for the work and for its application. We hope that you enjoy this book and through its use add another 'i' to the title, inspiration, as it is there where new beginnings are found and new discoveries made. And that is a journey we are all on.

References

Bartlett, R. and O'Connor, D. (2010) *Broadening the dementia debate: toward social citizenship.* London: The Policy Press.

Department of Health (2012) *Prime Minister's challenge on dementia: delivering major improvements in dementia care and research by 2015.* London: Department of Health.

Kitwood, T. (1997) *Dementia reconsidered: the person comes first.* Bucks: Open University Press.

Kontos, P. (2014) Musical embodiment, selfhood and dementia. In L.C. Hydén, H. Lindemann and J. Brockmeier (eds), *Beyond LOSS. Dementia, identity, personhood.* New York: Oxford University Press.

Sabat, S.R., Johnson, A., Swarbrick C. and Keady, J. (2011) The 'demented other' or simply 'a person'? Extending the philosophical discourse of Ursula Naue and Thilo Kroll through an appreciation of the situated self. *Nursing Philosophy*, 12: 282–292.

Ward, R., Campbell, S. and Keady, J. (2016) Assembling the salon: learning from alternative forms of body work in dementia care. *Sociology of Health and Illness*, 38(8): 1287–1302.

Zeilig, H., Killick, J. and Fox, C. (2014) The participative arts for people living with a dementia: a critical review. *International Journal of Ageing and Later Life*, 9(1): 7–34.

1 Developing the Co-researcher INvolvement and Engagement in Dementia model (COINED)

A co-operative inquiry

Caroline Swarbrick and Open Doors

Outline

This chapter outlines the development of the CO-researcher INvolvement and Engagement in Dementia (COINED) model using co-operative inquiry. The consultation stages of the development of COINED are shared together with how people living with dementia want to be involved in research and the challenges and opportunities that this presents for academics and organisations. The COINED model could be seen as a guiding frame for the book in the applied use of creative and social research methods that follow.

Introduction

Since the early 1990s, researching the lived experience of dementia has seen the researcher role evolve from one of detachment – where the researcher had control over the design, data collection, transcription and analytic process – to one of inclusion where the person(s) living with dementia is seen as an integral member of the research team and the authentic voice in representing shared meanings. This changing face of dementia studies has been manifest in many ways and in this opening chapter we will focus on one such journey which underpins work programme 1 of the NIHR/ESRC funded 'Neighbourhoods and Dementia: a mixed methods study' (referred to henceforward as the 'Neighbourhoods Study') – a five-year research study (2014–2019) as part of the first Prime Minister's Challenge on Dementia in the United Kingdom (UK) (Department of Health, 2012 and see Keady *et al.*, 2014; www.neighbourhoodsanddementia. org). Work programme 1 of the Neighbourhoods Study is all about people living with dementia as co-researchers and meets two of the overall Study aims, namely: (i) to learn from the process and praxis of making people living with dementia and their care partners; and (ii) to build capacity within the research community and the networks of people living with dementia and their care partners.

However, in beginning to address such fundamental aims it is important to establish what roles and ambitions people living with dementia themselves see as important in conducting research. Working alongside three of the activist/peer support groups attached to the Neighbourhoods Study – the Open Doors project (based in Salford, Greater Manchester, UK; http://dementiavoices.org.uk/group/open-doors-project/), the Scottish Dementia Working Group (based in Glasgow, UK; www.sdwg.org.uk/) and EDUCATE (based in Stockport, UK; www.educatestockport.org.uk/) – this chapter outlines the development of an innovative, participatory model of research involvement and engagement, the CO-researcher INvolvement and Engagement in Dementia model, or COINED for short (Swarbrick *et al.*, 2016). The development of the COINED model through the methodology of co-operative inquiry, and the shared vision and values that underpin it, represent the primary focus of this chapter, whilst also fostering the need to develop more creative social methods that promote full and participatory engagement of people living with dementia in research.

Co-research and co-operative inquiry

Whilst there are examples of generic 'involvement in research' frameworks, such as INVOLVE (www.invo.org.uk/), which is funded by the UK's National Institute for Health Research, its transferability into the dementia research field remains under-developed. Within the UK, one of the principle areas to involve people living with dementia as co-researchers[1] is in health service and social care provision, of which examples include service planning and design (Cantley *et al.*, 2005; Eley, 2016), service development (Cantley *et al.*, 2005; Litherland, 2014) and service evaluation (Cheston *et al.*, 2000; Litherland, 2014). Contemporaneous with such developments, are an increasing number of influential dementia working groups and networks, regionally and internationally, that aim to drive forward an empowerment and activist agenda as well as inform policy; see, for example: European Working Group of People living with dementia (www.alzheimer-europe.org/Alzheimer-Europe/Who-we-are/European-Working-Group-of-People-with-Dementia); Irish Dementia Working Group (http://dementiavoices.org.uk/group/irish-dementia-working-group/); Ontario Dementia Advisory Group (www.odag.ca/); and the Dementia Engagement and Empowerment Project (http://dementiavoices.org.uk/). As a further illustration, the involvement of people living with dementia through the medium of consultation has influenced dementia strategies at a local level (McCabe and Bradley, 2012) and a national level (Eley, 2016).

The implicit theoretical underpinnings of co-research are largely embedded within a co-operative inquiry methodology. Co-operative inquiry focuses on the lived experience, traditionally referred to as 'experiential research' (Heron, 1971). The purpose of co-operative inquiry is to develop mutually usable knowledge between contributors (Baldwin, 2001), particularly through innovative and creative practices with the emphasis on researching together (Reason, 1999; Heron and Reason, 2001). There are numerous examples of co-operative inquiry within wider health and social care fields, including mental health (Hummelvoll and Severinsson, 2005) and learning disabilities (Healy *et al.*, 2015); however, it has received limited research attention in dementia studies (Swarbrick, 2015). The potential of co-created knowledge to have far-reaching impact makes its relevance to research in dementia studies significant, most notably through its creative and empowering underpinnings and its aim to close 'the gap between research and everyday life' (Heron and Reason, 2001, p. 182). Co-operative inquiry is framed around four ways of 'knowing', which we now describe through the lived experience of dementia:

1   '*Experiential* knowing' relates to the experience of living with a diagnosis of dementia. Its inherent empathy and understanding particularly towards others who may also have a diagnosis is often represented through peer support.
2   '*Presentational* knowing' concerns the visual representation of the lived experience, expressed through a range of creative approaches, which do not necessarily depend on the written word. Examples include art, poetry, music and dance. Whilst such creative approaches are often referred to as 'interventions' within clinical and academic contexts, here we refer to them as enjoyable activities undertaken in everyday life.
3   '*Propositional* knowing' refers to the 'science behind the knowing', enabling us to make sense of our own experiences. It is the very essence of who we are, what we believe and how we understand and make sense of our world, and is embedded within our own life story.
4   '*Practical* knowing' brings together the underpinnings of *Experiential*, *Presentational* and *Propositional* knowing, and is demonstrated through skill or competence. Changes in cognition (experienced during trajectory of dementia) will invariably shape the performance and level of the skill or competence and it is the responsibility of all contributors to recognise that such skills may be demonstrated through creative, 'non-traditional' means (Heron, 1996; Reason 1998, p. 427; 1999).

These types of knowing are integral to the four phases of reflection and action, which form the basis of co-operative inquiry. These four phases are built on an iterative cycle of human experience, focusing on the interplay between reflective processes and practical application. Each phase is traditionally informed by an Inquiry group/s and members, who are referred to in the remainder of this chapter as 'Inquirers'.

Inquiry groups

The authors (Caroline Swarbrick – Facilitator; Open Doors – founding Inquiry group) worked alongside an additional two established groups of people living with dementia from the inception of the co-operative inquiry: EDUCATE and the Scottish Dementia Working Group. Due to geographical logistics, Open

Doors, EDUCATE and the Scottish Dementia Working Group met independently, but the Facilitator remained constant throughout the Inquiry. Despite the formality of an 'Inquiry group', relationships remained informal, peer and friendship-based (Heron and Reason, 2001). Inquiry group meetings ranged from four-18 members and met a total of eight times. This process will now be described in more detail.

Focus of inquiry (phase 1 – reflection)

All three Inquiry groups were research active groups and using this as a starting point, initial discussions (as led by Open Doors) focused on the representation of people living with dementia in research. It soon became clear that the viewpoint and experiences of research were regarded as something 'done to' rather than 'done alongside' people. Whilst the desire of Inquirers to be part of the wider research process was clearly evident, they acknowledged that opportunities for involvement beyond the realms of participant were very limited (*propositional* knowing). There were many parallels across group discussions with regards to the focus of inquiry, with the consensus on exploring ways of involving people living with dementia across the research process as co-researchers (*presentational* knowing).

Involvement in research (phase 2 – action)

Building on the key messages of phase one, phase two sought to identify practical ways of involving and integrating people living with dementia as co-researchers within and across the research process. Here, Inquirers took an active role in exploring the 'doings' of research in a practical, discussion-based format (*experiential* knowing). Open Doors and the Scottish Dementia Working Group took part in wider group discussions, whilst EDUCATE engaged in smaller group work activities (due to the numbers of people involved). The purpose was to develop a single framework which would be used as the basis of co-researcher involvement. Ideas were interchanged between Inquiry groups via the Facilitator, who remained the consistent link between all groups for the duration of the co-operative inquiry. Despite working independently, there was consensus amongst Inquiry groups with six common themes emerging to develop an initial draft framework of involvement, which mirrored INVOLVE's research cycle (INVOLVE, 2012, p. 40) (*practical* knowing). Inquirers were keen to use the initial ideas, as presented in Figure 1.1, as a platform to develop a more comprehensive model of involvement across the research process. In particular, Inquirers were also keen to identify specific areas of involvement with the aims of enriching the quality of the research process and integrating the lived experience within the dementia studies arena. Here, there was a natural progression into phase 3 of the co-operative inquiry.

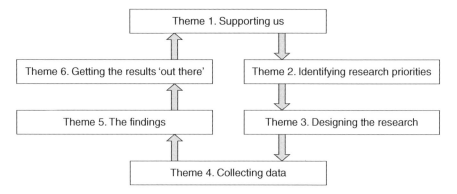

Figure 1.1   Initial involvement framework.

Developing the model (phase 3 – action)

The rebalancing of control within the research process was acknowledged by Inquirers as an important step forward in the integration of people living with dementia across the trajectory of the research process. Building on the initial framework outlined in Figure 1.1, Inquirers developed a more descriptive anthology of approaches (see Figure 1.2), which were generated collectively over the three groups, as led by Open Doors. Inquirers' understanding of the research process facilitated a shift from the initial stepped cyclical framework to an iterative pattern of action from an immersive approach (*practical* knowing).

Ongoing training and support

Inquirers unanimously agreed that ongoing training and support is fundamental to the involvement of people living with dementia as co-researchers. This works in two ways: first, training and support for people living with dementia as co-researchers; and second, training and support for academic researchers working alongside people living with dementia (*practical* knowing).

Ongoing consultation

In keeping with the ethos of 'nothing about us without us' (Bryden, 2015), Inquirers advocated that the voice of people living with dementia must remain central to *all* types of dementia research. Consequently, Inquirers recommended that the representation of the voice of people living with dementia must be embedded within steering and advisory groups as a continuous presence for the duration of the research. Furthermore, Inquirers emphasised the importance of peer support in providing a community network in maintaining their own well-being, self-confidence and sense of security within an ever-changing environment (*experiential* knowing).

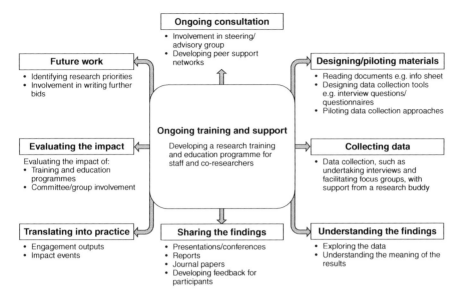

Figure 1.2 The CO-researcher INvolvement and Engagement in Dementia (COINED) model.

Source: Swarbrick *et al.* (2016). Reproduced with permission from Sage Publications.

Designing/piloting materials

Involvement in the design stage of the research was the most common experience of Inquirers. That said, it cannot be assumed that this was always a positive experience. With regards to reading study documentation, it was acknowledged that academic researchers have ethical constraints in terms of the amount of information which needs to be provided. However, Inquirers commented that the quantity and quality of the information is not always balanced appropriately taking into account the differing abilities and skill-base of the participants. Inquirers were fully supportive of their own involvement in schedule design (such as interviews and focus groups) and also in the piloting of materials, describing themselves as 'experts by experience' (*propositional* knowing).

Collecting data

There was a sense of discontent amongst Inquirers, which was located in their experiences as participants (research on) at the expense of opportunities for wider involvement in a co-researcher capacity (research alongside). Potential involvement as collectors of data was a focal point of discussion. Here, the ethical dilemma (as raised by several Inquirers) was the extent to which the shared experiences of the participant and co-researcher may influence participant responses. Here, questions centred on awareness and objectivity. Ultimately, the shared experience between the co-researcher and participant has the potential to unlock an empathetic level of knowledge and understanding, rich in detail and context (*propositional* knowing).

Understanding the findings

Making research findings meaningful and accessible – particularly the results of complex research studies – were discussion points across all of the Inquiry groups. Inquirers reported that key findings were often lost in the midst of multi-faceted reporting and ambitious assertions, whilst having limited relevance outside of the academic and healthcare world. Inquirers recommended that findings should be translatable and tangible, with a clear and meaningful message (*practical* knowing).

Sharing the findings

Numerous discussions centred on the communication of research findings and in particular, ways in which such findings are visually presented. Language and terminology were regarded as central to effective and respectful communication. The 'language of representation' is twofold: how a person living with dementia is represented or positioned in the context of the research findings; and the accessibility/meaningfulness of these findings for a person living with dementia. Several Inquirers were enthusiastic about social media as an instant avenue to 'getting the message out there', particularly for 'in the moment' information and updates. Sharing knowledge, particularly using creative methods, was pivotal in order to extend the present discourse (*presentational* knowing).

Translating into practice

Discussions around the practical application of research findings raised two fundamental questions: first, how might the research findings benefit people living with dementia; and, second, what difference does the research actually make to real life experiences. 'Research' and 'practice' were often regarded as separate entities, a responsibility largely attributed to the academic field. A co-research partnership attempts to address this disparity whilst focusing on the expressive methodologies used to translate its practical application (*practical* knowing).

Evaluating the impact

Given the different meanings and interpretations of the term 'impact', we agreed that we would use impact to refer to the effectiveness of the research or the self-defined effectiveness of the involvement of people living with dementia as co-researchers (Swarbrick *et al.*, 2016). Inquirers viewed the term 'evaluation' as a way of ensuring we are 'getting it right'. Consequently, the evaluation should function as a process of self-reflection and introspective learning which would con-tribute to and potentially shape future decision-making (*propositional* knowing).

Future work

Inquirers acknowledged the logistics and practicalities of the research culture and the need to identify research priorities which reflect the wider existing and changing landscape. Whilst this sometimes resulted in conflict and tension, par-ticularly as current priorities did not always resonate with the lived experience, re-positioning the roles of people living with dementia as centre-stage (Williams and Keady, 2012) aided in the attempt to re-balance of control and priority setting of research agendas (*practical* knowing).

The final cut (phase 4 – reflection)

Inquiry groups collectively agreed that the COINED model (see Figure 1.2) represents a wealth of opportunities that should be offered to people living with dementia as co-researchers in the field of dementia care (*presentational* and *propositional* knowing). Inquirers were also keen to emphasise that involvement and engagement must be facilitated in ways that are creative, meaningful and positive for all those involved (*presentational* knowing).

Ethical debates

The involvement of people living with dementia as co-researchers is not without its ethical debates. Such debates are largely underpinned by issues around capa-city, balancing legal constraints with moral rights and obligations. Members of Open Doors were keen to point out that 'good practice' dictates that all people, regardless of cognitive abilities, should be given the opportunity to be involved in research as participants and as co-researchers. It is the role of the Facilitator (academic researcher) to ensure that appropriate risk assessments and safeguard-ing are in place as well as peer and professional support networks. Whilst previous research that has involved people living with dementia as co-researchers has involved people with 'mild or moderate' dementia (Hanson *et al.*, 2007; Tanner, 2012), people living with dementia, in this study at least, argue that capacity should not be a barrier to co-researcher involvement.

As previously indicated, the anonymity and confidentiality of any individual providing 'data' must be safeguarded. Whilst UK academic researchers are bound by the Research Governance Framework for Health and Social Care (Department of Health, 2005), there are no parallel frameworks for co-researchers. Here, we put forward the need to formalise the expectations and responsibilities of the co-researcher role and that this should be regarded as an integral part of the co-research process, specific to each research project. Fur-thermore, whilst previous examples (see Tanner, 2012) question the ability of co-researchers to maintain objective, all parties must be cognisant of the variance between: co-researcher empathy towards participants; shared knowledge/experiences; and the potential to influence participant responses.

Discussion

By using a co-operative inquiry approach to develop the COINED model, we have demonstrated that this methodology can be effectively and appropriately applied to the field of dementia studies. Whilst discussions in the wider literature focus on whether people living with dementia (as co-researchers) are able to engage in a way meaningful to the research process (Tanner, 2012), our approach is to ensure that co-researcher involvement is, first and foremost, meaningful and a positive experience for the individuals themselves, thus respecting and empowering the personhood of people living with dementia (Kitwood, 1997). One of the key messages of the model is to ensure that its implementation allows for creative methods and expressive output and should not be constrained by traditional research methods and processes. For example, Lee and Adams (2011), Capstick (2011) and Bartlett (2012) all offer a collection of visual methods to engage co-researchers in the data collection domain of the research process. The range of research methods need to reflect the diversity and heterogeneity of the dementia community and most importantly, need to be a negotiation between all parties involved. It is this negotiation, sparked by the dynamic and creative social research methods that underpin the COINED model that could be seen as a cornerstone of this book and one way of defining such need.

Highlighted learning points from the method

- The importance of mutual relationship-building cannot be under-estimated. Take time to build up trust and rapport.
- Enabling and maintaining balance in joint decision-making is key to a successful Co-operative Inquiry.
- Co-operative Inquiry groups are made up of individuals with different needs and ways of communicating.
- Facilitating as an audience member is a skill that needs practice.
- As an academic researcher, it is important to minimise control during the Co-operative Inquiry and embrace the evolving process, whilst bringing the discussions back to group-led agendas.

Key references

- Alzheimer Europe. (2011). *The ethics of dementia research report*. Luxembourg: Alzheimer Europe.
  Provides a more generic overview of the ethics of dementia research, the section focusing on 'Involving people living with dementia' offers insightful way of involving people living with dementia in the research process.

- Swarbrick, C.M., Open Doors, Scottish Dementia Working Group, EDUCATE, Davis, K. and Keady, J. (2016 e-publication ahead of print). Visioning change: co-producing a model of involvement and engagement in research (Innovative Practice). *Dementia: The International Journal for Social Research and Practice.* DOI: 10.1177/1471301216674559.
  This article presents an overview of the COINED model and its role in a wider multi-site international study.

Recommended future reading

- Bryden, C. (2015). *Nothing about us without us! 20 years of dementia advocacy.* London: Jessica Kingsley Publishers.
- Jennings, L. (ed.) (2014). *Welcome to our world. A collection of life writing by people living with dementia.* Canterbury: Forget-Me-Nots.
- Reason, P. and Heron J. A short guide to Co-operative Inquiry. (Online) Available: www.human-inquiry.com/cishortg.htm (accessed 6 March 2017).
- Whitman, L. (2016). *People living with dementia speak out.* London: Jessica Kingsley.

Acknowledgements

The authors would like to thank everyone who has contributed and supported our work to date, especially all of the Inquirers for their time, wisdom and energy, and remembering those who are sadly no longer with us. The support of the Economic and Social Research Council (ESRC) and National Institute for Health Research (NIHR) is gratefully acknowledged. This work forms part of the ESRC/NIHR Neighbourhoods and Dementia: a mixed methods study (www. neighbourhoodsanddementia.org), work programme 1: member involvement.

Note

1 By co-research, we refer to a collaborative, cooperative and community-based approach in order to promote a more inclusive, diverse and empowered research agenda (Swarbrick *et al.*, 2016).

References

Alzheimer Europe. (2011). *The ethics of dementia research report.* Luxembourg: Alzheimer Europe.
Baldwin, M. (2001). Working together, learning together: co-operative inquiry in the development of complex practice by teams of social workers. In Reason, P. and Bradbury, H. (eds) *Handbook of action research. Participative inquiry and practice.* London: Sage Publications.
Bartlett, R. (2012). Modifying the diary interview method to research the lives of people living with dementia. *Qualitative Health Research*, 22(12): 1717–1726.

Bryden, C. (2015). *Nothing about us without us! 20 years of dementia advocacy.* London: Jessica Kingsley Publishers.

Cantley, C., Woodhouse, J. and Smith, M. (2005). *Listen to us: involving people living with dementia in planning and developing services.* Newcastle upon Tyne: Dementia North.

Capstick, A. (2011). Travels with a flipcam: bringing the community to people living with dementia in a day care setting through visual technology. *Visual Studies*, 26(2): 142–147.

Cheston, R., Bender, M. and Byatt, S. (2000). Involving people who have dementia in the evaluation of services: a review. *Journal of Mental Health*, 9(5): 471–479.

Department of Health (2005). *Research governance framework for health and social care (second edition).* (Online). Available: www.dh.gov.uk (accessed 19 January 2017).

Department of Health (2012). *Prime Minister's challenge on dementia: delivering major improvements in dementia care and research by 2015.* London: Department of Health.

Eley, R.M. (2016). Telling it like it is: involving people living with dementia and family caregivers in policy making, service design and workforce development. *Working with Older People*, 20(4): 219–222.

Hanson, E., Magnusson, L., Arvidsson, H., Claesson, A., Keady, J. and Nolan M. (2007). Working together with persons with early stage dementia and their family members to design a user-friendly technology-based support service. *Dementia: The International Journal for Social Research and Practice*, 6(3): 411–434.

Healy, J., Tillotston, N., Short, M. and Hearn C. (2015). Social work field education: believing in supervisors who are living with disabilities. *Disability and Society*, 30(7): 1087–1102.

Heron, J. (1996). *Co-operative inquiry.* London: Sage Publications.

Heron, J. (1971). *Experience and method: an inquiry into the concept of experiential research.* Guildford: The University of Surrey.

Heron, J. and Reason, P. (2001). The practice of co-operative inquiry: research 'with' rather than 'on' people. In Reason, P. and Bradbury, H. (eds) *Handbook of action research. Participative inquiry and practice.* London: Sage Publications.

Hummelvoll, J.K. and Severinsson, E. (2005). Researchers' experience of co-operative inquiry in acute mental health care. *Journal of Advanced Nursing*, 52(2): 180–188.

Keady, J., Clark, A., Ferguson-Coleman, E., Hellström, I., Hydén, L-C., Pendleton, N., Reilly, S., Swarbrick, C., Ward, R., and Young, A. (2014). Neighbourhoods and dementia. *Journal of Dementia Care*, 22(6): 16–17.

Kitwood, T. (1997). *Dementia reconsidered: the person comes first.* Buckingham: Open University Press.

Lee, H. and Adams, T. (eds) (2011). *Creative approaches in dementia care.* Basingstoke: Palgrave Macmillan.

Litherland, R. (2014). Involving people living with dementia in service development and evaluation. In Downs, M. and Bowers, B. (eds) *Excellence in dementia care.* Berkshire: Open University Press.

McCabe, L. and Bradley, B.E. (2012). Supporting user participation in local policy development: the Fife Dementia Strategy. *Social Policy and Society*, 11(2): 157–169.

Reason, P. (1998). Co-operative Inquiry as a discipline of professional practice. *Journal of Interprofessional Care*, 12(4): 419–436.

Reason, P. (1999). Integrating action and reflection through co-operative inquiry. *Management Learning*, 30(2): 207–226.

Swarbrick, C. (2015). The quest for a new methodology for dementia care research. *Dementia: The International Journal for Social Research and Practice*, 14(6): 713–715.

Swarbrick, C.M., Open Doors, Scottish Dementia Working Group, EDUCATE, Davis, K. and Keady, J. (2016). Visioning change: Co-producing a model of involvement and engagement in research (Innovative Practice). *Dementia: The International Journal for Social Research and Practice*. e-publication ahead of print.

Tanner, D. (2012). Co-research with older people living with dementia: experience and reflections. *Journal of Mental Health*, 21(3): 296–306.

Williams, S. and Keady, J. (2012). Centre stage diagramming: late-stage Parkinson's disease and Alzheimer's disease. *Journal of Aging Studies*, 26(2): 204–213.

Part I

Social research methods – participatory and visual media

The significance of the local environment

The neighbourhood is an everyday setting for all human beings and to be active outdoors has a significant impact on a person's health and sense of wellbeing (Gatrell, 2013; Mitchell, 2014; Mitchell and Burton, 2010). In a life course perspective, the home and one's neighbourhood environment may be even more important for people living with dementia due to the fact they will, more likely than not, spend a significant part of the day in such environments. To be able to continue to live in one's familiar place could be of great advantage for people living with dementia as it has been proved easier to navigate and way-find in well-known and familiar neighbourhoods (Sheehan *et al.*, 2006).

In a review, Keady and his colleagues (2012) found 'no research that sets out to enquire how people living with dementia might define their neighbourhood or that explores everyday neighbourhood practices for those affected by the condition' (p. 160). A participatory approach by researchers to involve people living with dementia is suggested with the aim of generating data in an 'unmapped everyday life site' helps to giving voice to neighbourhood-bound narratives and a better understanding about outdoor experiences (Keady *et al.*, 2012). This new research orientation towards mapping the complexity in everyday life for people living with dementia requires development of methods that takes account of both embodied and situated practices, and also accounts for sensory experiences undertaken in interaction with the local place of residence.

There is a broad scholarly literature about the links between the impact of environment (including both outdoor and indoor environment) in the later period of life. In the complex transition of getting older, the environmental conditions will be of central meaning corresponding to early work in environmental gerontology by Lawton and Nahemow (1973). They introduced a model called the Press-Competence Model. Central concepts in their framework on the interaction between environment and older people are the environmental press or demands put on the ageing person corresponding to his/her individual level of competence and level of adaptation (Nahemow and Lawton, 1973).

The Press-Competence model is based on thoughts concerning the importance of environment for health and wellbeing at an older age. A person's sense of control is related to the immediate outdoor environment and is connected to the level of wellbeing. Older people with a disability are expected to have reduced competence (in the model is level of competence related to an individual's physically and cognitive capacity) and are expected to be more sensitive to environmental stress than those with higher competence. To age-in-place and feel well is of value and presupposes a dynamic interaction between a person with his/her individual competence and the actual environment with its specific character (Shipp and Branch, 1999).

Lawton has been criticised for having a static and quantitative view on the interaction between the material and build environment and individual's competences (Scheidt and Norris-Baker, 2003). Lawton's person-environment model has been developed by Wahl *et al.* (2012) by putting more emphasis upon the interaction between a person and the immediate environment as a process. It is suggested that resources in the environment as well as personal resources are crucial to the sense of belonging and agency. More attention is needed into how personal experiences and a sense of belonging are perceived, as determinants about how a person acts and behaves in the actual environment are crucial in fostering a deeper understanding of connection (Wahl *et al.*, 2012). This is in line with other approaches on interaction with the outdoor environment that point out that it might not only be understood as physical-material but also as perceived and imagined (Lefebvre, 1991). Cummins and colleagues (2007) argue the need to always consider subjective perceptions, based on the specific meaning people give to their neighbourhoods, all dimensions that are always based on individual experiences, attachment to place, lengths of residence and local knowledge and so on. Macintyre and Ellaway (2003) stipulate that 'people create places, and places create people' (p. 26) and, further, Buffel *et al.* (2012) argues that there is a two-directed relationship between older people and their neighbourhood: 'Individuals are not only shaped by exchanges with places; people also shape and create the environment in everyday (inter)action' (p. 20). Thus, under the umbrella concept of mobile methods, interview techniques have developed that are place orientated.

Mobile methods in social research

An alternative methodology with point of departure in the mobility has been developed over the last few decades and shaped a new mobile paradigm (see, for example, Büscher and Urry, 2009; Hein *et al.*, 2008). The paradigm has its focus on the theoretical and empirical roots in social research perspectives applied to move in different ways in everyday life, since people in modern society become more mobile and moveable (Kusenbach, 2012). Hein *et al.* (2008) argues that mobile methods would give essential knowledge on embodiment and the significance of place. Further, a methodology where the researcher shares experiences together with the research participant would give rich data in a unique interview process (Hein *et al.*, 2008). The mobility itself brings the research outdoors to the environment of interest, either by foot or in any vehicle, in which the interaction between the participant and the researcher, as well as the interaction with the environment, becomes accessible for research (Jones *et al.*, 2008; Kusenbach, 2003).

In the reported study, we have conducted walking interviews driven by the idea that the neighbourhood lived space could inform us as to what people living with dementia perceive and experience and where, and when, those perceptions and experiences are situated in the neighbourhood. Here, we would like to draw attention to the ways conducting walking interviews helps us in gaining knowledge of how people living with dementia use their neighbourhood in everyday life practice and their interaction related to the neighbourhood. We wanted to collect data on embodied experiences in their neighbourhood in real time for people living with dementia. The empirical research is drawn from the international interdisciplinary project 'Neighbourhoods and Dementia – our People, our Places' funded as a work programme (4) under the NIHR/ESRC 'Neighbourhoods and Dementia: a mixed methods study' (Keady, 2014; and see www.neighbourhoodsanddementia.org). In this chapter, we report findings and discuss insights from walking interviews drawn in the Swedish field-site that is one of three field-sites; the other two field-sites are co-ordinated, separately, by researchers at Salford University/The University of Manchester and The University of Stirling.

Walking interviews as a research method

The purpose of mobile interviews, known also as walking interviews, go-along interviews or walk-along interviews, is driven by attempts to deepen the understanding of the participant's outdoor local context as it gives opportunities to both observe behaviour and listen to narratives at the same time. Such approaches have long been established in (other) academic disciplines outside of dementia studies (see, for example, Kusenbach, 2003; 2012) and walking interviews are often combined with data information from other sources, such as video, photographs, sit-down interviews and field notes (Pink, 2007).

When employing a participatory approach, Clark and Emmel (2010) argue that walking interviews are preferable to sit-down room-based interviews as they permit participants to reach a greater degree of control during the walk. Kusenbach (2012) suggests there is a difference between researchers conducting a go-along interview that connects to the participants' regular mobility performed in everyday life, compared to planned tours by the researcher. Furthermore, narratives produced whilst walking in such a context could be of greater value and contain more details if they are directly informed and situated in the neighbourhood, something that is difficult to achieve with traditional sit-down interviews (Kusenbach, 2012). Another important aspect of using walking interviews is that the experiences of the participant's senses are present in the direct interaction with the outdoor environment under study when moving outdoors. The experiences of the environment, such as social meetings that happen during the walking interview, are thereby shared with the researcher in the 'here and now', which is different compared to conducting sit-down interviews as noted by Emmel and Clark (2009). The influences and connections to a place can be seen as a process that is continually established as a mirror of the dynamic interactions between a person and a specific place (Massey, 2005).

Hall points out that mobile research methods like walking interviews go beyond the communication between the interviewer and interviewee as dimensions of interaction with the outdoor environment is added, in kind of three-way conversation (Hall, 2009). Indeed, to walk beside the interviewee has drawn researchers' attention in diverse field of academic disciplines, i.e. geography (Evans and Jones, 2011), sociology (Carpiano, 2009) and occupational therapy (Brorsson *et al.*, 2013). In addition, recent research has revealed that walking interviews are a promising participatory research method, that gives unique possibilities to promote and encourage the participant to be active (Garcia *et al.*,

2012) and to be a 'tour guide' for the researcher on the walk. Also, the practice of everyday walking could give opportunities to support abilities and empower the interviewee (Evans and Jones, 2011).

Walking interviews as a research method within the field of dementia research

People living with dementia have been excluded from research as, until fairly recently, they have not been seen as the primary source of information or the focal point of the research. It is, therefore, urgent that subjective knowledge and experiences are included in research as active participants and not as passive actors (Blackman *et al.*, 2003). To go for a walk and talk could potentially make the person living with dementia feel more at ease, as compared to sitting down and formulating verbal responses to questions posed by the researcher. Unfortunately, to date, there have only been a limited number of empirical studies that have addressed the outdoor environment practices of people living with dementia (Keady *et al.*, 2012). Accordingly, studies using any mobile research methods involving people living with dementia in outdoor spaces is in need of development and reporting (Brorsson *et al.*, 2013), especially in developing the knowledge base from the access of outdoor spaces connected to nursing homes and their gardens (see, for example, Schwartz and Rodiek, 2007) however important this restorative function may be.

Social research about public space for people living with dementia in their ordinary housing in the local community has only recently begun to develop. Brorsson and colleagues (2013) conducted participant observations walking alongside people living with dementia when they went out to do their daily grocery shopping. Several challenging situations were found relating to failing memory, wayfinding, heavy traffic situations and problems paying for the goods. The outdoor participant observations contributed essential information to the data that wouldn't have been the case if only sit-down interviews had been conducted. Despite the emergent question concerning 'a shrinking world' of people living with dementia as reported by Duggan (2008), places such as city centres and shopping malls risk becoming 'no go' areas that people living with dementia avoid as they do not feel at ease in the environment. The area in where people living with dementia experience independence tends to be cut down and the lengths of walking outdoors decreases as the cognitive impairment increases related to the condition (Duggan *et al.*, 2008). In situated talk with care-partners to people living with dementia about walking in their neighbourhood, rich data about the importance of face-to-face meetings in a familiar supportive environment can be collected. Moreover, the need of a social network for couples where one person is living with dementia has been recognised by researchers (Hellström and Torres, 2013). Ward and colleagues (2012) also pointed out the neighbourhood as a resource for social support to carers as well as people living with dementia (Ward *et al.*, 2012).

neighbourhood while walking, telling where friends and/or family were living. Participants often took the point of view of a visitor, telling the researcher what was coming along next. Most participants were also concerned that the researcher who walked behind with the video camera would feel comfortable during the walk.

The researchers' role in walking interviews

In traditional interview situations the researcher has the role of leading the session but in walking interviews this is not taken for granted. Van Hoven and Meijering (2011) observed that the risk of imbalance in the power relation between the participant and the researcher has the potential to develop in a more equal way in walk and talk interviews compared to sit-down indoor interviews. This is in line with what other researchers have noticed (Evans and Jones, 2011; Garcia *et al.*, 2012). An attitude of promoting the interviewee whilst walking alongside is an important prerequisite for empowerment in the situation. Also, the researcher experiences with all their senses what is happening in the neighbourhood during the walk and the open-ended format gives a good opportunity for a fluid conversation to develop, driven by the participant. The researcher had to listen carefully and follow up embodied as well as verbal information during the walk. Moreover, the researcher had to concentrate for long periods of time and needed sensitivity when conducting interviews to keep the conversational flow going (Bergeron *et al.*, 2014).

In our experience as a research team, it was an advantage to let one researcher walk with the participant while another was responsible for the video recording. Preferably, the researcher, or the person being interviewed, should wear a portable microphone for audio recording in addition to video recording; this, we found, helped in audio transcription. The researcher also had to share sensory impressions and personal perceptions and interact with the participant while moving around in the neighbourhood. The researcher had also to be aware of his/her own pre-understandings, attitudes and beliefs when interviewing the person living with dementia in their local community and, at times, be mindful of road safety especially when walking in an unfamiliar environment.

Insights gained from using the method

Walking interviews as a research method gives opportunities to share experiences with a person living with dementia in everyday outdoor situations. Furthermore, recording both non-verbal and verbal communication during the walk gives rare opportunities to gain knowledge about the interaction between the participant and their social and physical neighbourhood environment. Spending time together with the person living with dementia whilst walking within and throughout his/her neighbourhood allowed us to study ways of interaction and perceptions related to the everyday context. Immediately, at the start of the walk, participants began to communicate their local knowledge, the neighbourhood history and their experiences of specific places and social contacts, generating narratives that with high probability would not have been told if sitting down indoors. Further, non-verbal, embodied neighbourhood interaction was captured by using video during the walking interviews. The use of videotaping allowed for an analysis of different dimensions of communication during the walk: the body interaction with the environment (i.e. gestures and bodily orientation) and also social interaction with others in neighbourhood, as well as personal experiences and perceptions embedded in their neighbourhood.

The interview format offers the possibility for the interviewee to control and regulate the conversation by using pauses both in talk and walk. This is something that makes walking interviews preferable to sit-down interviews for people living with dementia, as there is less pressure to express oneself verbally. During the walks, often things happened that were not planned. For instance, it started to rain, the wind rustled in the trees, an aeroplane flew by, an animal or a traffic situation captured our attention for a while. All these situations fed in to the conversation. The participants had prepared themselves and seemed to have planned where to go. Most walks were part of the participants' everyday routines; for instance, a walk with the dog, going out for daily shopping or a regular walk aiming to be physical active to promote health and wellbeing. The interviewees living with dementia stated that they had chosen a route they usually walked and referred to meaningful parts and occasionally stopped to tell an episode coming up when walking past.

With respect to the fact that dementia is a neurological condition with well documented risk for problems with orientation and way-finding (WHO, 2012), it was interesting that only one participant expressed hesitation about the way back home. Participants seemed to feel at ease walking in their neighbourhood, and we understood that they felt proud to show their neighbourhood. Indeed, walking interviews as a research method was applicable to people living with different types of dementia, in a wide range of ages (62–87 years), living in different types of housing, either living alone or with a spouse, and in varying physical health status. Long lengths of living in their neighbourhood corresponded to safe navigation and high perceived sense of safety, i.e. trustfully saying hello in face-to-face contact when meeting neighbours or others during the walk. By conducting walking interviews, these subjective experiences of neighbourhood are given a voice and the embodiment of people living with dementia is given a context on the ground for narratives. By walking side-by-side with a person living with dementia a unique communication situation emerges that adds valuable dimensions and new knowledge of life with dementia, as it is difficult to capture such rich data about interactions within the neighbourhood in other ways. The method challenges the stereotypical view of people living with dementia as passive, as people living with dementia during the interview acted as active participants and showed us their neighbourhood as situated agents in their everyday life.

Walking interview and focus on embodied experience

The walking interview method provides an opportunity to understand the perspectives of embodied practice as applied to the experiences of people living with dementia (Martin *et al.*, 2013). The body is a resource for information and knowledge about life with dementia and walking facilitates research with embodied data information. Hydén (2013) explored storytelling in dementia and argue that data on embodied movement goes beyond the verbal expressions and is an interactive process worth to elucidate further. Walking interviews put less strain on verbal communication whereas the participants themselves control and regulate what they want to talk about and when and where they want to share their experiences and perceptions. Being in motion outdoors gives an opportunity to let the thoughts flow freely and topics of conversation can come spontaneously when passing by specific places in nature and landmarks. This is quite different from sit-down interviews in which the interviewee is expected to answer the questions primarily formulated by the researcher. The interactive process in the neighbourhood during the comfortable walking interview was supportive, participatory and less stressful which suited people living with a condition with cognitive problems. The participants described and shared what they saw, smelled, and heard or what their moving body experienced. Walking interviews add essential information and gives another basis for thought, whereas moving the body in their neighbourhood, on well-trodden paths; participant's senses were exposed to triggers in the environment that incited them to recall and to tell narratives and memories about the past, present and the future.

Walking interviews support wellbeing

The participants expressed that walking in their neighbourhood promoted health and wellbeing, irrespectively of less or more symptoms of their condition. Participants who had planned the walking tour beforehand tended to select the green spaces in their neighbourhood and nature was frequently the subject of narratives during the walks. Meaningful outdoor activities were conducted in the neighbourhood in all seasons of the year and were essential for maintaining a sense of independence and wellbeing among people living with dementia. Continuing to walk in the neighbourhood did not seem to be problematic and had an impact on the existential dimension of life. With impaired cognition, the ability to walk can be a resource that corresponds to strengthening of selfhood. The neighbourhood can be the point of departure for people's connection to the social world outdoors. Overall, the participants' ability to relate to others who we met during the walks was intact as they frequently said *hello* to others in a friendly manner. Just to see and meet others in a well-known environment where they were used to navigate in seemed to support their sense of coherence. It has to be mentioned that the walking interview probably primarily attracted participants who are used to being on foot in their neighbourhood as a routine of daily life.

Navigating in public space

The walks most frequently took place on a secure walking path for pedestrians with no motor vehicles present and just occasional bicyclists. However, some participants walked on streets with relatively heavy traffic but had no problem handling the traffic situation and they looked carefully before crossing the streets. Brorsson and colleagues (2013) explored the access to public space for people living with dementia and found that they had difficulties crossing streets with heavy traffic. After completing 19 walking interviews we noted that very few of the planned walks had been inhibited due to weather conditions irrespective of the time of year. None of the interviewees walked aimlessly or got lost.

Care implications of conducting walking interviews

In terms of a supportive environment for people living with dementia, healthcare professionals have mainly addressed the indoor architectural design and functionality (see, for example, Lee *et al.*, 2016). The experiences drawn from the walking interviews show that it is necessary for healthcare professionals to also focus on a person's outdoor environment. It is of great importance to facilitate easy access to the neighbourhood for people living with dementia. The outdoor environment needs to be treated as just as important as the indoor environment when taking care of people living with dementia, living either in ordinary or special forms of housing. The knowledge about the importance of physical activity for people living with dementia in all ages is well-documented (Balsamo *et al.*, 2013; Blankevoort *et al.*, 2010). This knowledge must be implemented in the care of people living with dementia. Our participants articulated that going outdoors to walk made them feel well. Developing the possibility for health professionals to walk and talk in the neighbourhood is a promising way of caring that is needed: walking as a physical activity, for instance, is good for the whole body, but especially for the brain.

Ethical reflections and implications

The walking interview methodology reported here has been based on participatory principles to involve people living with dementia as the primary source of knowledge. We have striven to produce the research data together with people living with dementia that has actively taken part in the outline of the walks (Scottish Dementia Working Group, 2014: see also the model in Chapter 1).

Researchers must carefully focus on the participant's actual state of health and clearly inform the participant about the research project, aim and the method used in every single meeting with the participant. Researchers informed participants that it was possible to cancel their participation at any time without any explanation.

During the walks the researcher(s) had to be aware of the participant's physical health as well as their perceived safety and interrupt if any problems occurred. As various conditions, such as the weather or temperature could affect the personal wellbeing of the interviewees rapidly, the health status of the interviewees must be observed continuously. Most participants were elderly and therefore the researchers had to be aware that their physical health status and capacity for decision-making could change rapidly during the walk.

When walking outdoors, the researcher also had to be prepared for problems with their own wayfinding. In addition, another situation that had to be talked about and discussed before conducting walking interviews is how the participant wanted to present the researcher in the case of meeting a neighbour or friend. Therefore, the method of video recording the walking interview had to be designed by the researcher so as to avoid filming other people.

Conclusion

Walking interviews are an applicable methods approach in dementia research. The data gained through walking interviews are informed by all senses and in real time, as compared to traditional sit-down interviews that are based on participant's memories and images about the outdoor space, which could be challenging for participants. In neighbourhood meaning-making and the development of a sense of place, personal biography and embodied experiences were essential and stimulated by putting the 'feet on the ground' and walking.

Acknowledgements

The support of the Economic and Social Research Council (ESRC) and National Institute for Health Research (NIHR) is gratefully acknowledged. This work forms part of the ESRC/NIHR Neighbourhoods and Dementia: a mixed methods study (www.neighbourhoodsanddementia.org) work programme 4: 'Neighbourhoods: our people, our places'.

Highlighted learning points from the method

- Walking interviews are part of a participatory method that offers people living with dementia the opportunity to have control over the research situation and the process over data being collected.
- Walking interviews are a helpful research method to operationalise the relational interaction to their neighbourhood, irrespectively of the social or physical environment.
- Walking interviews support participants to display local places that are important for them, not only talk about them. For people living with dementia, situated narratives based on their personal biography are more accessible when walking in their neighbourhood.
- In the field of dementia research, walking interviews offer an opportunity to add new perspectives to how people living with dementia define and make use of their neighbourhood.

Key references

- Blackman, T., Mitchell, L., Burton, E., Jenks, M., Parsons, M., Raman, S. and Williams, K. (2003). The accessibility of public spaces for people living with dementia: a new priority for the open city. *Disability Society*, 18: 357–371.
- Evans, J. and Jones, P. (2011). The walking interview: methodology, mobility and place. *Applied Geography*, 31: 849–858.
- Kusenbach, M. (2012). The Go-along Method. In S. Delamont (ed.) *Handbook of qualitative research in education* (pp. 252–264). London: Edward Elgar Publishing Limited.

Recommended future reading

- Ingold, T. and Vergunst, J.L. (2008). *Ways of walking: ethnography and practice on foot.* Burlington: Ashgate.
- Kaplan, S. and Kaplan, R. (1982). *Cognition and environment: functioning in an uncertain world.* USA: Praeger Publishers.
- Peace, S., Wahl, H.-W., Mollenkopf, H. and Oswald, F. (2007). Environment and ageing. In Bond, J., Peace, S., Dittman-Kohli, F. and Westerhof, G. (eds) *Ageing in society* (pp. 209–243). London: Sage Publications.
- Solnit, R. (2001). *Wanderlust: a history of walking.* United Kingdom: Penguin Books.
- Ulrich, R.S. (1981). Natural versus urban scenes: some psychophysiological effects. *Environment and Behavior*, 13(5): 523–556.
- Van Hoven, B. and Meijering, L. (2011). On the ground. In Del Casino, V.J., Thomas, M., Cloke, P and Panelli, R. (eds) *A companion to social geography* (pp. 161–180). London: Blackwell Publishing Ltd.

References

Balsamo, S., Willardson, J.M., de Santana, F.S., Prestes, J., Balsamo, D.C., Nascimento, D.C. and Nobrega, O.T. (2013). Effectiveness of exercise on cognitive impairment and Alzheimer's disease. *International Journal of General Medicine*, 6: 387–391.

Bergeron, J., Paquette, S. and Poullaouec-Gonidec, P. (2014). Uncovering landscape values and micro-geographies of meanings with the go-along method. *Landscape and Urban Planning*, 122: 108–121.

Blackman, T., Mitchell, L., Burton, E., Jenks, M., Parsons, M., Raman, S. and Williams, K. (2003). The accessibility of public spaces for people living with dementia: a new priority for the open city. *Disability Society*, 18: 357–371.

Blackman, T., van Schaik, P. and Martyr, A. (2007). Outdoor environments for people living with dementia: An exploratory study using virtual reality. *Ageing and Society*, 27: 811–825.

Blankevoort, C.G., Van Heuvelen, M.J.G., Boersma, F., Luning, H., De Jong, J. and Scherder, E.J.A. (2010). Review of effects of physical activity on strength, balance, mobility and ADL performance in elderly subjects with dementia. *Dementia and Geriatric Cognitive Disorders*, 30: 392–402.

Brorsson, A., Öhman, A., Cutchin, M. and Nygård, L. (2013). Managing critical incidents in grocery shopping by community-living people with Alzheimer's disease. *Scandinavian Journal of Occupational Therapy*, 20: 292–301.

Buffel, T., Verté, D., de Donder, L., de Witte, N., Dury, S., Vanwing, T. and Bolsenbroek, A. (2012). Theorising the relationship between older people and their immediate social living environment. *International Journal of Lifelong Education*, 31: 13–32.

Büscher, M. and Urry, J. (2009). Mobile methods and the empirical. *European Journal of Social Theory*, 12(1): 99–116.

Carpiano, R.M. (2009). Come take a walk with me: the 'Go-Along' interview as a novel method for studying the implications of place for health and well-being. *Health and Place*, 15: 263–272.

Clark, A. and Emmel, N. (2010). Using walking interviews. *ESRC National Centre for Research Methods. Realities*: 1–6.

Cummins, S., Curtis, S., Diez-Roux, A.V. and Macintyre, S. (2007). Understanding and representing 'place' in health research: a relational approach. *Social Science and Medicine*, 65: 1825–1838.

Day, K., Carreon, D. and Stump, C. (2000). The therapeutic design of environments for people living with dementia: a review of the empirical research. *Gerontologist*, 40: 397–416.

Duggan, S., Blackman, T., Martyr, A. and Van Schaik, P. (2008). The impact of early dementia on outdoor life: a 'shrinking world'? *Dementia: The International Journal of Social Research and Practice*, 7, 191–204.

Emmel, N. and Clark, A. (2009). *The methods used in connected lives: investigating networks, neighbourhoods and communities*. ESRC National Centre for Research Methods. NCRM Working paper series 06/09.

Evans, J. and Jones, P. (2011). The walking interview: methodology, mobility and place. *Applied Geography*, 31: 849–858.

Garcia, C.M., Eisenberg, M.E., Frerich, E.A., Lechner, K.E. and Lust, K. (2012). Conducting go-along interviews to understand context and promote health. *Qualitative Health Research*, 22: 1395–1403.

Gatrell, A.C. (2013). Therapeutic mobilities: walking and 'steps' to wellbeing and health. *Health and Place*, 22: 98–106.

Hall, T. (2009). Footwork: moving and knowing in local space(s). *Qualitative Research*, 9: 571–585.

Hein, J.R., Evans, J. and Jones, P. (2008). Mobile methodologies: theory, technology and practice. *Geography Compass*, 2: 1266–1285.

Hellström, I. and Torres, S. (2013). A wish to know but not always tell – couples living with dementia talk about disclosure preferences. *Aging and Mental Health*, 17: 157–167.

Hydén, L.C. (2013). Storytelling in dementia: Embodiment as a resource. *Dementia: The International Journal of Social Research and Practice*, 12: 359–367.

Jones, P., Bunce, G., Evans, J., Gibbs, H. and Hein, J.R. (2008). Exploring space and place with walking interviews. *Journal of Research Practice*, 4: 1–9.

Keady, J. (2014). Neighbourhoods and dementia. *Journal of Dementia Care*, 22: 16–17.

Keady, J., Campbell, S., Barnes, H., Ward, R., Li, X., Swarbrick, C. and Elvish, R. (2012). Neighbourhoods and dementia in the health and social care context: a realist review of the literature and implications for UK policy development. *Reviews in Clinical Gerontology*, 22: 150–163.

Kusenbach, M. (2003). The go-along as ethnographic research tool. *Ethnography*, 4: 455–485.

Kusenbach, M. (2012). The Go-along Method. In S. Delamont (ed.), *Handbook of qualitative research in education* (pp. 252–264). London: Edward Elgar Publishing Limited.

Lee, S.Y., Chaudhury, H. and Hung, L. (2016). Effects of physical environment on health and behaviors of residents with dementia in long-term care facilities: a longitudinal study. *Research in Gerontological Nursing*, 9: 81–91.

Lefebvre, H. (1991). *The production of space*. Oxford: Blackwell.

Macintyre, S. and Ellaway, A. (2003). Neighborhoods and health: an overview. In I. Kawachi and L. Berkman (eds), *Neighborhoods and health*. New York: Oxford University Press.

Martin, W., Kontos, P. and Ward, R. (2013). Embodiment and dementia. *Dementia: The International Journal of Social Research and Practice*, 12: 283–287.

Massey, D. (2005). *For space*. London: Sage Publications.

Mitchell, L. (2014). A step too far? Designing dementia-friendly neighbourhoods. In R. Cooper, E. Burton and C. Cooper (eds), *Wellbeing and the environment* (pp. 185–218). Oxford: Wiley Blackwell.

Mitchell, L. and Burton, E. (2010). Designing dementia-friendly neighbourhoods: helping people living with dementia to get out and about. *Journal of Integrated Care*, 18: 11–18.

Nahemow, L. and Lawton, P. (1973). Ecology and the aging process. In C. Eisdorfer (ed.), *The psychology of adult development and aging* (pp. 619–674). Washington, DC: American Psychological Association.

Pink, S. (2007). Walking with video. *Visual Studies*, 22: 240–252.

Scheidt, R.J. and Norris-Baker, C. (2003). The general ecological model revisited: evolution, current status, and continuing challenges. In H-W. Wahl, R. Scheidt and P. Windley (eds), *Environments, gerontology and old age. Annual review of gerontology and geriatrics 2003* (pp. 34–58). New York: Springer.

Schwartz, B. and Rodiek, S. (2007). *Outdoor environment for people with dementia*. New York: Routledge.

Scottish Dementia Working Group. (2014). Core principles for involving people living with dementia in research. *Dementia: The International Journal of Social Research and Practice*, 13, 680–685.

Sheehan, B., Burton, E. and Mitchell, L. (2006). Outdoor wayfinding in dementia. *Dementia: The International Journal of Social Research and Practice*, 5: 271–281.

Shipp, K.M. and Branch, L.G. (1999). The physical environment as a determinant of the health status of older populations. *Canadian Journal on Aging*, 18: 313–327.

van Hoven, B. and Meijering, L. (2011). On the ground. In V. Del Casino, J.M. Thomas and E.P. Cloke (eds), *A companion to social geography* (pp. 161–180). Oxford, UK: Wiley-Blackwell.

Wahl, H.W., Iwarsson, S. and Oswald, F. (2012). Aging well and the environment: toward an integrative model and research agenda for the future. *Gerontologist*, 52: 306–316.

Ward, R., Clark, A. and Hargreaves, M. (2012). What does 'neighbourhood' mean for carers of people living with dementia? *Journal of Dementia Care*, 20: 33–36.

WHO (2012). *Dementia: a public health priority. Report World Health Organization*, www.who.int

3 Audio recorded data as a method to understand encounters between people living with dementia and social workers

*Johannes H. Österholm and
Annika Taghizadeh Larsson*

Outline

This chapter provides an insight into the advantages of using *naturally occurring data* in the form of audio recorded conversations and outlines how such research could be conducted within the theoretical and methodological framework of *discourse analysis*. In the chapter the authors refer to their experiences from a research project based on audio recordings of assessment meetings where a social worker met a person living with dementia, and often their relatives, to assess and negotiate the person's need for social care services. The meetings took place within a legislative context where people living with dementia have the same right to self-determination, in relation to social care services, as every other adult citizen. A particular focus is placed on the benefits of the chosen methodological approach in exploring the participation of people living with dementia in the meetings.

Introduction

People living with dementia are usually described as a vulnerable group. This refers to those who have impaired abilities to understand information and who are at risk of being exploited. Therefore, extra concerns about research ethics must be taken into account when people living with dementia are involved. Within dementia research, there has been a tendency to exclude people living with dementia from research and instead focus on formal and informal caregivers. Hougham (2005) argues that research on vulnerable groups should be more widely facilitated. High thresholds that have been created to protect vulnerable groups from harm have unintended consequences in reduced advancement in knowledge about how to improve care for this population (Hougham, 2005), and the person's own experience of living with dementia is not widely recognised (Beard, 2004). This protectionist approach is especially found in research about how decisions about care services are made and experienced by those involved (Taghizadeh Larsson and Österholm, 2014). Therefore, little is known about these decisions and how the process to gain support can be adopted to suit people living with dementia.

Decisions on care services, such as relocation to special housing, are 'a milestone both in the progress of the dementia and in the relationship between the person, the family and the professionals involved' (McDonald, 2010, p. 1233). However, there are only a few studies on the participation, or scope for participation of people living with dementia, in the process of deciding on care services. The same applies to how communicative challenges associated with dementia actually matter and are managed in meetings with health and social care professionals. For example, the existing body of research that focuses on decisions on social care services involving people living with dementia is dominated by studies where relatives of the individual have been asked to share their experiences of the process (Taghizadeh Larsson and Österholm, 2014). There are few studies aiming to capture the experiences of the people living with dementia (e.g. Aminzadeh *et al.*, 2009; Fetherstonhaugh *et al.*, 2013; Tyrell *et al.*, 2006). Furthermore, the studies in this area tell more about the exclusion of people living with dementia from care decisions than providing examples about their actual involvement.

As we will illustrate and argue in this chapter, this is an understanding that is related not only to assumptions about the abilities of people living with dementia but also has to do with the methods used for generating data. Interviews are often used, but interviewees will only note and remember a small part of what happened in a specific situation. However, while interviews seem to be the preferred method of gathering data of many scholars, there are alternative methods of investigating the participation of people living with dementia.

This chapter aims to provide an insight of the advantages of using *naturally occurring data* in the form of audio recorded conversations. More specifically, we will describe and discuss how such research could be conducted in practice within the theoretical and methodological framework of *discourse analysis*. The chapter is based on the authors' experiences of using audio recordings in a research project. The material consists of 15 audio recordings of assessment meetings where a social worker meets a person living with dementia to assess the person's need for social care services; they also negotiate, decide on and plan for future care (Österholm, 2016; Österholm and Hydén, 2016; Österholm *et al.*, 2015).

In the chapter, we will first introduce the theoretical and methodological framework of discourse analysis as well as naturally occurring data. Referring to our experiences from the research process in question, we will then describe how such data could be generated within the framework of discourse analysis and reflect on ethical issues encountered during the data collection phase. After that, we will provide insight into specific analytical approaches and focus that could be adopted in such a study. Lastly, we will summarise what we consider to be the benefits of using audio recorded conversations and discourse analysis and discuss possible implications for policy and practice for the knowledge provided.

Introduction to discourse analysis and naturally occurring data

Discourse analysis is an umbrella concept which has its origins in the social constructionist perspective. At the core of discourse analysis, which is both a theory and a method for analysis, is the notion that talk and text can be conceived of as social practices or actions that are part of social interaction (Potter, 2004; Potter and Wetherell, 1987). This means that language does not merely mirror phenomena or objects in the world, but rather helps to construct these phenomena. The meaning of different things, such as objects, previous happenings, attitudes, and opinions is constructed, negotiated and given meaning by the interlocutors in conversations (Nikander, 2008; Wetherell and Potter, 1992). It is important to underline that discourse analysis cannot (and should not) be used to identify who is 'wrong' and who is 'right' in the conversation or to describe for instance individuals' cognitive processes (Potter and Wetherell, 1987). Rather, within discourse analysis '[d]iscourse is treated as a potent, action-oriented medium, not a transparent information channel' (Potter and Wetherell, 1987, p. 160). These negotiations are built on the participants previous (shared or private) understanding of the phenomenon discussed. In discourse analysis a core assumption is that social actions are embedded in talk (Hutchby and Wooffitt, 2008).

Naturally occurring data (Silverman, 2013) – that is, recordings of activities that unfolds and are situated as far as possible in the ordinary course of people's lives (Hutchby and Wooffitt, 2008) – provides a basis for studying and understanding how people interact. Naturalistic material, such as audio recorded conversations, makes it possible to study how the interaction took place and how the participants oriented themselves to each other. In other words, naturally occurring data preserves the phenomenon that are subject for research (Edwards, 1997; Wetherell and Potter, 1992). It is important to remember that the interaction between the participants most probably will be affected in some way by the presence of a researcher and audio recording of the ongoing talk. Thus, the data will never be 'pure', uncontaminated by the researcher or the research process.

In the following section, we will describe how naturally occurring data could be generated within the framework of discourse analysis. We will also present and discuss some decisions made throughout our research process, including how we handled some of the ethical concerns that we encountered.

Generating naturally occurring data within the framework of discourse analysis

Audio recordings of naturally occurring talk could be generated and approached in many ways. In discourse analysis, the researcher starts with a set of discursive phenomena that are assumed to be interesting and relevant for the ongoing project. It is the researcher's aims that guide the collection of data and the analysis.

The research on which this chapter is based constitutes the first author's PhD project; he also conducted most of the actual work in generating, coding and analysing the data. The project started with a broad aim: 'to explore and understand how people living with dementia use their remaining resources to invoke, negotiate, and use their rights as citizens in the institutional context where their care needs are assessed' (Österholm, 2016, p. 12). When the aim was set, we contacted two different local social welfare offices where assessment of people living with dementia care needs was conducted. After some negotiations with the two social welfare offices we obtained the possibility of collecting data.

The first author was present at the welfare offices during the data collection phase to facilitate the contact with the participating social workers, to remind them that there was a research project going on, but also to get a deeper understanding of the work conducted by the social workers. In the data collection phase, the first author followed seven social workers in 15 assessment meetings. When everybody was gathered in the room where the meeting was going to take place, the first author started the audio recorder and then remained in the room during the whole meeting. It is not that uncommon that the researcher leaves the room after the audio recording has started to avoid unnecessary influence on the material. The decision to stay was made to get a better understanding of non-verbal interaction – for instance, body language, eye gazes and so forth. Ethnographic field notes were written about these interactional events and a clear reference was made to where in the conversation they happened in terms of what the participants said at that very same moment.

As stated in the introduction, people living with dementia are usually not included in research about the decision-making process surrounding care services. A reason for excluding people living with dementia from research has often to do with perceived competence in relation to the possibility of informed consent (Cubit, 2010). Informed consent is required from all who participate in research according to the Declaration of Helsinki (last revision 2013). Informed consent in our research has been given as a multistage consent process. Information about the study has first been given by telephone, by mail and then face-to-face to all participants. This multistage consent process has the benefit of allowing all participants several opportunities to be informed and to withdraw their consent to participate. This increases the chance that their decision to participate is a fully informed one (Hellström *et al.*, 2007).

The Swedish legislation governing our research project (SFS, 2003:460) allows relatives to give consent for vulnerable people so that they can participate in research. At any rate, the cornerstones of informed consent cannot be disregarded: the person living with dementia, as well as her or his proxies, must give their consent. When we were contacting the potential participants for our project, some of the participants' adult children expressed that they did not consent to participate with a reference to the person's with dementia values, such as respect for privacy. In other cases, the adult children argued that they would consent to participate with reference to their parent's previous willingness to participate in research.

When a surrogate decision maker gave their consent to participate, we tried to be extra sensitive to how the person living with dementia reacted, both when information was given and during the data collection. If there were any signs that the person did not wish to participate, the collection of data was terminated at once in order to respect the person's right to self-determination. On two occasions, we decided not to collect data because the potential participants appeared to be distressed or uncomfortable, i.e. had concerns with the audio recorder or did not recognise memory problems. On these two occasions, we expressed our gratitude for them letting us meet them and then left before the meeting began in order to influence the meeting as little as possible.

The audio recordings were then transcribed verbatim, including hesitations, partial wording, pauses, repetitions, unintelligible syllables and so forth. This was a very time consuming part of the work, and it was challenging to transcribe conversations with multiple participants. However, detailed and accurate transcriptions are a prerequisite for any type of discourse analysis. Also, transcribing the audio recordings makes it easier to work with the analysis: when transcribing, you get familiarised with your data (Guendouzi and Müller, 2006) and interesting phenomena will most probably be noticed. When encountering interesting phenomena, it is important to record your ideas so you do not forget them.

The analysis proceeded in several steps. The involved researchers listened to the audio recordings repeatedly and the transcriptions were read several times, in order to get a sufficient overview and understanding of the data material. In the next step, sequences involving phenomena of interest were identified and extracted from the data. This procedure was undertaken to get a smaller corpus of data to work with.

Within these extracted sequences, the interaction and the consequences of these actions were coded. Each extracted sequence was coded, with one or several codes, in relation to what the participants accomplished through different utterances. These codes were then used to identify different patterns in the interaction, in relation to our research questions. At this stage, theoretical understandings of what occurred should have as little significance as possible to remain open to what is actually happening in the interaction. It is what is made significant by the participants in the interaction that is of interest and what interaction functions they have in the ongoing conversation (Nikander, 2008; Potter, 2004). Thus, a single utterance cannot be analysed separately. The utterance is a part of a greater whole and should be analysed regarding its contexts; what has previously been said and what actions followed the utterance. Here, another finding could be that the utterance was (partly) lacking context if it was not noticed or picked up by the other interlocutors.

Examining the participation of people living with dementia

Margaret Wetherell (2001), a prominent scholar within the field of discourse analysis, presents three domains of studies on social interaction in discourse research. The first domain is about social action and interactional order and concerns the organisation of talk as a joint activity. Focus on this analytical domain involves how people coordinate their talk and how mutual understanding is reached (Wetherell, 2001). In the second domain, focus is on the production of social actors, including how sense making is accomplished and how constructions of identities are conducted and affirmed in talk-in-interaction (Schegloff, 1992; Wetherell, 2001). The third and final domain concerns the study of discourse in relation to culture, history, and the institutional features of discourse (Wetherell, 2001).

In the following section we will refer to, and present, these three domains further as we have used them (see Österholm, 2016), to clarify how the participation of people living with dementia could be examined using audio recorded conversations and discourse analysis. In doing so, we will provide empirical findings from our research and discuss our experience gained from using this method.

Contribution in the conversation

One way to understand and investigate the participation of people living with dementia in meetings with social and health care professionals is to focus on how the participants coordinate their talk (the first analytical domain). This can be accomplished by looking at each participant's contribution in the conversation. One of our research questions was directed at the ability of people living with dementia to take part in negotiations for formal support (Österholm and Hydén, 2014). We were interested in the organisation of talk and how the participants coordinated their talk, but also how mutual understanding was reached between different participants in these meetings. Here, the analysis was conducted in relation to the question whether the person living with dementia was able to take part in these types of institutional conversations, and if they were positioned as a competent interlocutor whose opinion mattered.

This analysis was accomplished by calculating each participant's discursive contributions in the assessment meeting, measured in number of words per turn. First, all utterances were sorted to the person who uttered them. All words and all turns each participant had in the conversations were counted. The total amount of words spoken by each participant was divided by the amount of turns they had uttered to get the average number of words per turn. The calculation of each participant's participation in relation to words, turns, and word per turn is presented in Table 3.1.

From Table 3.1, it is possible to see that the relative difference between the social workers average of words per turn compared to the person living with dementia's average of word per turn differs between the meetings. Thus, based upon this calculation, it is possible to say that the participation of people living with dementia is heterogeneous – some people living with dementia are taking part to a greater extent than others in the assessment meetings.

Hence, by using naturalistic data we could show that in all cases, except for case 1, people living with dementia participated actively in the conversation.

Table 3.1 Contributions to the assessment meetings ordered from lowest relative difference between social worker and PWD in terms of mean of words/turn to highest

Case	Participants	Number of words	Number of turns	Words per turn	Relative difference
8	SW/PWD/B/DR	1190/2401/748/657	84/174/61/57	14.2/13.8/12.3/11.5	0.4
3	SW/RN/PWD	3125/977/3180	207/81/235	15.1/12.1/13.5	1.6
5	SW/PWD/W	4806/852/4475	400/95/403	12/9/11.1	3.0
6	SW/PWD/S/DL	1276/927/975/617	87/83/73/44	14.7/11.2/13.4/14	3.5
11	SW/PWD/D	4579/1139/2769	376/165/266	12.2/6.9/10.4	5.3
10	SW/PWD/W	1258/653/749	93/82/38	13.5/8/19.7	5.5
4	SW/PWD/S	5029/3847/1076	218/222/73	23.1/17.3/14.7	5.8
2	SW/PWD/H/D	3146/722/1613/1707	217/102/186/148	14.5/7.1/8.7/11.5	7.4
9	SW/PWD/S/D	3782/1484/560/1484	227/205/51/150	16.7/7.2/11/9.9	9.5
7	SW/AN/PWD/W/D	1437/1166/168/1164/625	103/70/43/112/46	14/16.7/3.9/10.4/13.6	10.1
1	SW/S	2061/1253	125/123	16.5/10.2	16.5
Sum	Prof13/PWD10/Rel15	33832/15373/19219	2288/1406/1831	195.3/97.9/182.4	
Mean		2603/1537/1281	176/141/122	15/10/12	6.2

Notes
SW = social worker, RN = registered nurse, AN = assistant nurse, PWD = person living with dementia, H = husband, W = wife, S = son, D = daughter, B = brother, DL = daughter-in-law, DR = distant relative, Prof = professionals, Rel = relatives.

Nevertheless, the word count says nothing about what the talk was about, and if the person living with dementia participated in the decision making of social care services. But from the table above, it is very clear that people living with dementia can and do engage in the conversation when their care needs and potential support is assessed and negotiated. Some possible ways to study the person's participation in more detail will be presented in the following section.

Discursive strategies

One possible way to study the participation of people living with dementia in meetings with social and health care professionals is to focus on the professionals' discursive strategies and their consequences in terms of the participation of the person living with dementia. This was our analytical focus in relation to a research question dealing with how social workers handle the dilemma between self-determination as stipulated in the Swedish social services act (2001:453) and cognitive impairment (Österholm *et al.*, 2015). In this case the analysis addressed the two domains of how people coordinate their talk, and how institutional features are used in institutional talk. Discursive institutional features – that is, talk that is used in a specific institutional context by the professional to conduct their everyday work – used by social workers were studied, as well as how changes in their talk could facilitate for the people living with dementia to part take in decision-making. We use a broad definition of discursive strategy; it involves, for example, utterances made by the social worker, or allowing others to speak for the person living with dementia. A discursive strategy, referred to as a strategy, is thereby defined as a discursive action made by the social worker. This action had consequences on the participation of the person living with dementia in the negotiation of support. From this set of data, we do not know whether or not these strategies were used deliberately to affect the participation of the person living with dementia.

We found three main strategies that social workers used to handle the dilemma. The first strategy involved social workers engaging the people living with dementia in the assessment of needs and wishes by asking closed questions. This strategy allowed the people living with dementia to voice their needs and preferences in relation to the issues under discussion. In the second strategy, social workers turned their investigation of the needs and preferences towards the person's relatives, thereby excluding the person living with dementia from taking part in this discussion. Nevertheless, the person living with dementia was then either engaged in the arrangement of services or informed about the outcome of the discussion. In the third and last strategy, both the people living with dementia and their relatives were engaged in the assessment of needs and wishes. This was accomplished by the social worker by either making sure that relatives' preferences were in accordance with the client's preferences, or by allowing relatives to remind them about previous preferences.

Our analysis of naturalistic data allowed for identifying the discursive strategies used by the social workers in the assessment meetings and to shed light on

details of more overarching strategies related to autonomy that have been identified in previous research on assessment meetings concerning older clients based
on interviews: to coax, guide, and let time take its course. For example, to pose
closed questions or remind the client about previous preferences could be considered as specific and diverse ways of guiding (cf. Nordström, 1998).

Example 1 is used to discuss our analytical arguments and how to give references to examples in the writing of the findings in discourse analysis. Transparency is vital in discourse analysis giving the readers the possibility to make their
own judgements about the findings (Peräkulä, 2011; Potter and Wetherell, 1987;
Silverman, 2013). Therefore, longer examples from the data are presented along
with detailed interpretations where analytical claims are linked to specific parts
of the extracts (Hutchby and Wooffitt, 2008; Potter and Wetherell, 1987).

Example 1 is extracted from case 2 and shows how the social worker
excluded the person living with dementia from discussions on needs and preferences, but then involved the person living with dementia in the arrangement of
decided services. Those present at the meeting were the social worker, the person
living with dementia, her husband and her daughter. Before this sequence, the
husband and daughter, who handled the negotiation of services with the social
worker, had agreed to accept home care once a week to help the person living
with dementia to take a shower. The person living with dementia had great difficulties engaging in the conversation (see Table 3.1) and during the meeting,
she seemed to be more interested in the coffee cups and thermos in front of her.

Example 1: SW = Social worker, PWD = Person living with dementia, H =
Husband, D = Daughter

 1   SW: yes, that's right, once a week then
 2   H: yes
 3   D: mm
 4   SW: mm that's right
 5   PWD: is that something you've decided now
 6   D: yes, what do you think then
 7   PWD: yes, I won't intervene in this
 8   H: surely it's good that someone will come and help you shower
 9   D: yes mm
10   PWD: I hope that the boys don't come
11   D: no
12   SW: no, oh no, you don't want that
13   PWD: it's just you who'll be coming, right
14   D: no, now staff from that residential care facility will come
15   PWD: aha
16   D: but we can tell them that it should be girls, it's mostly girls who
        work there
17   H: yes, yes I think so
18   D: yes, but there's a man who works nights, and we don't need him

19   SW: yes, yes, it's so different in different places, but I'm pointing it out so
that no men come, because it's a little different

This sequence starts with a conclusion by the social worker about what has been
decided previously in the conversation, namely, that the home helper should help
the person living with dementia to shower once a week. This decision is acknowledged by the husband and daughter in the subsequent turns, but the person
living with dementia asks in line 5 if they have decided anything. This utterance
indicates that she has not been able to participate in the conversation held before,
but that she has understood that a decision might have been reached. In our analysis, this was coded as an exclusion of the person living with dementia from the
decisions on social care services. But then something else happened: the person
living with dementia's husband explained the situation for her, that it would be
good if someone could come and help her to take a shower. This clarification
specified what had been decided and the person living with dementia can engage
in the organisation of how the support should be given: that there will be no
males coming to help her to shower. This part of the sequence was coded in our
analysis as participating in the organisation of services. These two codes, in the
same sequence, create something together that is more than exclusion of the
person and less than self-determination in relation to social care services. These
nuances of participation and support for participation would most probably have
been missed in research without a naturalistic material where the person living
with dementia would most likely have been seen as excluded from the decision-
making process since the formal decision to accept care services were made by
her relatives.

Autobiographical stories

Another question in our research project concerned how autobiographical stories
were used and what function stories have in assessment meetings (Österholm
and Hydén, 2016). Here, all three domains were addressed. With a special focus
on stories and narration, we analysed how identities were constructed through
various discursive practices. First, we looked at who was positioned as the narrator and how stories were used to position the person in the meetings in relation
to credibility, need of social care services, competence and so forth. Second, the
ways the institutional context influence the participation of the person living
with dementia. All transcripts were scrutinised to identify and extract stories that
were told in these assessment meetings as presented above.

Ochs and Capps' (2001) perspective of living narratives was used – that
stories are told in conversation as a social phenomenon that occurs in social
exchanges amongst multiple storytellers. Labov and Waletzky's (1997) definition of narrative was used to some extent, stating that narratives are organised
around previous events. The studied meetings aimed at identifying needs that the
person must manage their everyday activities. One way to identify the person's
care needs is to let them talk about previous happenings in their everyday lives

(Payne, 2012). The analysis focused on talk about previous events that happened to any of the participants in the meetings.

First, we found that all participants in the included assessment meetings were narrators of stories and engaged in the storytelling in different ways. The people living with dementia, their relatives and professionals told stories, either alone, in pairs, or all together. The constellations of narrators in relation to cases and stories told are presented in Table 3.2.

Table 3.2 presents how talk was coordinated amongst the participants. Co-narration occurs in different constellations and both social workers, people living with dementia, and relatives, construct narratives on their own in assessment meetings.

Three different functions of stories were found. These included: (1) justification of why social care services were needed; (2) description of experiences about previous social care services or accounts of how previous discussions about social care services had unfolded; as well as (3) providing a good working climate amongst the participants. Stories told to justify why social care services were needed involved stories where the person's abilities were in focus, showing that her or his abilities were insufficient to manage everyday activities. It also involved illness narratives to justify the need for care; this was accomplished by telling stories about previous operations, strokes and meetings with other health care professionals. By narrating these stories, the person living with dementia either positioned him- or herself, or was positioned by others, as in need of social care services.

Describing previous experiences and discussions about social care services made it possible for different participants to voice their own or some other person's wishes or opinions about social care services. Stories were also told about previous experiences of social care services. By telling these stories the narrator ruled out services that had been unsuccessfully used in the past, or in other cases argued for the continuation of services that had been successfully implemented before. These stories were about social care services rather than needs that existed. When stories were used to provide a good working climate the shortcomings of the person were not in focus. Social workers could also tell the other

Table 3.2 Constellations of narrators in relation to cases and stories told

Narrator(s)	Number of cases	Total number of narratives
Relatives	10	17
Relatives and person living with dementia	6	15
Person living with dementia	6	13
Relatives and professionals	5	6
Professionals	5	8
Person living with dementia and professionals	4	5
Everyone together	6	17

participants about personal things, such as where they had lived before or what they had worked with earlier. When social workers told such stories, the formal format of the meeting was lightened up.

The naturalistic data gave us the possibility to categorise the functions of narratives in talk-in-interaction. One striking thing with our results is that stories had little impact on the personalisation of social care services for people living with dementia.

Example 2 is used to exemplify our discourse analysis of narratives of naturalistic audio recorded data. In the example the person living with dementia is the main narrator, and tells a story to justify his need of care services. He wants to get help from the social worker to secure a place at a residential care facility. This example occurs early in the conversation. During the assessment meeting the social worker judges the person to be too healthy for a place at a residential care facility, and instead encourages him to contact landlords who have apartments close to a meeting place for older people, to accept food distribution from the municipality, and so forth. All alternative services offered to him are declined. Participants at this meeting were the person living with dementia, his son, and the social worker.

Example 2: SW = Social worker, PWD = Person living with dementia, S = Son

1 SW: how is it with the health and such (,) when it comes to your health
2 PWD: it could be a little better
3 SW: it could be better
4 PWD: I'll tell you what it's about (small laugh)
5 SW: yes please do
6 PWD: yes, it's like this that I have a little
7 SW: I need something to write on
8 PWD: difficult to walk outside (,) ehh I went down to (.) e (.) to ICA [grocery store] down here about three weeks ago
9 SW: mm
10 PWD: and it was okay getting there (,) slow and steady one step at a time
11 SW: mm
12 PWD: I rolled along (,) then when I were to go home again then I came to a sudden stop then my legs began to go like this
13 SW: yes
14 PWD: and then and then I sank down on the street (,) and there I lay
15 SW: okay
16 PWD: then two ladies came along and helped me up they probably thought I was drunk
17 S: (laugh)
18 SW: yes
19 PWD: so she looked at me for quite a while then she came over and asked me how are you can you manage to get up if I can lie here a while and rest so I lay there and rested and got better then I got up on my knees (little laugh) then

20 SW: mm
21 PWD: and then I looked around so I had or the next place and walk there then
22 SW: mm
23 PWD: and then there was a fence five meters away yes I can walk there I thought(,) I can walk there then there was a tree that I walked to so I walked five meters at a time like that
24 SW: mm
25 PWD: finally I got home (.)
26 SW: okay how do you feel about going out now
27 PWD: no I don't dare go out now
28 SW: you don't dare go out no
29 PWD: because I don't want to r- run into those ladies again (laugh)
30 SW: (laugh) it was the ladies that were the problem
31 PWD: yes that was the question yes
32 SW: yes okay
33 PWD: well, well, that's the way it is

The story started as a response to a question asked by the social worker, directed towards the person living with dementia, about his health status. The story is directed to the social worker, as the person living with dementia opens the story with a statement that 'I'll tell you'. By using the first-person pronoun (the Swedish 'jag'/'I') he also positions himself as a competent interlocutor who knows his own needs and that he should present them himself. His introduction also suggests that his story is one example of many when his health has had consequences in his everyday life. The social worker confirms her position as the one to whom the story is directed, and acts as though what will come is important for her in her assessment by encouraging him to tell his story and by stating that she must have something to take notes on. Throughout the telling of the story, the person living with dementia is the main narrator and the social worker acknowledges her listening by giving minimal responses (such as 'mm') to his story. The person living with dementia recapitulates what happened to him when he walked home from the local grocery store. Within the story there is information that positions him as vulnerable and in need of support. By telling this story he supports his agenda that he needs a place in a residential care facility since he is unable to accomplish everyday activities such as grocery shopping on his own.

The story is not sufficient for the social worker to decide about residential care, and in line 26, she asks how he feels about leaving his home nowadays. To feel unsafe in one's own home or surroundings is one of several criteria for a place at a residential care facility. Thus, this question makes the person living with dementia's story relevant in the needs assessment process. His response is that he does not dare to go out any longer and he continues with something that could be understood as a joke, but takes away the seriousness in his response about feeling unsafe (line 29): that he does not want to run into those two ladies again. This story, and other justifications given by him, was not enough to get an offer regarding residential care from the social worker, who judged that his needs could be satisfied by other supportive services, which the person living with dementia declined.

Implications for policy and practice

One of the strengths of the detailed analysis of a naturalistic material that we have conducted is that it enables us to identify what's 'really' occurring in these meetings and not only what is presented in accounts given in interviews. Participation in decisions about care services varies and takes different forms and is affected by all parties' actions. The use of audio-recorded data has made it possible to identify specific and various forms of participation by the person living with dementia in the assessment meeting and in the shaping of different care services. We have identified different strategies used by social workers to facilitate for the person to participate in decisions. Different obstacles for the person to act as an agent have also been identified. In addition, the use of a naturalistic audio-recorded material made it possible to expand our understanding of what functions stories have in assessment meetings. This has been overlooked in previous research based on interviews.

There are several implications for policy and practice from using discourse analysis conducted on a naturalistic audio-recorded data material involving people living with dementia. It is important to understand that research conducted with a discursive approach 'does not lie well with input/output style evaluations' (Wiggins and Hepburn, 2007, p. 281). Therefore, practical implications rising from discourse analysis should be seen as suggestions of how to handle the situation, and not necessarily the only way. Based on our analysis and our data material we found that people living with dementia participate in negotiations about care services in different degrees and that communicative challenges can be solved if social workers do not intervene too quickly. Different discursive strategies, such as using closed questions, and informing the person living with dementia about the outcome of decisions on social care services to stimulate a reaction from the person being assessed for support could be used to facilitate for people living with dementia to participate in the negotiation about care services. Further, stories in assessment meetings can be used to justify why social care services are needed, to describe experiences about previous care services, to give accounts of how previous discussions about different social care services had unfolded, and to provide a good working climate amongst the participants. When using stories in assessment meetings, social workers need to differentiate between those who present these stories and try to support the person living with dementia to present their own stories as far as possible.

The use of a naturalistic material to research different institutional conversations sheds light on how these meetings proceed for those who are unfamiliar with these situations, such as politicians, executives at social welfare offices, and members of the general public. This insight makes it possible to develop guidelines of how the process could be advanced, for example to get an understanding of how the Social Services Act (2001, p. 453) is transformed into practice – how to prepare oneself for the meeting when social care services are applied for and so forth. It might be hard or even impossible to get the same information about the proceedings of the meeting through other data material such as interviews or quantitative measures of different variables. Most probably it could be even more challenging when the primary subject for research is a person living with dementia who, due to cognitive impairments, may not be able to participate in research interviews or questionnaire studies, or might not even recall the meeting subject for research. Thus, there is a potential risk that the person living with dementia is marginalised in research or even excluded. Using naturalistic audio-recordings the person and her or his actions in meetings can be studied and the result would most probably be more nuanced and accurate to what occurs in these meetings.

There are also educational implications of the chosen method in relation to those who usually participate in these types of meetings (in our research, social workers). By taking part in detailed studies of discursive practices in assessment meetings social workers get an opportunity to monitor consequences of different actions in conversations. These results can be used by them to reflect on their own discursive patterns and their thoughts and beliefs about people living with dementia of which they previously might not have been aware. Furthermore, these results can be used as a basis for discussions amongst colleagues of how to tackle difficult situations, for example how to handle the dilemma that arises between the ideal of self-determination and cognitive impairments. The use of audio-recorded naturalistic data can also give students (in our research, primarily social work students) an insight into how social workers handle clients with dementia, but also how people living with dementia and/or their relatives might behave in these meetings. This offers them the possibility of avoiding negative discursive practices, creating different conversational strategies to promote participation for people living with dementia or finding ways of using stories in their forthcoming work as social workers.

Highlighted learning points from the method

- A core notion of discourse analysis is that talk and texts can be conceived of as social practices or actions that are part of social interaction.
- Discourse analysis is not about identifying who is 'wrong' and who is 'right', it's rather about understanding how people create a common understanding of different situations or phenomena.
- Utterances in conversations are part of a greater whole, and thus single utterances should not be analysed separately.
- Naturalistic data preserves the phenomenon of interest and makes it possible to study how interaction took place and how interlocutors oriented themselves to each other.
- Practical implications arising from discourse analysis should be seen as suggestions as to how to handle the situation, and not as necessarily the only way.

Key references

- Potter, J. and Wetherell, M. (1987). *Discourse and social psychology: beyond attitudes and behaviour.* London: Sage Publications.
- Österholm, J.H. (2016). *Assessment meetings between care managers and persons living with dementia: citizenship as practice.* Norrköping: Linköping University, Department of Social and Welfare Studies, 2016 (Linköping Studies in Arts and Science: 684).
- Österholm, J.H. and Hydén, L-C. (2016). Citizenship as practice: handling communication problems in encounters between persons with dementia and social workers. *Dementia: The International Journal of Social Research and Practice,* 15(6): 1457–1473.
- Österholm, J.H., Taghizadeh Larsson, A. and Olaison, A. (2015). Handling the dilemma of self-determination and dementia: a study of case managers' discursive strategies in assessment meetings. *Journal of Gerontological Social Work,* 58(6): 613–636.

Recommended future reading

- Guendouzi, J.A. and Müller, N. (2006). *Approaches to discourse in dementia.* Mahwah, NJ: Lawrence Erlbaum.
- Hutchby, I. and Wooffitt, R. (2008). *Conversation analysis.* Cambridge: Polity Press.
- Wetherell, M. (ed.) (2001). *Discourse theory and practice.* London: Sage Publications, in association with the Open University.
- Wetherell, M. and Potter, J. (1992). *Mapping the language of racism: discourse and the legitimation of exploitation.* New York: Columbia University Press.

References

Aminzadeh, F., Dalziel, W.B., Molnar, F.J. and Garcia, L.J. (2009). Symbolic meaning of relocation to a residential care facility for persons with dementia. *Aging and Mental Health,* 13: 487–496.

Beard, R. (2004). In their voices: identity preservation and experiences of Alzheimer's disease. *Journal of Aging Studies,* 18(4): 415–428.

Cubit, K. (2010). Informed consent for research involving people living with dementia: a grey area. *Contemporary Nurse,* 34(2): 230–236.

Declaration of Helsinki (2013). *Ethical principles for medical research involving human subjects.* World Medical Association.

Edwards, D. (1997). *Discourse and cognition.* London: Sage Publications.

Fetherstonhaugh, D., Tarzia, L. and Nay, R. (2013). Being central to decision making means I am still here! The essence of decision making for people living with dementia. *Journal of Aging Studies,* 27: 143–150.

Guendouzi, J.A. and Müller, N. (2006). *Approaches to discourse in dementia.* Mahwah, NJ: Lawrence Erlbaum Associates.

Hellström, I., Nolan, M., Nordenfelt, L. and Lundh, U. (2007). Ethical and methodological issues in interviewing persons with dementia. *Nursing Ethics*, 14(5): 608–619.

Hougham, G. (2005). Waste not, want not: cognitive impairment should not preclude research participation. *American Journal of Bioethics*, 5(1): 36–37.

Hutchby, I. and Wooffitt, R. (2008). *Conversation analysis.* Cambridge: Polity Press.

Labov, W. and Waletzky, J. (1997). Narrative analysis: oral versions of personal experience. *Journal of Narrative and Life History*, 7(1–4): 3–38.

McDonald, A.A. (2010). The impact of the 2005 Mental Capacity Act on social workers' decision making and approaches to the assessment of risk. *British Journal of Social Work*, 40(4), 1229–1246.

Nikander, P. (2008) Constructionism and discourse analysis. In J. Holstein and J.F. Gubrium (eds) *Handbook of constructionist research* (pp. 413–428). New York: Guilford Press.

Nordström, M. (1998). *Yttre villkor och inre möten: Hemtjänsten som organisation* [External conditions and internal meetings: the home help services as an organisation] (Dissertation). Gothenburg University, Gothenburg, Sweden.

Ochs, E. and Capps, L. (2001). *Living narrative: creating lives in everyday storytelling.* Cambridge, MA: Harvard University Press.

Österholm, J.H. (2016). *Assessment meetings between care managers and persons living with dementia: citizenship as practice.* Norrköping: Linköping University, Department of Social and Welfare Studies, 2016 (Linköping Studies in Arts and Science: 684).

Österholm, J.H. and Hydén, L-C. (2014). Citizenship as practice: handling communication problems in encounters between persons with dementia and social workers. *Dementia: The International Journal of Social Research and Practice*, 15(6): 1457–1473.

Österholm, J.H. and Hydén, L-C. (2016). Autobiographical occasions in assessment meetings involving persons with dementia. *Journal of Qualitative Social Work* (online).

Österholm, J.H., Taghizadeh Larsson, A. and Olaison, A. (2015). Handling the dilemma of self-determination and dementia: a study of case managers' discursive strategies in assessment meetings. *Journal of Gerontological Social Work*, 58(6): 613–636.

Payne, M. (2012). *Citizenship social work with older people.* Bristol: Policy Press.

Peräkulä, A. (2011). Validity in research on naturally occurring social interaction. In D. Silverman (ed.) *Qualitative research* (pp. 365–382). London: Sage Publications.

Potter, J. (2004). Discourse analysis. In M.A. Hardy and A. Bryman (eds) *Handbook of data analysis* (pp. 607–624). London: Sage Publications.

Potter, J. and Wetherell, M. (1987). *Discourse and social psychology: beyond attitudes and behaviour.* London: Sage Publications.

Schegloff, E.A. (1992). Repair after next turn: the last structurally provided for place for the defense of intersubjectivity in conversation. *American Journal of Sociology*, 95(5): 1295–1345.

Silverman, D. (2013). *Doing qualitative research.* Thousand Oaks, CA: Sage Publications.

Svensk författningssamling (SFS) [Swedish Code of Statutes]. (2001:453). *Socialtjänstlagen* [Social Services Act] (2001; 453).

Svensk författningssamling (SFS) [Swedish Code of Statutes]. (2003:460) *Lag om etikprövning av forskning som avser människor* [Act concerning the ethical review of research involving humans] (2003: 460).

Taghizadeh Larsson, A. and H. Österholm, J. (2014). How are decisions on care services for people living with dementia made and experienced? A systematic review and qualitative synthesis of recent empirical findings. *International Psychogeriatrics, 26:* 1849–1862.

Tyrrell, J., Genin, N. and Myslinski, M. (2006). Freedom of choice and decision-making in health and social care: views of older patients with early-stage dementia and their carers. *Dementia: The International Journal of Social Research and Practice*, 5: 479–502.

Wetherell, M. (2001). Editor's introduction. In M. Wetherell, T. Stephanie and S.J. Yates (eds) *Discourse theory and practice* (pp. 1–8). London: Sage Publications, in association with the Open University.

Wetherell, M. and Potter, J. (1992). *Mapping the language of racism: discourse and the legitimation of exploitation.* New York: Columbia University Press.

Wiggins, S. and Hepburn, A. (2007). Discursive research: applications and implications. In A. Hepburn and S. Wiggins (eds) *Discursive research in practice. New approaches to psychology and interaction* (pp. 281–291). Cambridge: Cambridge University Press.

4 Video data as a method to understand non-verbal communication in couples where one person is living with dementia

Ali Reza Majlesi, Elin Nilsson and Anna Ekström

Outline

This chapter outlines the use of video recordings as a way to analyse and gain knowledge about collaborative aspects of the arrangement of tellership in storytelling by couples where one person is living with dementia. It describes how video recording can be used to explore the intricate interplay within couples in a particular context of an interview, and it also provides a brief description of conversation analytic methodology and its development regarding video analysis. In addition, the chapter discusses the significance of detailed analyses of talk and other resources in interaction including gaze, gestures, body movements, etc.

Introduction

This chapter discusses the use of video recordings as a way to analyse and gain knowledge about collaborative aspects of the arrangement of tellership in storytelling by couples where one person is living with dementia in interview situations: a theme that is continued in the next two chapters of the book. The key to this collaboration lies in the ability of people living with dementia to exploit the co-presence of his/her partner when contributing to talk-in-interaction and also to employ various resources including talk, gaze, gestures, body movements, etc. (Hydén, 2013; Majlesi and Ekström, 2016).

As frequently debated, the resources used for communication (talk, gesture, gaze, etc.) ought to be understood as mutually supportive and co-dependent systems working together when conveying meaning rather than distinctive, self-containing meaning-making systems (Goodwin, 2000; 2007; 2013). By drawing on the conversation analytic method (Sacks, 1992; Schegloff, 2007) in doing the analysis of video captured face-to-face interaction (Mondada, 2016; Goodwin, 2013), the chapter describes how video recording can be used to explore the intricate interplay within couples in a particular context of an interview. Telling a story together with a spouse is an activity that contributes to, as well as draws from, the couple's shared experiences and common ground (Hydén and Nilsson, 2015). In this chapter, we focus on storytelling where the role of the person living with dementia and his or her partner in the tellership – as a main teller or consociate – is organised. Our purpose is to show that the unique possibility of audio-visual recordings to capture both vocal and embodied conduct constitutes an important resource to study the interactive organisation of social activities involving people living with dementia. The chapter will also provide a brief description of conversation analytic methodology and its development regarding video analysis, and will also discuss some important aspects related to using video data.

Conversation analysis

Having roots in interaction studies (see Goffman, 1956; 1963; 1967; 1974; 1981) and Ethnomethodology (see Garfinkel, 1967; 2002), conversation analysis emerged as a research domain in the lectures given by Harvey Sacks in the 1960s and the 1970s (Sacks, 1992). Aiming at studying talk-in-interaction with all its details in its organisation, conversation analysis soon became a discipline in its own right with its own theory and methodology (Heritage, 1984). Conversation analysis attends to the details of unfolding interaction, to the sequentiality and temporality of the production of talk (turn-taking, opening, closing and the course of actions in between, etc.) and action formation through sequencing (see Schegloff, 2007) all by studying *naturally occurring interaction* as data.

Sacks' lectures (1992) show that his interest in talk-in-interaction was oriented – albeit not limited – to two questions: what the 'machinery' of talk-in-interaction consists of, i.e. how it works, and what people do with such a 'machinery' in the social organisation of their interactional activities. The main interest of conversation analysis is not thus conversations and language in itself but rather the organisation of social interaction. Therefore, the term conversation analysis after all seems to be a 'misnomer' (Psathas, 1995, p. 2). Nonetheless, for the purpose of studying the organisation of social order, conversations make a convenient object of study, being both a pervasive form of social action and easily accessible for detailed, repeated analysis (Watson, 1994). Moreover, talk-in-interaction is considered to be a primordial site for human sociality (Schegloff, 1986).

In its principles, conversation analysis has its roots in Garfinkel's Ethnomethodology programme (1967; 2002). Some of these methodological principles are: research on talk-in-interaction must be driven by data in order to demonstrate evidence-based practices, and the analysis must also be derived from data with no a priori theories (see also Sacks, 1984). The analyst adopts the participants' views, i.e. the analyst understands them as they understand each other. S/he does it by attending to the 'procedural consequentiality' of context, which means attending to how context is reflexively shaped and reshaped by the participants themselves (see Schegloff, 1991;[1] Duranti and Goodwin, 1992). Just as the term ethnomethodology does not refer to a specific *method* but rather a sociological approach or a programme with its interest in social order as an empirical phenomenon, and in people's practices for doing social life, conversation analysis does also designate a topic, which could be described as 'interlocutor's own conjoint and culturally methodical analysis of their conversational actions' (Watson, 1994, p. 178). According to Watson (1994) language and culture was for Sacks a toolkit for everyday business and his approach was designed to 'empirically, observationally address that foundational sociological question "How is social order possible?"' (Watson, 1994, p. 180) which shows conversation analysis' close relation to ethnomethodology.

Incorporating the analysis of embodiment in conversation analysis: a multimodal approach

Based on its principles, some of which we only touched upon in the previous section,[2] conversation analysis began to explore the mechanisms used in the organisation of talk-in-interaction, mechanisms such as turn-taking (Sacks *et al.*, 1974), the organisation of correction and repair in talk (Schegloff *et al.*, 1977), the organisation of preference at talk (Sacks and Schegloff, 1979), assessments (Pomerantz, 1984), and sequencing, projecting, positioning, among many others. And since the late 1970s and the early 1980s, research on talk-in-interaction took interest in nonverbal conduct partly owing to the observable fact that verbal conduct in interaction is almost always concomitant with nonverbal conduct (see Kendon, 1970; 1977; 1990; C. Goodwin, 1979; 1981; M.H. Goodwin, 1980; Schegloff, 1984; Goodwin and Goodwin, 1986; Heath, 1984), and partly because of the development of technology of video-recording that made it possible that such observations could be turned into workable and presentable data.

Very soon embodied actions (the combination of talk with gaze, gesture, body movements, etc.) were spotlighted as constitutive of the underlying organisation of talk-in-interaction (see C. Goodwin, 1979, 1981; M.H. Goodwin, 1980). The systematic design of talk proposed by Sacks and his colleagues actually maps onto the exchange of other semiotic resources as well. The results of the investigations on the use of non-verbal conduct in interaction have also shown the systematic orderliness in the use of embodiment in interaction, the speakership and the recipientship, the management of the engagement and disengagement in interaction, mutual understanding, meaning making, etc. (for a review see Sidnell and Stivers, 2013).

As conversation analysis has broadened its domain of analysis from talk to embodiment (see Deppermann, 2013), its area of research has also expanded to both ordinary conversations, and institutional talks (Drew and Heritage, 1992), and also to atypical conversations, that is conversations with people with communicative and cognitive impairments, or with competences unmatched with their interactional partners (e.g. Wilkinson, 2007; Peräkylä *et al.*, 2008), which, also, includes interaction with people living with dementia.

There is a growing body of research on interaction with people living with dementia particularly from a conversation analysis perspective (see e.g. Plejert *et al.*, 2015; Jones *et al.*, 2016; Peel, 2015, for a review; and also Chapter 5 in this book). The basic principles of sequential analysis of talk-in-interaction (analysing the basic turn-taking system and action formations in social interactions) and searching for regularities in practices of exchanging verbal units have lent themselves to the quest for regularities and rationalities also in the use of nonverbal conduct in interaction with people with various communicative abilities (see Goodwin, 2003). The research has shown that people living with dementia use body movements as a compensatory strategy to communicate what they mean in various types of activities, especially when some of their communicative abilities are diminished (e.g. in joint activities, Hydén, 2013; see also Majlesi and Ekström, 2016). However, our knowledge about the details of the mobilisation of different communicative resources in interaction with people living with dementia is still limited. Video analysis of communication with people living with dementia may help unravel the hidden patterns of behaviour and the ways that various communicative resources are used in interaction, something that would be inaccessible otherwise.

Using video data: prospects and consequences

Participant observation has been established as a way of conducting research in different fields and is an alternative to video recording, if video recording is not a viable option. However, using direct observation as the only method bears some difficulties. One of the shortcomings of a mere direct field observation is that the researchers' notes are, at best, a description of the reported events and not the events themselves. In other words, in direct field observation, as Mehan (1979, p. 72) once described it, there is the danger of relying on the 'anecdotal' quality of the field notes, the 'tabular or summary form' of the observation, without having retrievable and re-examinable data. Therefore, it is not easy to consider any alternative interpretations of the same data. This problem was also highlighted by Harvey Sacks (1992a, p. 28), when he called for 'building an observational study' that can use sociological data as objects of study in a way that the material and the claims can be rechecked, or tested again.

Tape-recording was the solution that Sacks and his colleagues came up with when conducting research on telephone conversations to preserve the collected data that could be checked, typed out, and repeatedly worked on (Sacks, 1992a, p. 622). Attending to both verbal and nonverbal conduct in social activities, however, requires a documentation technique that can use images as well as sounds as its research objects.

Video cameras have shown to be excellent sources for preserving data for the study of everyday social activities. Even though photo-cameras and audiotape-recorders are still part of the equipment that field researchers use,[3] video-recording is the only way to collect retrievable data when it comes to a detailed study of nonverbal behaviour.

Using video as a methodological tool, however, is not without its problems. As Mondada (2006) argues, the ways that videos are produced are usually based on biased choices, that is, they simply do not allow the researchers to transparently see the entire social field vis-à-vis the participant-observation 'out there' in the setting. That is why direct observation, and even interview data is not only complementary to video data but it is also sometimes necessary to gain inside knowledge – as participants in an activity have – to understand the activity in hand or the participants' ways of going about their business.

Moreover, the recording technique may be considered intrusive. That is, the presence of cameras in the field might be disturbing if the participants feel uncomfortable in front of the recording devices, and/or the setting does not keep its naturalness intact in their presence (the argument can also be made about the presence of any participant-observer in the field; see Labov, 1972, on 'observer's paradox' regarding unavoidable changes in the setting and the very phenomenon under study because of the presence of the observer).

There are indeed ways to minimise the intrusiveness of recording devices in the setting with smaller devices and the ways they are positioned in the setting. In short, with all their influences on the settings, cameras have nonetheless some undeniable benefits. The transcribed talk and other embodied conduct annotated with direct observations can visually bring some details before analysts that could be missed otherwise. To have the ability of re-playing the recorded events, to use slow motion, or to rewind or zoom the shots, etc. are among the advantages of video data (Luff *et al.*, 2011, p. 215; see also Mondada 2014; 2016). For such reasons, we'll simply trade off the possible influence of the camera on the field for the benefit of capturing more precise data on the tapes as the data is preserved for repeated observations and re-examinations.

Some ethical considerations

The data set out of which the material is presented here is interview data collected by researchers at the Centre for Dementia Research (CEDER) at Linköping University, Sweden. Before the process of data collection began, after receiving ethical approval from the regional ethical vetting committee, we have also received informed consents from the participants, i.e. both from people living with dementia and their partners. The co-presence of the partners/spouses to people living with dementia would also help to guarantee that all those involved have understood the purpose of the research, and the reason for video recording the interviews. For extra cautions, information providing and consent receiving were repeated at every occasion of data collection. The anonymity of the identity of the participants was guaranteed and the materials have been kept, observed and analysed only for research purposes.

Data

Our data used for this chapter consists of two excerpts out of the interview data with couples where one person is living with dementia. The interview was led by one of the authors (Elin Nilsson) together with another colleague (Lars-Christer Hydén) in two different memory clinics in Sweden. There are two cameras used to video-record the interview, one focusing on interviewers and the other on the

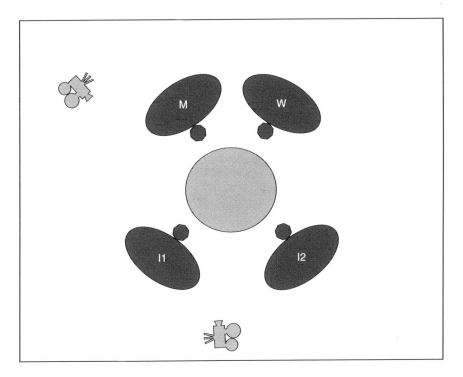

Figure 4.1 The configuration of the setting.

couples. Figure 4.1 shows the participants' configuration and the placement of the cameras in the interview setting.

The interviews were designed to be the occasions to provide interactional spaces where the couples could talk about their experiences regarding living with dementia and it occasionally is the case that they tell their biographical events in a form of narratives. These narratives or stories based on shared events and experiences are often told in a turn-taking basis and thus co-constructed by the couples together (see Hydén, 2011).

Storytelling as a co-operative action

The early systematic analyses of storytelling would base their formal and structural analysis on the contributions of the teller – and the story itself – (Labov and Waletzky, 1967; cf. Propp, 1958) and not much on the account of storytelling as a communicative event (Sacks, 1972/1992: Lecture 2; cf. Goffman, 1974, p. 503). Analysing the communicative aspects of storytelling would emphasise the interactional and collaborative interplay of interactants in talk-in-interaction (e.g. Jefferson, 1978; Goodwin and Goodwin, 1986; Lerner, 1992; Hydén, 2011). Collaboration in storytelling makes it a coherent conversational event where the story is co-constructed not just by a main teller but also by other inter-actants in the social situation. This makes storytelling an extended series of turns at talk which are 'locally occasioned' and 'sequentially built' (Jefferson, 1978, p. 219; cf. e.g. Sacks, 1972/1992, Lecture 2). Enacted as a social activity, then, storytelling may have sequential contexts of 'initiation', 'delivery' and 'recep-tion' (see Lerner, 1992) which are dialogical at all points.

It is within this dialogical (interaction and contextual) activity of telling that we can also point to co-telling (Lerner, 1992; cf. M.H. Goodwin, 1980) or the co-authorship of stories by interactants (cf. C. Goodwin, 1986). This may occur often in the joint storytelling of couples in our data set when they collaborate with each other to tell about their biographical stories as shared experienced events (Hydén, 2011) and thus displaying what may be called their 'couplehood' (Mandelbaum, 1987; Kaplan, 2001; Hellström, 2005; Hydén and Nilsson, 2015). When one of the partners (spouses) talks, the other one does not just take the role of a listener who may only contribute to the narrative by signs of apprecia-tion (see Goffman, 1974, p. 503; Sacks, 1971/1992: Fall, Lecture 1). They may adopt the role of a consociate (Schutz, 1973) to become a co-teller. However, the arrangement of tellership is a matter of interactional organisation, that is how the story begins and proceeds to its end and how telling the story is distributed by the distribution of turns at talk (cf. Lerner, 1992). Organising the roles in the telling may arise right from the initiation of the telling where we are focusing in this chapter.

Co-operation in initial story prefaces

As Lerner (1992, p. 255) shows us, the arrangement of tellership starts right from the course of the preface of storytelling where the roles of the storyteller and the consociate in the telling are interactionally organised. The story preface such as 'have you heard what happened to x?' not only signals that a story about x is going to be delivered, it also provides an interactional space for the recipi-ents to demonstrate their acknowledgement of accepting the role of recipientship (e.g. by providing a next turn in the sequence to be a go-ahead signal for the story to begin). It also gives the opportunity (or even obligation – see Lerner, 1992, p. 250) for the 'knowing recipients' to show their possible knowledge about the event.

The preface sequence could also be a place for the potential co-teller(s) of the story to enter in the telling and assist the storyteller in the course of the telling. As Lerner (1992, pp. 251–255) exemplifies, the initial assistance for storytelling may include 'story prompts', 'story provocations' (e.g. through teasing) and 'reminiscence recognition solicit'. In the two cases that we are presenting here, both story prompts and reminiscence solicitation are used as devices in the dis-tributions of the roles. The story prompts could be instantiated in multiparty talk where one party encourages another to tell a story, e.g. 'how did you two meet?' The reminiscence device would be an example such as 'do you remember how it happened?'

In the case of the interviews in our data, the prompts for storytelling stems directly from the question asked by the interviewer. There are some questions that the couples are asked which are consistent throughout the data set, across the occasions of interviewing the couples, the questions such as 'I/we would like you to tell us about how you (pl.) met each other for the first time?' or 'how did it come about that you got examined and received a diagnosis?' These questions seem to initiate a multiunit turn (or turns in co-telling) as response with the features consistent with storytelling (see Labov and Waletzky, 1967).

Let's consider the first example (Example 4.1) where the interviewer asks about the diagnosis procedure. In this example, the man is diagnosed with Alzheimer's disease four years prior to the interview and has lived with the condition possibly even a year before the diagnosis (according to the interview). With the focus of this chapter in mind, we would like to draw attention to the way the role of the teller and the consociate are organised right in the beginning of the telling.

In the transcript, we show the latching between turns with '=', smile with '&', pauses in parentheses, and emphasis with underlining (the details of the transcription conventions you can find in the Appendix to this chapter):

Example 4.1 (coup0901 (10:02–10:25))
Participants: Interviewer (I), Woman (W), Man (M)

```
1   I:  hur kom de sej att (0.2) du: då- s- (.) >blev undersökt å fick en
2   diagnos?<
3   How did it come about that (0.2) you (.)>got examined 'n received
4   a diagnosis
5   W:  ((sniffs))
6   (0.7)
7   M:  .hh ja: hur va de egen[tligen?
8   .hh yea:h how was it really?
9   W:  [.hh hh: (1) a: de va ju- börja me på en
10  [.hh hh: (1) yeah: it was [PART] began at a
11  vårdcentral (0.8) att dom kom på att han hade ett högt blodtryck,
12  a clinic(0.8)that they found out that he had a high blood pressure
13  (0.3)
14  M:  >s:å vare. ja<=
15  >that's right. yeah<=
16  W:  =a:, (0.5)
17  =yeah, (0.5)
18  W:  å så fick han en blodtrycksmedicin (1)
19  'n then he received medicine for the blood pressure (1)
20  som han blev personlighetsförändrad av
21  by which his personality changed
```

Providing assistance in the delivery of stories can range from providing signals of continuation or any forms of showing appreciation (including laughter,

Lerner, 1992, p. 259), and also entering in the course of the telling by either self-selection or receiving the floor for the entry, something that we can see in Example 4:1. The main recipient of the question (line 1 and 2) is the person living with dementia (M) who is addressed to respond the question about the past events concerning his diagnosis. But right from the story preface (after the question, line 7) when the initiation for the telling began, M asks, '.hh yea:h how was it really?'.

Now with transcription, which is quite detailed in itself, one cannot say for sure if the question was self-addressed or other-addressed. However, we can observe how M's question (line 7) is received as soliciting help from his wife. W takes the opportunity to enter into the conversation and, in fact, takes the role of the main recipient and responds to the question herself. So, right from the beginning, there is a change in the participation framework (Goffman, 1981) where the position of the wife of the person living with dementia changes from a non-recipient participant to a recipient participant who takes over the floor to tell the story.

With this brief description, there is a 'danger' that the analysis would show how a person living with dementia is being side-lined by his wife not just in terms of losing the floor of the talk to her, but also being almost a third party in the conversation as she addresses him as a third person when talking to the interviewer (pay attention to line 11 where the woman talks about his husband as 'he'). The picture seems to be consistent with the studies who insist that communicative problems with people living with dementia in talk-in-interaction would lead to their social marginalisation not just because of their incapacities, but due to 'disempowering' imposed on them in interpersonal relations (for example see Kitwood, 1990 on malignant social psychology; cf. Sabat, 1994).

However, looking at the video, incorporating images into the transcription, and annotating the details of embodiment in interaction – i.e. transcribing the event multi-modally as regards talk, gesture, gaze, body movements, handling any artefacts, etc. – would change that image. If we take a look at the first three turns and how the distribution of gaze and head movements are organised, then we would see a more complicated interaction where interactants react not just to each other's verbal contributions but also to each other's concomitant nonverbal behaviour.

Let's now consider a very sketchy model of the exchange of the participants' gaze in the beginning of the excerpt:

1   I: question
     I direct his gaze towards M
2   W: ((sniffs)) *and directs her gaze towards M*
3   M: question
     M directs his gaze down and then towards W; M and W have mutual gaze
4   W: answer
     W direct his gaze towards I
     I direct his gaze towards W

To be more exact, we have tried to align the precise moment of gaze orientations and head movements with the talk in the following transcription. We use the sign such as '*' to show the exact moment of the onset and the retraction of the non-verbal actions in relation to talk. For the interviewer we use '*', for M, we use '✧' and for W, we use '☻', and *gz* is a short form for gaze (for other conventions please see the Appendix).

Example 4.1 (coup0901 (10:02–10:25) – Multimodal version)
Participants: Interviewer (I), Woman (W), Man (M)

```
1   I:  ✧hur kom de sej att (0.2) du: då- s- (.) >blev undersökt å fick en
2   diagnos?<
      ✧ ... gz to M, tilted head (Fig.4:2)–>
```

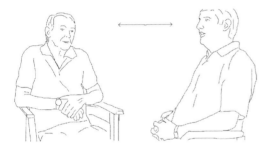

Figure 4.2 (M on the left).

```
3   How did it come about that (0.2) you (.)>got examined 'n received
4   a diagnosis
5   W:  * ☻ ((sniffs))
      ☻ ... gz to M–>
      * ... gz down–>(Fig. 4:3)
```

Figure 4.3 (W on the right).

```
6   (0.7)
```

7 M: *.hh ja: hur va de ✧ egen[tligen?
8 **.hh yea:h how was it really?**
    ->* ... *gz to* –>>*(Fig.4:4)*
    -> ✧ *gz to W*–>

Figure 4.4 (M turns towards W).

9 W: [◉.hh hh: (1) a: de va ju- börja me på en
10 **[.hh hh: (1) yeah: it was [PART] began at a**
    -> ◉ ... *gz away* –>
11 vård ◉central (0.8) att dom kom på att han hade ett högt blodtryck,
12 **a clinic(0.8) that they found out that he had a high blood pressure**
    -> ◉ ... *gz to I* –>>
13 (0.3)
14 M: >s:å vare. ja<=
15 **>that's right. yeah<=**

With the details of embodied actions manifested in the transcripts, now one can see that without doubt, the interviewer's question both verbally and bodily is directed to M. After the question and during the pause in line 6, M manifestly adopts a thinking face (Goodwin and Goodwin, 1986) with gaze averted from the interviewer down to the corner of the room (Figure 4.3). This follows the question that M poses in response to the interviewer in line 7, which is also manifestly designed as a direct request for assistance in the telling of the past event (cf. Lerner, 1992) to his wife. In the beginning of his turn in line 7, M turns his torso and head towards W and holds his gaze on W even during W's subsequent talk to I.

We can therefore restate the description of how the story preface is organised in the example above: the person living with dementia uses the question as a reminiscence soliciting device (cf. Lerner, 1992) and relies on the competence of his partner/wife to remind him of the course of events in the past. He competently manages his failure to provide the answer to I's question by passing the turn to his wife and inviting her to be the main storyteller; however, he remains a co-teller as he ratifies what is being said when confirming the wife's telling:

'>that's right. yeah<' (line 14). In this way, he also signals his own ability to recollect the story right from the beginning.

To emphasise the significance of attending to embodiment in analysing talk-in-interaction and also the importance of video data to make such an analysis possible, in what follows, we provide a second example from the same data set but with a different couple. In the example below (Example 4.2), the interviewer asks a couple about their first meeting and he specifically tells them that they are free to tell about the event in any way they want (lines 16 and 20). In this example, the woman is diagnosed with Alzheimer's disease four years prior to the interview and has lived with memory problems quite some time before the diagnosis (possibly around the past ten years according to the interview).

Example 4.2 (coup0101a (02:16–02:47))
Participants: Interviewer (I), Woman (W), Man (M)
I: den första frågan (0.3) som som jag skulle vilja be er

```
 1  the first question that that I would like to ask you(pl.)
 2  W:  mm
 3  I:  att berätta om (0.3) det är lite (.) hur ni (0.4)träffades,
 4  to tell about (0.3) it is a bit (.) how you(pl.) (0.4) met each other,
 5  I:  (1) å (0.4) när å var var[e
 6  (1)'n (0.4) when 'n where was [that
 7  M:  [ja
 8  [Yeah
 9  (0.4)
10  I:  e: å [vad som hände sen [egentligen å ni å då-
11  e: 'n[what happened then[actually and you(pl.) å then-
12  W:  [hihihihihihihihihi
13  M:  [ja
14  [yeah
15  I:  får själv välja
16  may choose yourself
17  W:  &a:&=
18  &yeah&:=
19  I:  =precis vad ni vill: (.) berätta (.)ja ä bara lite
20  =exactly what you(pl.) would like (.) to tell (.) I am just a little
21  I:  (0.9) nyfik[en på (.) på: >ja< vilka ni ä (0.5)
22  (0.9) curious about (.) abou:t >yeah< who you(pl.) are (0.5)
23  W:  [&a&
24  [&yeah&
25  W:  &aha&
26  M:  jasså,
27  aha,
28  I:  s- som par °s[å att säga°
29  s- as a couple °s[o to speak°
```

```
30   W:   [.jha[a ((inhaled affirmative))
31        |.yuh
32        [ja
33        |yeah
34   W:   a:,
35        alright:,
36        (0.7)
37   M:   he,- &ska ja(h)g bö(h)[rja(h) e(h)ll(h)er? Hihihih&=
38        &should I(h)b(h)e|gi(h)n o(h)r? Hihihih&=
39   W:   [&ja&
40        |&yeah&
41   W:   =&de ä du som [(hänga) hahahaha&
42        =&this is you who (keeps up) hahahaha&
43   M:   &jag [kommer ihåg dethehehehehe&
44        &I |remember thathehehehehe&
```

This quite long spate of talk which only encompasses the preliminary talk before the storytelling may also be reduced grossly to the following model:

First sequence
1. I: question (a multiunit turn accompanied by the continuers provided by the recipients, lines 1–29)
2. M AND W: response (showing understanding conjointly produced by the couple, lines 31–35)

Second sequence (a side sequence, see Jefferson, 1972)
1. M: question (a self-invitation to tell the story, line 38)
2. W: response (a confirmation of leaving the floor to M, lines 40–42)
3. M: an increment (a comment on his remembering the event, line 44)

After posing the question (regarding the events about the couple's meeting for the first time) which takes the interviewer a few rounds of talk in exchange to formulate it (lines 1–29), the couples do not begin with immediate response to the request to tell the story, although they respond to the question by receipt tokens such as 'mm' or 'Yeah' (e.g. lines 3, 8, 14). However, after receiving the question, they engage in what may be called a side-sequence (Jefferson, 1972) and negotiate who will tell about the event. Our focus here is on this negotiation where the couple organise the issue of the tellership. Again with only the verbal transcript at hand, albeit its detailed description, one may wonder about how the role of the husband as a main teller during the second sequence is established. In other words, one may wonder how M's self-selection (line 38) to tell the story comes about.

As it is shown in the transcript, after the interviewer is done with his question (line 30) there comes a couple of receipt-token-exchange between M and W (lines 31–34), which is followed by a pause (line 37). After the pause (line 37), M does a self-selection move to take the floor (line 38) and one may wonder whether something occasions such a self-selection before or during the pause or M's action is just as abrupt as it seems to be. To have a better understanding (seeing what participants see in interaction – '*members' view*', see Garfinkel, 1967; also Sacks, 1966/1992: Part III, Lecture 33), we rely once more on our video data and try to incorporate the participants' relevant embodied moves into the transcription. Because of the limited space in the chapter, we constrain ourselves just to the part where the couple manage the tellership after I's question, right before the pause in line 37:

Example 4.2 (coup0101a (02:16–02:47) – Multimodal version)
Participants: Interviewer (I), Woman (W), Man (M)

```
1   I:  den första frågan (0.3) som som jag skulle vilja be er
2       the first question that that I would like to ask you(pl.)
3   W:  mm
4   I:  att berätta om (0.3) det är lite (.) hur ni (0.4)träffades,
5       to tell about (0.3) it is a bit (.) how you(pl.) (0.4) met each other,
```

((some lines omitted))

```
35  W:  *a: ☻,
36      alright:,
        * ... gz to M–>
        ☻ ... gz to W –> mutual gz M,W (Fig.4:5)
37  (0.7)
```

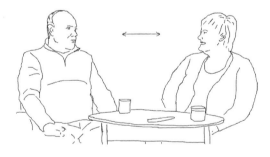

Figure 4.5 (W on the right).

```
38  M:  he,- &ska ja(h)g bö(h)*[rja(h) e(h)ll(h)er? ⊘Hihihih&=
39      &should I(h)b(h)e |gi(h)n o(h)r? Hihihih&=
        ->*,,, ... gz down ->⊘ ... gz away–>
40  W:  [&ja&
41      [&yeah&
42  W:  =&de ä du ☻som [(hänga) hahahaha&
43      =&it's you who (keeps up) hahahaha&
        ->☻,,, ... gz to W
```

44 M: &jag [kommer *ihåg dethehehehehe♡&
45 **&I |remember thathehehehe&**
    -> *,,, ... *gz to M(mutual gz)*
    ->♡,,, ... *gz to I*

As it is now manifested in the transcript, the exchange of gaze before and during
the pause (line 37) is decisive in terms of providing account as how interaction
unfolds. The exchange of gaze, in fact, together with the production of 'a:,' by
W *projects* that M and W are going to address the interviewer's question prior to
M's self-selection to tell the story (line 38). Directed to M, 'a:,' seems not to be
just the token of receipt or a continuer in relation to the prior turn but together
with the gaze and the head movement towards M, it seems that 'a:,' and the affil-
iative mutual gaze (Figure 4.5) are doing also another job. The embodied actions
produced by the person living with dementia initiate the side-sequence for negotiation and the organisation of the tellership in the continuation of the sequence.
In other words, with that gaze towards M, and receiving the returning gaze from
M, now W and M are in a preliminary phase of deciding over the main tellership
and the consociate role, which could be verbalised otherwise in a format like
'who's going to start now?' (cf. examples of preliminary sequences in Schegloff,
1980, p. 107, such as 'Tell me something', 'Listen to this', etc.).

The self-selection of M does not therefore happen as an abrupt move against
the will of the person living with dementia but in collaboration with her. In fact,
the first move in terms of engaging in a mutual agreement over what should be
done next comes from the person living with dementia as she turns towards her
husband, M, gazes at him while articulating the token of 'a:,'. The whole multimodal gestalt (Mondada, 2014) produced by W is loaded with recognisable elements signalling that there is a transition space before the upcoming activity (see
pre-beginning elements, Schegloff, 1996) where she is explicitly requesting her
husband for help and thus co-participation.

Therefore, M's suggestion to take up the role of the main teller (line 38) is
built upon a preliminary interactional engagement and his initiation for engagement is built through a carefully designed interactional move. After he receives
the signal for his co-participation from his wife, he poses a question format with
a less serious tone, combined with inserted laughter particles (an utterance combined with *within-speech-laughter*, Jefferson, 1979, p. 82). His utterance (line
38) begins with a guttural out-breath with the combination of exhalation during
the speech production and is turned into a recognisable louder laughter at the end
(*post-positioned laughter*, see Shaw *et al.*, 2013), which is also reciprocated by
W. The use of laughter in this way could be a sign of a mitigating action for a
situation projectable as non-preferred – displaying the problematic nature of
current talk – such as a trouble in interaction or something embarrassing (see
more discussion on modulating action through laughter in Shaw *et al.*, 2013; cf.
Adelswärd, 1989; Wilkinson, 2007).

Although M's action design signals the production a dis-preferred action that
is being softened through laughter, nonetheless there is no sign of treating his

proposal as dis-preferred by his interactional partner (see Pomerantz, 1984). As a matter of fact, W's rushing in and accepting the proposal in an overlap with M's utterance (line 40) is a sign of co-participation and agreement. She even provides an account for such an agreement in the next turn ('**it's you who (keeps up) hahahaha**', line 42) while she laughs along with M. The interaction at the end of this sequence evidently exhibits that both participants are aligning and affiliating with each other over the course of upcoming activity and its initiation.

Conclusion

In this chapter, we have shown the significance of using video data in analysing communication with people living with dementia. We suggest that conversation analysis and its unique methodology of approaching interactional data with its fine-grained sequential analysis would allow us to see the interplay of talk with other embodied resources such as gaze and head movements in the organisation of talk-in-interaction. The level of interpretation of data would also oscillate considering the method of observation, with or without video. We have argued that video-recording together with the detailed transcription of embodied movements would provide crucial information about participants' exchange of actions. Without attending to the complex multimodal – interactional – gestalts used in the business of interchange between the participants, the analyst may come to some unfounded results which do not do justice to the data. This could be witnessed in the analyses in this chapter in the interpretation of the competence of people living with dementia in regard to the social organisation of talk and their capability of using their partner to manage their own and their partner's roles in interaction. The contribution of the interactional partners to people living with dementia could also be misconstrued as disempowering and imposing on their partners/spouses. With or without attending to the video data, one could come to discrepant results.

Finally, by using video recordings of communication and interaction involving people living with dementia, it is possible to detect habits, routines and practices that are unnoticed by the participants involved – the 'tacit' aspects of communication. This means that it is possible to reveal both beneficial communicative strategies as well as problematic communicative patterns previously not made aware to the participants.

Highlighted learning points from the method

- Video-data enables a deeper understanding of the interactions that couples build together where one person is living with dementia.
- Video data highlights the details of the interactional competence of people living with dementia in managing the sensitive issue of role assumptions in storytelling.
- Analysing video data shows the active participation of people living with dementia in co-tellership rather than their passiveness or exclusion from interaction.

- Video data also opens up possibilities of studying other embodied conducts besides talk and understanding communicative activities as coupled to material contexts.
- A multimodal transcription of video data provides fine-grained details of interaction for further analysis.

Key references

- Mondada, L. (2006). Video recordings as the reflective preservation and configuration of phenomenal features for analysis. In H. Knoblauch, H-G. Soeffner, J. Raab and B. Schnettler (eds), *Video analysis* (pp. 51–68). Bern: Lang. *This paper discusses methodological benefits of using video recordings and the consequence of such a method in scientific analysis of a studied phenomenon.*
- Schegloff, E.A. (2007). *Sequence organization in interaction: a primer in conversation analysis*, vol. 1. Cambridge: Cambridge University Press. *This book provides a fully elaborated analysis of sequencing in talk-in-interaction.*
- Hydén, L.C. (2011). Narrative collaboration and scaffolding in dementia. *Journal of Aging Studies*, 25: 339–347. *This paper provides knowledge about ways of collaboration in the joint activity of storytelling with people with dementia and the significance of scaffolding that partners to people living with dementia may provide for them to remain as active participants in interaction.*
- Goodwin, C. (2013). The co-operative, transformative organisation of human action and knowledge. *Journal of Pragmatics*, 46: 8–23. *This paper provides knowledge about using multimodal approach to interaction analysis and how action is co-constructed and knowledge is organised in human interaction.*
- Mondada, L. (2016). Challenges of multimodality: language and body in social interaction. *Journal of Sociolinguistics*, 20(3): 336–366. *This paper gives a thorough picture on using multimodal data to analyse human interaction in various types of situations.*

Recommended future reading

- Goodwin, C. (2003). *Conversation and brain damage.* Oxford: Oxford University Press.
- Kendon, A. (2004). *Gesture: visible action as utterance.* Cambridge: Cambridge University Press
- Streeck, J., Goodwin, C. and LeBaron, C. (2011). *Embodied interaction: language and body in the material world.* Cambridge, MA: Cambridge University Press
- Heath, C., Hindmarsh, J. and Luff, P. (2010). *Video in qualitative research.* London: Sage Publications
- Sidnell, J. and Stivers, T. (2013). *Conversation analysis.* Malden, MA: Wiley-Blackwell

Appendix transcription symbols

Symbols	Explanation
[	Left square bracket: a point of overlap onset
=	Equal signs: (1) two lines are connected (2) one turn is latched by another
(0.5)	Numbers in parentheses: silence, represented in tenths of a second
(.)	A dot in parentheses: a micro-pause (usually less than 0.2 seconds)
.	Period: falling intonation
?	Question mark: rising intonation of the whole syllable
,	Comma: a little rise in the intonation of the terminal sound(s)
::	Colons: prolongation or stretching of the sound
-	Hyphen: after a word or part of a word indicates a cut-off or self-interruption
Word	Underlining: stress or emphasis by increased loudness or higher pitch
WOR	All capital letters: much louder than the surrounding words
° °	Degree signs: the word is markedly quiet or soft
> <	More than, less than: with a jump-start, said in rush quickly
< >	Less than, more than: is markedly slowed or drawn out
Hhh	Out-breath: (1) laughter in voice, (2) in parentheses (h) indicates guttural outbreath within speech productions
.hhh	In-breath
(())	Double parentheses: transcriber's comments
(word)	Utterance in parentheses: transcription is not certain
(x)	Something is being said, but no hearing can be achieved (the number of syllables is indicated by the number of x)
...	Described gesture's preparation
–	Gesture's preparation apex is reached and maintained
,,,,	Gesture's retraction
* *	Asterisks and similar symbols (⊚ or ✧) indicate the position of an embodied action – with the beginning and the end – within a turn at talk
->	Embodied action described continues across subsequent lines
->*	The embodied action continued from the previous lines ends here
->>	Embodied action described continues until and after excerpt's end
>>	The action described begins before the excerpt's beginning

Notes

1 As Schegloff puts it: '*what is the mechanism by which the context-so-understood has determinate consequences for the talk*' (Schegloff, 1991: 53, emphasis in the original).
2 The list presented here is just a sketch of some CA principles. For further information, please see Heritage, 1984; Sidnell and Stivers, 2013, among others.
3 To review the history of using videos in social research, please see Erickson, 2011.

References

Adelswärd, V. (1989). Laughter in dialogue: the social significance of laughter in institutional discourse. *Nordic Journal of Linguistics*, 12: 107–136.
Deppermann, A. (2013). Turn-design at turn-beginnings: multimodal resources to deal with tasks of turn-construction in German. *Journal of Pragmatics*, 46: 91–121.
Drew, P. and Heritage, J. (1992). *Talk at work – interaction in institutional settings*. Cambridge: Cambridge University Press.

Duranti A. and Goodwin, C. (1992), *Rethinking context.* Cambridge: Cambridge University Press.

Garfinkel, H. (1967). *Studies in ethnomethodology.* New Jersey: Prentice Hall Inc.

Garfinkel, H. (2002). *Ethnomethodology's program: working out Durkheim's aphorism.* Lanham, Maryland: Rowman and Littlefield Publishers.

Goffman, E. (1956). *Presentation of self in everyday life.* Edinburgh: University of Edinburgh.

Goffman, E. (1963). *Behavior in public places.* New York: Free Press.

Goffman, E. (1967). *Interaction ritual: essays in face-to-face behavior.* Philadelphia: University of Pennsylvania Press.

Goffman, E. (1974). *Frame analysis.* New York: Harper and Row.

Goffman, E. (1981). *Forms of talk.* Philadelphia: University of Pennsylvania Press.

Goodwin, C. (1979). The interactive construction of a sentence in natural conversation. In G. Psathas (ed.), *Everyday language: studies in ethnomethodology* (pp. 97–121). New York: Irvington Publishers.

Goodwin, C. (1981). *Conversational organization – interaction between speakers and hearers.* New York: Academic Press.

Goodwin, C. (1986). Audience diversity, participation and interpretation. *Text*, 6: 283–316.

Goodwin, C. (2000). Action and embodiment within situated human interaction. *Journal of Pragmatics*, 32: 1489–1522.

Goodwin, C. (2003). *Conversation and brain damage.* Oxford: Oxford University Press.

Goodwin, C. (2007). Environmentally coupled gesture. In S.D. Duncan, J. Cassell and E.T. Levy (eds), *Gesture and the dynamic dimension of language* (pp. 195–212). Amsterdam: John Benjamins.

Goodwin, C. (2013). The co-operative, transformative organization of human action and knowledge. *Journal of Pragmatics*, 46: 8–23.

Goodwin, C. and Goodwin, M.H. (1986). Gesture and coparticipation in the activity of searching for a word. *Semiotica*, 62: 51–75.

Goodwin, M.H. (1980). Processes of mutual monitoring implicated in the production of description sequences. *Sociological Inquiry*, 50: 303–317.

Heath, C. (1984). Talk and recipiency: sequential organization in speech and body movement. In M. Atkinson and J. Heritage (eds), *Structures of social action – studies in conversation analysis* (pp. 247–265). Cambridge: Cambridge University Press.

Hellström, I. (2005). Exploring 'couplehood' in dementia: a constructivist grounded theory study. Dissertation, Linköping University.

Heritage, J. (1984). *Garfinkel and ethnomethodology.* Cambridge: Polity Press.

Hydén, L.C. (2011). Narrative collaboration and scaffolding in dementia. *Journal of Aging Studies*, 25: 339–347.

Hydén, L.C. (2013). Storytelling in dementia: embodiment as a resource. *Dementia: The International Journal of Social Research and Practice*, 12, 359–367.

Hydén, L.C. and Nilsson, E. (2015). Couples with dementia: positioning the 'we'. *Dementia: The International Journal of Social Research and Practice*, 14: 716–733.

Jefferson, G. (1972). Side sequences. In D. Sundow (ed.), *Studies in social interaction* (pp. 294–451). New York: The Free Press.

Jefferson, G. (1978). Sequential aspects of storytelling in conversation. In J. Schenkein (ed.), *Studies in the organization of conversational interaction* (pp. 219–248). New York: Academic Press.

Jefferson, G. (1979). A technique for inviting laughter and its subsequent acceptance declination. In G. Psathas (ed.), *Everyday language: studies in ethnomethodology* (pp. 79–96). New York: Irvington Publishers.

Jones, D., Drew, P. Elsey, C., Blackburn, D., Wakefield, S., Harkness, K. and Reuber, M. (2016). Conversational assessment in memory clinic encounters: interactional profiling for differentiating dementia from functional memory disorders. *Aging and Mental Health*, 20: 500–509.

Kaplan, L. (2001). A couplehood typology for spouses of institutionalized persons with Alzheimer's disease: perceptions of 'We'–'I'. *Family Relations*, 50: 87–98.

Kendon, A. (1970). Movement coordination in social interaction: some examples described. *Acta Psychologica*, 32: 100–125.

Kendon, A. (1977). *Studies in the behavior of social interaction*. Bloomington: Indiana University Press.

Kendon, A. (1990). *Conducting interaction – patterns of behavior in focused encounters*. Cambridge: Cambridge University Press.

Kitwood, T. (1990). The dialects of dementia: with particular reference to Alzheimer's disease. *Ageing and Society*, 10: 177–196.

Labov, W. (1972). Some principles in linguistic methodology. *Language in Society*, 1(1): 97–120.

Labov, W. and Waletzky, J. (1967). Narrative analysis: oral versions of personal experience. *Journal of Narrative and Life History*, 7: 3–38.

Lerner, G.H. (1992). Assisted storytelling: deploying shared knowledge as a practical matter. *Qualitative Sociology*, 15: 247–271.

Luff, P., Heath, C. and Pitsch, K. (2011). Indefinite precision: the use of artefacts-in-interaction in design word. In C. Jewitt (ed.), *The Routledge handbook of multimodal analysis*, (pp. 213–222). London: Routledge.

Majlesi, A R. and Ekström, A. (2016). Baking together: the coordination of actions in activities involving people living with dementia. *Journal of Aging Studies*, 38: 37–46.

Mandelbaum, J. (1987). Couples sharing stories. *Communication Quarterly*, 35: 144–170.

Mehan, H. (1979). *Learning lessons: social organization in the classroom*. Cambridge: Cambridge University Press.

Mondada, L. (2006). Video recordings as the reflective preservation and configuration of phenomenal features for analysis. In H. Knoblauch, H-G. Soeffner, J. Raab and B. Schnettler (eds), *Video analysis* (pp. 51–68). Bern: Lang.

Mondada, L. (2014). The local constitution of multimodal resources for social interaction. *Journal of Pragmatics*, 65: 137–156.

Mondada, L. (2016). Challenges of multimodality: language and body in social interaction. *Journal of Sociolinguistics*, 20: 336–366.

Peel, E. (2015). Diagnostic communication in the memory clinic: a conversation analytic perspective. *Aging and Mental Health*, 19: 1123–1130.

Peräkylä, A., Antaki, C., Vehviläinen, S. and Leudar, I. (2008). *Conversation analysis and psychotherapy*. Cambridge: Cambridge University Press.

Plejert, L., Antelius, E., Yazdanpanah, M. and Nielsen, T.R. (2015). 'There is a letter called ef' on challenges and repair in interpreter-mediated tests of cognitive functioning in dementia evaluations: a case study. *Journal of Cross Cultural Gerontology*, 30: 163–187.

Pomerantz, A. (1984). Agreeing and disagreeing with assessments: some features of preferred/dispreferred turn shapes. In J.M. Atkinson and J. Heritage (eds), *Structures of social action* (pp. 57–101). Cambridge: Cambridge University Press.

Propp, V. (1958). *Morphology of folktale*. Bloomington: American Folklore Society.

Psathas, G. (1995). *Conversation analysis: the study of talk-in-interaction*. Thousand Oaks, CA: Sage Publications.

Sabat, S.R. (1994). Excess disability and malignant social psychology: a case study of Alzheimer's disease. *Journal of Community and Applied Social Psychology*, 4: 157–166.

Sacks, H. (1984). Notes on methodology. In M.J. Atkinson and J. Heritage (eds), *Structures of social action: studies in conversation analysis* (pp. 21–27). Cambridge: Cambridge University Press.

Sacks, H. (1992, 1966, 1971, 1972). *Lectures on conversation*, vol. 1 and 2. Oxford: Blackwell.

Sacks, H. and Schegloff, E.A. (1979). Two preferences in the organization of reference to persons in conversation and their interaction. In G. Psathas (ed.), *Everyday language: studies in ethnomethodology* (pp. 15–21). New York: Irvington Publishers.

Sacks, H., Schegloff, E.A. and Jefferson, G. (1974). A simplest systematics for the organization of turn taking for conversation. *Language*, 50: 696–735.

Schegloff, E.A. (1980). Preliminaries to preliminaries: 'can I ask you a question'. *Sociological Inquiries*, 50: 104–152.

Schegloff, E.A. (1984). On some gestures' relation to talk. In J.M. Atkinson and J. Heritage (eds), *Structures of social action. Studies in conversation analysis* (pp. 266–296). Cambridge: Cambridge University Press.

Schegloff, E.A. (1986). The routine as achievement. *Human Studies*, 9(2/3): 111–151.

Schegloff, E.A. (1991). Reflections on talk and social structure. In D. Boden and D. Zimmerman (eds), *Talk and social structure* (pp. 44–70). Cambridge: Polity Press.

Schegloff, E.A. (1996). Turn organization: one intersection of grammar and interaction. In E. Ochs, E.A. Schegloff and S. Thompson (eds), *Interaction and grammar* (pp. 52–133). Cambridge: Cambridge University Press.

Schegloff, E.A. (2007). *Sequence organization in interaction: a primer in conversation analysis*, vol. 1. Cambridge: Cambridge University Press.

Schegloff, E.A., Jefferson, G. and Sacks, H. (1977). The preference for self-correction in the organization of repair in conversation. *Language*, 53: 361–382.

Schutz, A. (1973). *Collected papers vol. 1. The problem of social reality*. The Hague: Martinus Nijhoff.

Shaw, C., Hepburn, A. and Potter, J. (2013). Having the last laugh: on post-completion laughter particles. In E. Holt and P.J. Glenn (eds), *Studies of laughter in interaction* (pp. 91–106). London: Bloomsbury Academic.

Sidnell, J. and Stivers, T. (2013). *Conversation analysis*. Malden, MA: Wiley-Blackwell.

Watson, R. (1994). Harvey Sacks's sociology of mind in action. *Theory, Culture and Society*, 11: 169–186.

Wilkinson, R. (2007). Managing linguistic incompetence as a delicate issue in aphasic talk-in-interaction: on the use of laughter in prolonged repair sequences. *Journal of Pragmatics*, 39: 542–569.

5 Video data and biographical music as a method to record and explore interaction in semantic dementia

Jackie Kindell and Ray Wilkinson

Outline

This chapter describes details from a study where a novel combination of conversation analysis and narrative analysis was used to explore everyday interaction in a study into semantic dementia and plan individualised intervention. The chapter will first outline the features of semantic dementia and this will be followed by a description of conversation analysis and of narrative analysis including the reasons for them being combined in this research. Results from the study will be presented and the case made for the strengths of this combination of methods – which we term here 'interaction-focused life story work' – within dementia assessment and intervention.

Introduction

Semantic dementia is a rarer dementia that presents the individual concerned and their family members with particular challenges in communication. In terms of classification the condition may be referred to as one of the subtypes of fronto-temporal dementia (Neary *et al.*, 1998) or particularly within the North American and Australian literature, as the semantic variant of primary progressive aphasia (Gorno-Tempini *et al.*, 2011). Frontotemporal dementia is thought to account for between 5–10 per cent of all cases of dementia (Alzheimer's Disease International, 2009), however, the condition is more common in those presenting with a younger onset dementia (Onyike and Diehl-Schmid, 2013).

Semantic dementia presents with a different pattern of cognitive change to more common dementias such as Alzheimer's disease. For example, initial challenges are not with memory but with language, involving both expression and understanding, and although episodic memory does become impaired with time, recent memory is preserved in the early stages with difficulties described in long term memory as the condition progresses (Hodges and Patterson, 2007). Whilst the cognitive deficits displayed within test situations have been well documented (Gorno-Tempini *et al.*, 2011; Hodges and Patterson, 2007), very little research has been directed at how semantic dementia affects everyday interaction in the home or how therapeutic strategies might support such needs in a real world setting. For example, to our knowledge there is currently only one study examining everyday conversation in this condition (Kindell *et al.*, 2013).

In terms of intervention, much of the research has focused on the language disorder, with a number of studies examining the potential of word relearning strategies to enhance word retrieval (Jokel *et al.*, 2014). More broadly, there is little or no guidance in the literature explaining how, or if, therapies currently used across the general field of dementia care can be applied to semantic dementia. The coupling of communication difficulties and long term memory change, for example, means that popular approaches such as reminiscence and life story work may need to be adapted in this condition (Frontotemporal Dementia Toolkit, 2014; Kindell *et al.*, 2014a). In terms of the latter, life story work has been described as 'an approach to working with a person and/or their family to find out about their life, recording that information in some way and then using the information with the person in their care' (McKeown *et al.*, 2015, p. 239). One common way to deliver this in practice is to make a life story book of the person living with dementia's life and use this to facilitate interaction (Kindell *et al.*, 2014b). There is currently no research examining this in semantic dementia. In addition, whilst there appear to be many positive attributes to life story work, research approaches so far have found exploring the in-the-moment effects, including those with respect to communication, challenging (Gridley *et al.*, 2016; Subramaniamay *et al.*, 2014). Moreover, whilst the wider literature exploring conversational storytelling in dementia has direct relevance to life story work (Davis and Maclagan, 2014; Hamilton, 2008; Hydén, 2013; Hydén and Orulv, 2009) further work is required in using this knowledge to shape effective clinical practice in this area. The focus of this study (the first author's PhD study) was everyday interaction in semantic dementia and how this could be facilitated through life story work.

Study methods and rationale

The study focused on five families living with semantic dementia, with Jackie visiting them at home over a period ranging from seven to 18 months. The study had the following aims:

i   To gain in-depth insight into each family's everyday experiences at home around interaction.
ii To use this knowledge to plan and deliver an individually tailored intervention to enhance interaction in the home situation drawing from previous research into life story work in dementia (McKeown *et al.*, 2015) and interaction-focused therapy in aphasia (Wilkinson, 2010).
iii To explore the effects of the intervention on interaction and participation.

To meet these aims, a case study design (Yin, 2009) was chosen using a mixed methods approach combining conversation analysis and narrative analysis. As far as we are aware, these methods have not been used together previously in a design of this nature. Conversation analysis was chosen to directly observe and analyse interaction at home in each family, with narrative analysis used alongside to understand the broader family context in which such interactions took place, including the changes in their lives that semantic dementia had brought.

As also shared in the preceding chapter, conversation analysis is a naturalistic observation-based, qualitative research method described as 'a systematic procedure for the analysis of recorded, naturally occurring talk produced in everyday human interaction' (Beeke *et al.*, 2007, p. 137). The method is underpinned by a clear theoretical model, described as the 'cumulative science of conversation' (Silverman, 1998, p. 41) and this allows not just the exploration of conversation, but the description of recurring practices and behaviours evident within such conversations (Sidnell, 2010). In common with other qualitative methods, conversation analysis begins with the data and is not constrained by a pre-existing theory; accordingly, anything within the data is potentially of interest (Sidnell, 2010). This is particularly important for an area where little is known about everyday communication, such as semantic dementia.

Conversation analysis examines the part that all parties play in creating meaningful and coherent conversation within a given communicative context (Schegloff, 2003) and, therefore, offers an ideal way to explore the natural communicative behaviours of both the person with semantic dementia and their family members (Perkins *et al.*, 1998). In addition, in contrast to many quantitative approaches used to study language in dementia, the focus is not necessarily solely on communication breakdown but also highlights communicative success (Kindell *et al.*, 2013). Potential patterns in the data may uncover either, or both, of these phenomena (Perkins *et al.*, 1998). This is important for an intervention study because the behaviour of others in conversation may be crucial in scaffolding the conversation abilities of the person living with dementia (Kindell *et al.*, 2016a), or indeed in making conversation more problematic or difficult for the person living with dementia. Conversation analysis has been used successfully to drive interaction-focused therapies in a number of fields, including aphasia post stroke (Lock *et al.*, 2001; Simmons-Mackie *et al.*, 2014). Therapy of this nature can deliver individually targeted intervention that takes account of individual need in real life settings and current helpful and unhelpful conversational strategies, as well as examining outcomes for both parties (Simmons-Mackie *et al.*, 2014; Wilkinson, 2010). This is in contrast to current communication intervention approaches in the literature for semantic dementia which often target only the person living with dementia (Taylor *et al.*, 2009). Conversation analysis has also been used to explore training in using a life story resource (Spilkin and Bethlehem, 2003) and the use of a tablet computer for life story work (Ekström *et al.*, 2015).

As discussed previously, narrative analysis was used alongside conversation analysis. Williams and Keady (2008) advise that 'narrative research and analysis is about asking for people's stories, listening and making sense of them and establishing how individual stories are part of a wider "storied" narrative of people's lives' (p. 331). In this way, narrative research can be used to make sense of the interrelationship between identity, self and the social world (Williams and Keady, 2008). Narrative inquiry 'is grounded in the study of the particular' (Radley and Chamberlain, 2001, p. 331) and, therefore, enables exploration of in-depth experiences within case study research (Yin, 2009). This is important in an intervention study, such as this, where the aim is to focus on individual experiences within the context of couple and family relationships and tailor intervention to this individual need. Narrative analysis began in the assessment phase and continued into the intervention stage as part of individualised life story work. There were three related reasons why we chose to combine narrative analysis with conversation analysis:

To provide an understanding of the lived experience of each couple to support the conversation analysis

When conversation analysis has been mixed with other approaches, ethnography is most often the methodology of choice, as evident in the work of the Social Relations in Frontotemporal Dementia Group (Mates *et al.*, 2010). The rationale for this is generally to enhance the conversation analysis, particularly in less familiar settings where a more in-depth understanding of various activities may be needed. Torrisi (2010) justifies the use of ethnography combined with conversation analysis, saying 'through immersion in patients' daily activities and observing them in a variety of contexts one develops a more accurate sense of which behaviours and traits are characteristic or salient' (p. 27). We also felt an understanding of the lives of each couple would help us to understand why certain conversation features evident in the data might be significant in their lives. However, the following reasons outline why, for our study, we chose narrative analysis.

To ensure that psychosocial factors were appropriately considered in therapy

Traditionally, conversation analytic approaches avoid interpretations of speaker's private psychological states and intentions, preferring to focus on descriptions of talk and other forms of social conduct and how others respond to that talk/conduct (Smith, 2010). However, interventions aiming to change conversation practices provide additional challenges that may require engaging with psychological or psychosocial issues and, for this reason, in aphasia practice psychosocial aspects, in particular, are often addressed within interaction-focused therapy (Lock *et al.*, 2001). A narrative approach was, therefore, used to understand the broader psychosocial aspect of living with this condition for the person with semantic dementia and their spouse. Narrative methods can enable people living with dementia to convey their own experiences of living with dementia (Keady *et al.*, 2007; Surr, 2006) and help understand relationship and family contexts (Roach *et al.*, 2014). Understanding these psychosocial issues embeds intervention into a context that takes account of relationship issues, past and present, and the broader day-to-day issues of living with semantic dementia.

To explore how personally related interests might influence interaction

Lastly, the literature describes a number of features in the conversation of people with semantic dementia where individual biography may be of relevance. For example, people with semantic dementia have a tendency to have particular personally related topics that they like to talk about, described as thematic perseverations (Kertesz *et al.*, 2010). In addition, personally relevant vocabulary may be maintained longer into the condition than other vocabulary items (Julien *et al.*, 2010; Snowden, 2015). We, therefore, needed a flexible way to capture and explore issues of personal relevance and topic choice within conversation; for example, why the topics an individual with semantic dementia chose to talk about might be important in their lives. Given that such areas are highly unique to each individual and their life story, only narrative analysis delivered a method adequate for this task.

Ethical challenges

The study required two levels of approval, as is practice with research carried out in the National Health Service in England and Wales. The first level of approval was from a National Health Service Registered Ethics Committee designated to consider studies where participants may lack capacity to consent for themselves. The committee, therefore, had full understanding of the relevant legislature, including the Mental Capacity Act (2005) and the research application was required to comply with this in terms of seeking understanding and consent from people living with dementia and their family members. The study also required research governance approval from each National Health Service local organisation from where participants would be recruited. The relative rarity of semantic dementia meant that for this study this consisted of approval from a further four area committees. The study, therefore, presented a number of bureaucratic challenges.

All the ethical issues were outlined in a 46-page ethical application. As well as challenges with consent, another area that required particular attention was the use of video to collect data. For example, because video data can mean that study participants are identifiable, the committee required particular assurances in terms of how the video data would be transferred and stored both in the short and long term. Participants were required to consent in writing whether they allowed for their videos to be used once the research had been completed for: (i) further research studies; (ii) for dissemination of the study outcomes; and (iii) for teaching health and social care staff in training. Another area that the committee requested clarification about was the potential for video to document instances of potential abuse and that the research participant information sheets should reflect the process of events should this occur, including procedures for the protection of vulnerable adults. This, therefore, required careful wording on the information sheets to both outline the process whilst not appearing to alarm potential participants. Ethics and the use of video are also outlined in Chapters 6 and 9 of this book.

Data collection

It was the original intention that video recordings of conversation should be made at home with researchers not present when the recordings took place. However, two of the five couples were reluctant to record on their own, reporting that they felt awkward, necessitating flexibility in approach. Therefore, three couples engaged in their own recording using a small camcorder placed on a tripod in a position where participants identified conversation would take place, e.g. at the kitchen table or sitting on the sofa. Participants were free to record whenever they felt comfortable and could choose any topic of conversation they wished. Participants were given practice time and advice on using the camcorder. At the next visit we discussed how recording had proceeded and gave any necessary advice on camera use. This process was repeated twice more aiming for approximately 60 minutes of conversation. For the two couples reluctant to use the camera themselves, the video camera was taken along later, at a mutually convenient session, to record conversation with the couple and Jackie together. In these instances, narrative interviews were used as a start to prompt conversation with the conversation evolving freely as participants dictated.

In terms of the narrative analysis, semi-structured narrative interviews were carried out to explore the participants' lives both before and now living with semantic dementia. All interviews were audio-recorded. Whilst a brief outline of questions had been prepared in order to structure the interviews, in practice it was most helpful to ask participants to talk about their lives and follow their lead. Interviews were carried out with each couple together in all cases. Additional interviews took place with the carer separately in four cases and the person living with dementia on their own in a further two. For the remaining three people living with dementia, the person themselves either requested their spouse to be present or their communication difficulties meant that support from the spouse to facilitate interaction was helpful.

Following intervention, where possible, participants were video recorded engaging in life story work and using life story resources. This was analysed using conversation analysis and provided a method to analyse the 'in-the-moment' effects of life story on interaction. The patterns evident in interaction with and without the life story resource could be compared. This was not to ascertain which was best but to explore how the life story resource influenced interaction, including offering alternative choices to support conversation.

Insights and challenges: data analysis

In common with all studies involving mixed methods, the stage of data analysis presented both insights and challenges. Examination of the different data strands provided a holistic and in-depth insight into the experiences of the participants concerned and this in turn enabled intervention to be tailored to individual need. During the planning stages of this project, we had consulted a group of speech and language therapists who specialised in working with people living with dementia. One of their concerns was the need to understand the 'backstory' of people's lives when planning communication interventions in dementia. They felt this was a requirement in dementia care because of the progressive impact of the condition, including the differences in how individuals adapted to the changes dementia brought to their lives and the effects of this on their relationships. We felt that the mixed methods approach met this aim: it enabled us to explore different aspects of interaction, including the strengths and challenges within it for the person with semantic dementia and their carer, as well develop an understanding of the broader 'backstory' of how such issues played out in the participants lives.

The project, however, required a considerable degree of organisation to manage and analyse the amount and variety of data gathered. Both narrative analysis and conversation analysis are time consuming methods and, with a time limited reporting deadline, there is always the danger that inadequate time is given to either method. In addition, time was also required in this study to deliver and analyse the interventions offered. For this reason, it was only possible to work with five families.

Analysis began with appropriate transcription of the data. For the narrative interviews all the audio data was transcribed in full using a professional transcription service. Transcription of the video data was more challenging because conversation analysis transcription is a highly specialised and time consuming approach. Therefore, whilst all the video data was viewed on a number of occasions only certain sections of video were chosen for in-depth conversation analytic transcription. Particular sections were chosen where:

- Participants appeared natural in their interactions. Sections were excluded where participants appeared self-conscious or particularly aware of the presence of the camera.
- A range of conversational issues were displayed.
- Issues raised by the person with semantic dementia or the family carer during narrative interviews were displayed, therefore triangulating the data.

Transcription of data used an agreed system of transcription for conversation analysis (Jefferson, 2005). Where necessary, transcription of nonverbal behaviours, such as eye gaze and gesture also took place. Repeated viewings of data were required therefore to achieve this level of detail (Beeke *et al.*, 2007). In the earlier stages of the research the first author carried out all stages of the conversation analysis transcription. However, in the later stages the audio files were lifted from the identified extracts of the video and sent to a professional transcribing service with a request for a verbatim transcription. This was then taken by the first author and further developed into a conversation analysis transcription, thus saving time within the process.

NVivo was used as a tool to help analyse and manage the different data strands in a methodical and structured manner. Transcripts of conversation data were analysed via NVivo 10 for recurring and striking conversation features using initial broad descriptive codes. Video and audio data were played alongside transcripts to ensure data was viewed accurately. Conversation practices from these descriptions were then examined further outside of NVivo using the procedures of conversation analysis. This study followed the stages described by Hutchby and Wooffitt (2008) to study recurring patterns and practices in the data:

1   Highlight and then make a collection of examples of a particular practice within the data.
2   Analyse and describe one particular occurrence in detail.
3   Return to the data to see if other instances of the practice can be analysed and described in this way.

In addition, extracts of video from each couple were viewed jointly by the research team and discussed to further explore and refine this analysis.

Transcripts of interviews and field notes were read and analysed on a case by case basis initially and were analysed alongside the conversation data to provide a within case analysis. This process began by repeated reading of the transcripts, listening to the recorded interviews and viewing any visual data presented as part of the process, such as the viewing of photographs, objects, paintings etc. that illustrated the participant's life story (Keady *et al.*, 2009). Analysis was further guided by the approach suggested by Reissman (2008) where narratives were broken down into stories to create a sense of the whole. Transcripts were explored line by line and given a code that referred to a particular sequence within the text. Sequences chosen referred to a significant story, incident, or issue. Sections of interviews were also read separately by researchers and codes were compared and discussed.

At a later stage, once analysis of all cases had been completed narrative codes were compared and grouped in a hierarchical manner (Charmaz, 2006) to uncover recurring themes across the data set as described. As before, coding and emergent themes were discussed and explored. Likewise conversation practices across case studies were compared and examined to uncover recurring practices and issues with interaction. These conversation issues were charted in table format. This method is that advised by Yin (2009) to display the data from the individual cases 'according to some uniform framework' (p. 156) as is advised in cross-case synthesis in case study work

As far as we are aware, using NVivo 10 as the first part of the process is not a common practice in research using conversation analysis. However, given the amount and mix of data sources, this was an efficient practice to manage the large data set. In addition, having all the evidence in one place helped maintain one of Yin's (2009) principles in collecting case study research: maintain a chain of evidence. This principle is to allow clear cross referencing of evidence within the case study and into the case study report. Therefore, whilst descriptive conversation codes were kept separate from thematic narrative codes, comparison across codes could easily be made to explore recurring themes and linkages in the different strands of data efficiently triangulate data sources at an in-depth level for both individual and cross-case analysis.

Insights gained from interaction-focused life story work

The mixed methods analysis allowed for an in-depth description of the observed abilities of the person with semantic dementia, the challenges they and their spouse faced, and the level of scaffolding provided by the spouse. In addition, how such moments influenced, or were influenced by, their broader everyday lives, was uncovered. This information was of direct use in planning intervention because in each case, different issues with conversation were described and therapy, therefore, needed to be tailored appropriately and individually. This related both to the different issues with conversation presented and how family members managed these issues.

In terms of challenges with conversation, three carers reported that a lack of conversation was the issue of most concern to them, whereas one carer, Brian, reported that his wife, Ruby, talked at length and would not relinquish the conversational floor, thus presenting the opposite challenge. Other issues observed were a reduced repertoire of topics of conversation and repetitive questions, most often about the routine of the day.

With regard to adaptation to these changing abilities in conversation, there were differences in the data. In some instances, family members appeared to have adapted well and had developed their own strategies to manage the difficulties presented. For example, Reg not only tolerated Sarah's repetitive topics of conversation, he was observed in the video data to actively encourage them. In the narrative interviews he described his motivations for this, saying that Sarah did not initiate conversation herself and so he used certain triggers that he knew well to encourage her to talk; moreover, he reported 'I think if I don't give her those, what has she got? Because she won't come up with something herself.' As Reg had heard these stories many times, these particular conversations were not about information transfer but about encouraging interaction and being together in the moment. In contrast, however, some carers were struggling to adapt to changing need and engaging in practices within conversation that caused observable frustration for the person with semantic dementia and themselves, thus requiring support and advice. The mixed methods approach, therefore, provided an understanding of how each couple were adapting to changes in interaction and this in turn was placed in the context of broader adaptation to life with semantic dementia. It was the role of intervention to foster further adaptation where possible. In all cases life story work was delivered but tailored in approach and format to individual need. Life story formats included a small portable life story pocket book, life story topic books, a music DVD, a sheet summarising ways to 'make connections' and in one case the individual concerned, Ken, completed his own life story work on his computer.

Peter found his portable life story pocket book useful to take out with him and was able to read words aloud that he often struggled to find in open conversation. He would spontaneously show visitors to the house and others at day care his book, pointing to the pictures, such as his favourite football team, and read out the words 'Manchester United!' As a result he found the books engaging and helpful. The following example is taken from the video data and illustrates Peter showing one of his books to Jackie, in this instance pointing to where he was born on a map.

Picture 5.1 I was born here. Joanna, Peter and Jackie.

Some participants already had life story books made earlier in their dementia. However, whilst these were reported as helpful at that stage, in some instances the books were observed currently to offer little as a tool to facilitate interaction. Sarah, for example, did not recognise many of the photos in her book and even with prompting could not recall many of the associated long term memories (see Extract 1).

Extract 1 – parties at our house

Here Sarah is looking at her life story book with Jackie and her responses are minimal or quiet in volume.

001   J: *((Turns page))* ↑oh look at this lot *((pointing*
002   *at page))*

003 S: °parties° *((reading this))* ↑oh (1.0)
004 J: yeah
005 S: m
006 J: So parties with the girls
007   S: m
008   (4.0)
009 J: These look quite good
010 S: °ye-°
011   (2.0)
012 J: All dressed up you look like you're all dressed
013   there
014 S: mm
015 J: Did you get all dressed up for when you went to
016   parties
017 S: Oh yeah *((turns to Reg))* °I did didn't I°
018   *((looks back down at page))*
019 R: mm

Sarah reads the word 'parties' (003) and looks at the photos, but neither these stimuli nor Jackie's attempts encourage her to talk about these events. For example, 'so parties with the girls' (006) and 'these look good' (009) are both met with minimal acknowledgements, e.g. 'm' (007); 'ye-' (010) with considerable pauses in the conversation (008 and 011). When asked about getting dressed up for parties (015–016), despite the pictures clearly indicating this is the case, Sarah appears unsure and has to ask Reg: 'I did didn't I' (017). Therefore, in this instance despite the pictures, written cues and Jackie's attempts e.g. 'you look like you're all dressed there' (012) this does not cue any memories, or any conversation, from Sarah.

The same was true for Doug, who became agitated when required to sit and look through his book. This indicated that whilst the books had been helpful earlier on as a tool to encourage interaction a different format and approach within interaction-focused life story work was now required.

Narrative interviews indicated that music and singing had been a very important part of Sarah's identity with her often saying 'I've always been a singer'. A life story music DVD was co-produced with her and her family and Sarah was video recorded making and watching this resource. This revealed strikingly different abilities, illustrating that the DVD was a resource for encouraging verbal, emotional and embodied connections that reinforced Sarah's longstanding identity as a singer and performer (Kindell *et al.*, 2016b). Sarah, for example, initiated interaction by commenting on the lyrics of the song or by making jokes. She also used eye contact and touch to interact with her family and played on the responses of those around her ('the audience'). Whereas in conversation she often took a more passive role, she was centre stage when using the life story music resource. The following extracts illustrate how Sarah used the lyrics as a resource to interaction with Harriet and made up her own lyrics whilst singing.

Extract 2 – interaction arising from lyrics

Here Harriet (H) and Sarah (S) are singing to 'the Lady in Red' (M = music). Harriet sings 'I've never seen you looking so gorgeous as you did tonight' and in line 007 Sarah responds with a 'oh thank you', as though the lyrics Harriet has been singing are a compliment directed at Sarah. The effect is humorous and also indicates Sarah is processing the meaning of the words. Here singing is in bold text.

```
001   M: ⌈I've never seen you looking so gorgeous⌉
002   H: ⌊I've never seen you looking so gorgeous⌋
003   S: ⌊ ((clicking fingers)) ⌋
004   M: ⌈as you did tonight⌉
005   H: ⌊as you did tonight⌋
006   S: ⌊ ((eye contact, smiling)) ⌋
007   S: oh thank you
```

Extract 3 – making up own lyrics

Sarah would sometimes make up her own lyrics, for example, in this extract again from Tina Turner, Sarah is singing in tune to the music, but with her own words, telling Harriet that she loves her (lines 003 and 006).

```
001   S: better than all the rest hhh
002   M: ⌈ ((music still playing)) ⌉
003   S: ⌊ah ah I love you any⌈time of day⌋
004   H: ⌊              ((kisses S)) ⌋
005   M: ⌈ ((music still playing)) ⌉
006   S: ⌊I can't stay awake I love⌈you so oh oh oh o: ⌉
007   H: ⌊              ((kisses S)) ⌋
008   S: oh lovely thank you
```

In response to Sarah's singing, Harriet kisses Sarah twice (004 and 007) and Sarah responds with a positive assessment of this 'oh lovely thank you' (008).

The following photograph is taken from the video data, illustrating the resulting embodied connection between Sarah and Harriet, after singing the line 'dancing cheek to cheek' (Chris De Burgh).

The life story work with Doug focused on advice to his new care home on ways to encourage his interaction using the specific skills still available to him. We had worked with Doug on a previous project and reported on his skills with enactment (Kindell *et al.*, 2013). Some three years on from this, Doug's language difficulties had progressed but he still retained many skills with enactment within interaction. One of these skills was his ability to talk in an upper class English accent. This meant that when spoken to using this accent, Doug would respond by joking along also using this accent. Despite his speech being almost

Picture 5.2 Dancing cheek to cheek. Sarah and Harriet.

impossible to follow in terms of information exchange, the resulting interaction was a warm, humorous and engaging encounter as the following extract reveals.

Extract 4 – upper class accent

In the following extract, Doug (D) is in conversation with Karina (K) and Jackie (J), talking about a friend who is 'posh' (upper class). Here Doug can be seen to act out this accent, manipulating the phonetic aspects of speech, including extended vowel sounds along with an exaggerated gesture, facial expression and nose upwards, as upper class mannerisms are often acted out. Bold text here represents the upper class accent.

001 K: Jim is terribly very posh
002 D: **there's terribly see de de very easily see ree**
003   **round there I mean you can't go a<u>rou</u>nd not**
004   **doing anything at a:ll and you need a bit <u>mo:</u>re**
005   **you might do a little <u>more</u> than you're doing**
006   **now** *((shrugs shoulders))* **but just go slowly**
007   **round around** *((hands up & out & nose upwards))*
008   **I'll take you around** *((leans forward))* **and I'll**

009   tell you later in about <u>yes</u>terday I'll have
010   more than that thank you tush tush*((throwing*
011   *gesture))*
012   J: off you go
013   K: was that Jim
014   D: yes

His wife Karina reported that there had been a longstanding family joke, arising from Doug's mother's view that the family were of a distinguished class, often acted out with this accent. This retained skill observed in the conversation data, therefore, had a particular biographical connection within the family and illustrated how the two data strands linked together. Whilst life story work has generally focused on physical resources such as life story books or memory boxes (Kindell *et al.*, 2014b), in Doug's case the resource was a summary sheet, 'Making Connections' and this along with discussion with the care staff aimed to provide them with biographical interactional knowledge. The sheet, for example, explained that conversation did not have to make sense, it was the social connections that were important for Doug and it encouraged them to facilitate his upper class accent within interactions during the day, e.g. as they passed him wandering about the care home. True to the aims of life story work, such biographical information could be used in his care to facilitate interaction.

Conclusions

The mixed methods approach used in this study proved to be a useful way to assess abilities and tailor intervention to the particular needs of those concerned. A range of interactional issues were present in the five case studies illustrating the complexities of daily life with semantic dementia. The methods were helpful to directly observe the interaction and also to understand the impact of this on the person concerned and their family, as well as to understand why certain interactional behaviours were personally meaningful.

Life story work can be delivered in various ways with a range of intended outcomes or connections (Kindell *et al.*, 2014b). This study aimed to explore how this approach could be used with a particular focus on interaction and so we have termed this 'interaction-focused life story work'. The mix of direct observation of interaction analysed through conversation analysis and the narrative interviews helped us explore and develop this novel form of intervention. Developing methods to explore in-the-moment use of life story resources presents as an important step for practice orientated research and one which we hope to further refine. This helped us to explore the development and use of traditional resources such as life story books as well as creative resources such as a life story music DVD. In some instances the 'resource' was not a physical one but unique knowledge about how to scaffold interaction for the particular individual concerned. In addition, whilst the life story literature has often focused on conveying information in conversation, or transaction, this method allowed us to explore broader interactional skills including turn taking, tone of voice, facial expression etc. that foster in-the-moment connections.

Highlighted learning points from the method

- Pairing of narrative analysis and conversation analysis allowed for triangulation of data strands giving a rich understanding of both interaction and the lived experience of the person with semantic dementia and their family members.
- Examining video and audio data was a key part of assessment and planning interventions focused on interaction, rather than a sole focus on gathering factual aspects of life story information or photographic material.
- There is potential for video to explore the outcomes of life story interventions as part of in-the-moment analysis of participation in interaction using conversation analysis. Such analyses present as a gap in knowledge for life story practice.
- Greater focus on the goals of life story work is required in practice. This study aimed to develop 'interaction-focused life story work' and therefore methods to directly examine participation in interaction are required for both assessment and exploration of outcomes.

Key references

- Hydén, L.C. (2013). Storytelling in dementia: embodiment .as a resource. *Dementia: The International Journal of Social Research and Practice*, 12(3): 359–367.
  Using video data this study demonstrates how storytelling is scaffolded in dementia, including how body movement and other skills beyond verbal abilities are facilitated.
- Kindell, J., Keady, J., Sage, K. and Wilkinson, R. (2016). Everyday conversation in dementia: a review of the literature to inform research and practice. *International Journal of Language and Communication Disorders.* Published on-line ahead of print.
  A review of 50 journal articles and book chapters exploring conversation in dementia.
- Kindell, J., Sage, K., Keady, J. and Wilkinson, R. (2013). Adapting to conversation with semantic dementia: using enactment as a compensatory strategy in everyday social interaction. *International Journal of Language and Communication Disorders*, 48: 497–507.
  A study using conversation analysis to explore skills within interaction shown by 'Doug' a man living with semantic dementia and signifianct language difficulties.
- Mates, A.W., Mikesell, L. and Smith, M.S. (eds) (2010). *Language, interaction and frontotemporal dementia.* Oakville, CT: Equinox.
  A book reporting a collection of studies exploring interaction in frontotemporal dementia using conversation analysis and ethnography.

- McKeown, J., Ryan, T. and Clarke, A. (2015). 'You have to be mindful of whose story it is': the challenges of undertaking life story work with people living with dementia and their family carers. *Dementia: The International Journal of Social Research and Practice*, 14(2): 238–256.
  Building on an earlier review McKeown et al. present a study outlining some of the challenges of life story work in clinical practice.

Recommended future reading

- Ekström, A., Ferm, U. and Samuelsson, C. (2015). Digital communication support and Alzheimer's disease. *Dementia: The International Journal of Social Research and Practice*. Published online ahead of print.
- Hamilton, H.E. (2008). Narrative as snapshot: glimpses into the past in Alzheimer's discourse. *Narrative Inquiry*, 18(1): 53–82.
- McKeown, J., Ryan, T., Button, L., Galloway, S., Wattam, M., Jepson, C. and Rimmer, K. (2013). 'Told in South Yorkshire – life story work and people living with dementia'. Available at: www.toldinsouthyorkshire.co.uk
- Mikesell, L. (2009). Conversational practices of a frontotemporal dementia patient and his interlocutors. *Research on Language and Social Interaction*, 42(2): 135–162.
- Spilkin, M.L. and Bethlehem, D. (2003). A conversation analysis approach to facilitating communication with memory books. *Advances in Speech-Language Pathology*, 5, 105–118.

Transcription symbols

Symbols	Explanation
⌈	A large left-hand bracket links overlapping utterances or non-verbal
⌊	Actions at the point where the overlap begins
⌉	A large right-hand bracket marks where overlapping
⌋	Utterances or simultaneous non-verbal actions stop overlapping. For example:
	01 PR how have you been since I last saw ⌈you⌉
	02 AM ⌊not⌋ so good
(0.6)	Silences are marked in seconds and tenths of seconds, i.e. (0.6) is six tenths of a second; (1.2) is one second and two tenths of a second
oh:	A colon indicates an extension of the sound or syllable it follows (more colons prolong the stretch)
↑↓	Marked rising and falling shifts in intonation are indicated by upward and downward pointing arrows immediately *prior* to the rise or fall
stress	Underlining indicates emphasis
°no°	Degree signs indicate talk which is *quieter* than surrounding talk
((nods))	Double brackets represent a gloss or description of some non-verbal aspect of the talk
Bold	Bold type in this reporting structure indicates singing

References

Alzheimer's Disease International (2009). World Alzheimer's Report. London: Alzheimer's Disease International.

Beeke, S., Maxim, J. and Wilkinson, R. (2007). Conversation analysis in aphasia. *Seminars in Speech and Language*, 28: 136–147.

Charmaz, K.C. (2006). *Constructing grounded theory: a practical guide through qualitative analysis*. London: Sage Publications.

Davis, B. and Maclagan, M. (2014). Talking with Maureen: Extenders and formulaic language in small stories and canonical narratives. In Schrauf, R. and Müller, N. (eds), *Dialogue and Dementia: Cognitive and Communicative Resources for Engagement*. New York: Psychology Press.

Ekström, A., Ferm, U. and Samuelsson, C. (2015). Digital communication support and Alzheimer's disease. *Dementia: The International Journal of Social Research and Practice*. Published online ahead of print.

Frontotemporal Dementia Toolkit (Eastern Cognitive Disorders Clinic Australia (2014). Available: http://ecdc.org.au/ (accessed 15 April 2017).

Gorno-Tempini, M.L., Hillis, A.E., Weintraub, S., Kertesz, A., Mendez, M., Cappa, S.F., Ogar, J.M., Rohrer, J.D., Black, S., Boeve, B.F., Manes, F., Dronkers, N.F., Vandenberghe, R.M.D., Rascovsky, K., Patterson, K., Miller, B.L., Knopman, D.S., Hodges, J.R., Mesulam, M.M. and Grossman, M. (2011). Classification of primary progressive aphasia and its variants. *Neurology*, 76: 1006–1014.

Gridley, K., Brooks, J., Birks, Y., Baxter, K. and Parker, G. (2016). Improving care for people living with dementia: development and initial feasibility study for evaluation of life story work in dementia care. *Health Services and Delivery Research*, 4: 23.

Hamilton, H.E. (2008). Narrative as snapshot: glimpses into the past in Alzheimer's discourse. *Narrative Inquiry*, 18: 53–82.

Hodges, J.R. and Patterson, K. (2007). Semantic dementia: a unique clinicopathological syndrome. *Lancet Neurol*, 6: 1004–1014.

Hutchby, I. and Woofitt, R. (2008). *Conversation analysis*. Cambridge: Polity Press.

Hydén, L.C. (2013). Storytelling in dementia: embodiment as a resource. *Dementia: The International Journal of Social Research and Practice*, 12: 359–367.

Hydén, L.C. and Orulv, L. (2009). Narrative and identity in Alzheimer's disease: a case study. *Journal of Aging Studies*, 23: 205–214.

Jefferson, G. (2005). Glossary of transcript symbols with an introduction. In Lerner, G. (ed.), *Conversation analysis: studies from the first generation*. Amsterdam: John Benjamins.

Jokel, R., Graham, N., Leonard, C. and Rochon, E. (2014). Word retrieval therapies in primary progressive aphasia. *Aphasiology*, 28: 1038–1068.

Julien, C.L., Neary, D. and Snowden, J.L. (2010). Personal experience and arithmetic meaning in semantic dementia. *Neuropsychologia*, 48: 278–287.

Keady, J., Clarke, C.L., Wilkinson, H., Gibb, C.E., Williams, L., Luce, A. and Cook, A. (2009). Alcohol related brain damage: narrative storylines and risk constructions. *Health, Risk and Society*, 11: 321–340.

Keady, J., Williams, S. and Hughes-Roberts, J. (2007). 'Making mistakes' using co-constructed inquiry to illuminate meaning and relationships in the early adjustment to Alzheimer's disease – a single case study approach. *Dementia: The International Journal of Social Research and Practice*, 6: 343–364.

Kertesz, A., Jesso, S., Harciarek, M., Blair, M. and McMonagle, P. (2010). What is semantic dementia? A cohort study of diagnostic and clinical boundaries. *Archives of Neurology*, 67: 483–489.

Kindell, J., Sage, K., Keady, J. and Wilkinson, R. (2013). Adapting to conversation with semantic dementia: using enactment as a compensatory strategy in everyday social interaction. *International Journal of Language and Communication Disorders*, 48: 497–507.

Kindell, J., Sage, K., Wilkinson, R. and Keady, J. (2014a). Living with semantic dementia: a case study of one family's experience. *Qualitative Health Research*, 24: 401–411.

Kindell, J., Burrow, S., Wilkinson, R. and Keady, J. (2014b). Life story resources in dementia care: a review. *Quality in Ageing and Older Adults*, 15: 151–161.

Kindell, J., Keady, J., Sage, K. and Wilkinson, R. (2016a). Everyday conversation in dementia: a review of the literature to inform research and practice. *International Journal of Language and Communication Disorders*. Published on-line ahead of print.

Kindell, J., Wilkinson, R., Sage, K. and Keady, J. (2016b). Combining music and life story to enhance participation in family interaction in semantic dementia: a longitudinal study of one family's experience. *In preparation*.

Lock, S., Wilkinson, R. and Bryan, K. (2001). *Supporting partners of people with aphasia in relationships and conversation*. Milton Keynes, UK: Speechmark Publishing Ltd.

Mates, A.W., Mikesell, L. and Smith, M.S. (eds) (2010). *Language, interaction and frontotemporal dementia*. Oakville, CT: Equinox.

McKeown, J., Ryan, T. and Clarke, A. (2015). 'You have to be mindful of whose story it is': the challenges of undertaking life story work with people living with dementia and their family carers. *Dementia: The International Journal of Social Research and Practice*, 14: 238–256.

Mental Capacity Act. (2005). *Code of practice*. London: HMSO.

Neary, D., Snowden, J.S., Gustafson, L., Passant, U., Stuss, D., Black, S., Freedman, M., Kertesz, A., Robert, P.H., Albert, M., Boone, K., Miller, B.L., Cummings, J. and Benson, D.F. (1998). Frontotemporal lobar degeneration: a consensus on clinical diagnostic criteria. *Neurology*, 51: 1546–1554.

Onyike, C.U. and Diehl-Schmid, J. (2013). The epidemiology of frontotemporal dementia. *International Reviews in Psychiatry*, 25: 130–137.

Perkins, L., Whitworth, A. and Lesser, R. (1998). Conversing in dementia: a conversation analytic approach. *Journal of Neurolinguistics*, 11: 33–55.

Radley, A. and Chamberlain, K. (2001). Health psychology and the study of the case: from method to analytic concern. *Social Science and Medicine*, 53: 321–332.

Riessman, C.K. (2008). *Narrative methods for the human sciences*. Thousand Oaks CA: Sage Publications.

Roach, P., Keady, J., Bee, P. and Williams, S. (2014). 'We can't keep going on like this': identifying family storylines in young onset dementia. *Ageing and Society*, 34: 1397–1426.

Schegloff, E.A. (2003). Conversation analysis and communication disorders. In Goodwin, C. (ed.), *Conversation analysis and communication disorders*. Oxford: Oxford University Press.

Sidnell, J. (2010). *Conversation analysis: an introduction*. Chichester, West Sussex: Wiley-Blackwell.

Silverman, D. (1998). *Harvey Sacks: social science and conversation analysis*. Oxford: Oxford University Press.

Simmons-Mackie, N., Savage, M.C. and Worrall, L. (2014). Conversation therapy for aphasia: a qualitative review of the literature. *International Journal of Language and Communication Disorders*, 49: 511–526.

Smith, S.S. (2010). Exploring the moral bases of frontotemporal dementia through social action. In Mates, A.W., Mikesell, L. and Smith, M.S. (eds), *Language, interaction and frontotemporal dementia: reverse engineering the social mind.* Oakville, CT: Equinox.

Snowden, J. (2015). Semantic memory. In Wright, J.D. (ed.), *International encyclopedia of the social and behavioural sciences* (2nd edition). Amsterdam: Elsevier.

Spilkin, M.L. and Bethlehem, D. (2003). A conversation analysis approach to facilitating communication with memory books. *Advances in Speech-Language Pathology*, 5: 105–118.

Subramaniamay, P., Woods, B. and Whitaker, C. (2014). Life review and life story books for people with mild to moderate dementia: a randomised controlled trial. *Aging and Mental Health*, 18: 363–375.

Surr, C. (2006). The role of interpretive biographical methodology in dementia research. *Dementia: The International Journal of Social Research and Practice*, 5: 284–290.

Taylor, C., Kingma, R., Croot, K. and Nickels, L. (2009). Speech pathology services for primary progressive aphasia: exploring an emerging area of practice. *Aphasiology*, 23: 161–174.

Torrisi, S. (2010). Social regulation in frontotemporal dementia: a case study. In Mates, A.W., Mikesell, L. and Smith, M.S. (eds), *Language, interaction and frontotemporal dementia.* Oakville, CT: Equinox.

Wilkinson, R. (2010). Interaction-focused intervention: a conversation analytic approach to aphasia therapy. *Journal of Interactional Research in Communication Disorders*, 1: 45–68.

Williams, S. and Keady, J. (2008). Narrative research and analysis. In Watson, R., McKenna, H., Cowman, S. and Keady, J. (eds), *Nursing research designs and methods.* Philadelphia: Churchill Livingstone Elsevier.

Yin, R.K. (2009). *Case study research: design and methods.* California: Sage Publications.

6 Video and observation data as a method to document practice and performances of gender in the dementia care-based hair salon

Practices and processes

Sarah Campbell and Richard Ward

Outline

This chapter outlines the use of videography as a data collection tool within an ESRC funded study (RES-061–25–0484) exploring the role of appearance in the lives of people living with dementia, particularly through the lens of care-based hairdressing services, colloquially known as 'The Hair and Care Project'. The study took place between November 2010 and November 2013. It will present an overview of video as a data collection method within dementia studies before unpacking the ways that the method was used in this study and the opportunities and challenges that this afforded us as researchers.

Introduction

The Hair and Care Project (https://thehairandcareproject.wordpress.com/) was a mixed methods qualitative study that sought to explore the role of appearance in the lives of people living with dementia. Arguably, this topic is a neglected area of health and social care research due to the perception that appearance has lacked importance in social gerontology (Ward *et al.*, 2016a and 2016b). To date, appearance has more often than not been considered as an endpoint of care, a notion emphasised in the work of Lee-Treweek (1994) in her much cited example of 'lounge standard residents'. Here, Lee-Treweek (1994) tells of how the work undertaken by care workers – sometimes coercively – happens 'back stage' (Goffman, 1978) to create people that are presentable to the outside world and can be brought 'front stage' to the communal sitting areas of the care settings and presented as 'lounge standard' residents who are similarly attired and groomed.

In the social sciences there has been a so-called 'visual turn' which has seen the rise of visual based methods that have included video and different types of photography or photo voice methods. Film work has been undertaken in many different settings and has formed different types of data. In more recent years due to the improvement of technology and the decrease in the cost of equipment there has been a steady growth in the use of video as a tool for social research (Erickson, 2011). Sarah Pink, an anthropologist whose work is at the forefront of this 'visual turn' and whose work has been a major influence on our study, argues that film works as a method which can gain insight into the embodied everyday experiences of people lives, hence its relevance for our work (Pink, 2007; 2012; 2013). Her work informs our research design in developing methods that enabled us to capture experiences that were multi-sensory, and where the practices of salon life can be shown rather than simply told.

Clark and Morriss (2015) suggest that using all kinds of visual methods are as much about the process as the outcome and that visual methodologies often engage with the power dimensions of the research process in attempting to find ways to engage and include the research participant in the process. This was particularly significant in our own work where we wished to include and involve people living with dementia, including those who were more advanced in their condition and may no longer use spoken language.

Dementia and videography

The use of video within 'Dementia Studies' is beginning to emerge as a method and to date video has been used by a small number of social researchers. In this field video has not only been used within social science but also by more biomedical studies (Snow *et al.*, 2004; Husebo *et al.*, 2009; Karaman *et al.*, 2010); however, these studies have tended not to engage reflexively with the method beyond its ability to collect data. For example, in the case of Karaman and colleagues (2010), although they reflect on their use of video they describe video as an 'objective' form of data collection. In contrast, in this chapter, we will argue that the method provides a tool for knowledge construction rather than one that can provide objective insights.

For those working in dementia studies within the social sciences video has been selected by researchers because of the opportunity it provides for a more meaningful approach to engaging participants in research (Cook, 2003; Capstick and Ludwin, 2015; Capstick *et al.*, 2016). It has also been perceived as a particularly useful method for use in research that is exploring interaction and communication (Offord *et al.*, 2006; Ward *et al.*, 2008; Yokokawa, 2012; Kindell *et al.*, 2013). The currently small numbers of researchers using this method may be related to a number of challenges that are connected to this particular method such as gaining ethical approvals, time constraints and resources. However, within dementia research the need for finding new methodologies that engage in more participatory and full-bodied ways with the experience of living with dementia has seen the emergence of innovation within the field (see Bartlett, 2012; 2014; Buse and Twigg, 2015; 2016; Swarbrick, 2015; Ward and Campbell, 2013b). The use of video has been cited as a particularly useful method to enable the inclusion of people whose 'voices' may otherwise be neglected from research (Cook, 2003; Ward *et al.*, 2005; 2008; Ward and Campbell, 2013a and 2013b; Capstick, 2011, 2012; Capstick and Ludwin, 2015; Ludwin and Capstick, 2015). Many of the studies described here have used videography alongside other types of data collection methods (see Gallagher-Thompson *et al.*, 1997; Örulv and Nikku, 2007; Ward *et al.*, 2008; de Mederios *et al.*, 2011; Yokokawa, 2012; Ward and Campbell, 2013b).

One argument that has been pivotal in our consideration for including video is that it allows a more multi-dimensional approach to data collection because aspects other than the spoken narratives of participants can be captured. This is of great value when considering research including people living with dementia and for those whose dementia is more advanced and/or who have limited verbal language. Video allows the capturing of the non-verbal in terms of behaviours, practices and actions in everyday life; sometimes participants may say one thing, but this may not be played out in their actions. In a study on friendship, the video was able to capture relationships that could be seen in everyday practice but had not been described in interviews with research participants (de Mederios *et al.*, 2011). The idea of video enabling studies to capture what can be shown – rather than simply told – was of particular value when entering into a space such as the care-based hair salon which could enable us to provide a description of the work carried out in these environments. Video also has the ability to capture elements that are not easily seen, or described, such as responses to smells, temperatures, or to the sensory 'feel' of something. In the Hair and Care Project this was another key criterion for using video in order to have a method that opened-up these aspects of the multi-sensory salon space. It provided the means to capture responses to the olfactory, haptic and auditory experiences of attending the care-based hair salon, such as the smells of the hair products, the feel of the setting lotion and the experience of being under the dryer and the touch of the hairdresser.

Researchers in dementia studies using video have also used it also in particular ways to engage participants more fully in the process of conducting research. As Cook (2003) notes, this is particularly important when there may be some difficulties to achieve informed consent due to capacity issues. She argues that using film invites participants to be active in their capacity within the research study, and gives them a chance to 'show' their best side. She noted that participants in her study, whilst not fully understanding what she was doing when she was note-taking, were much more aware of the camera and of 'being on film' when she undertook the video observation. This acknowledges the research process as an event and so, rather than the researcher attempting to fade into the background, the researcher and video camera are an integral part of the process. This virtual and visual impact on the research process is an important methodological point: film supports an engagement with the researcher constructing knowledge whilst in the field and beyond. Cook also states that her participants enjoyed the filming process, or were able to tell her when to stop, because it was clear that she was 'doing something' and the video camera made that process visible and transparent. In the study, Cook also describes someone with dementia having the capacity to tell her to stop filming when they became uncomfortable about the camera which was focused upon them. She notes that as a method it was less successful when she showed film back to her participants for comment and suggests that this does not work because it is no longer 'in the moment'. In other words, it is the 'in the moment' quality that is especially valuable when using film as a data collection method as viewing the film back is expecting participants with dementia to remember something, to recall the process in some way, which may, of course, be challenging for the person.

For many dementia studies researchers using video, one of the most important aspects was the opportunity to involve participants who may otherwise not be included in research activities. Capstick and colleagues study engaged with participants in order to make films (Capstick, 2011, 2012; Capstick and Ludwin, 2015; Ludwin and Capstick, 2015). The aim of the study was to explore opportunities for more focused and inclusive person-centred care. Participants were involved in the creation of digital life stories in the medium of a film. Although many of the participants were not able to operate the video camera and conduct filming themselves, they were able to help build narratives, find a focus for the film and select images and sound for their films. Capstick and colleagues show how, given the opportunity and using methods that are flexible and adaptive, people living with advanced dementia can be engaged and involved in film-making and research.

Videography: the sensory and embodied salon space

The challenge for our work within the Hair and Care Project was in attempting to capture embodied and sensory experiences within the previously unarticulated practice of 'care-based hairdressing'. In particular, we wished to include participants within the study who were more advanced in their dementia and were sometimes not able to use language to tell us about the experience or to reflect upon what was meaningful about having their hair done. Moreover, participants were not always able to tell us what they felt was important – or not – about their appearance. The challenge in the research design and conduct was to be able to include experiences that were both non-verbal and in the moment and did not rely on participants reflecting back to an experience. Videography provided the opportunity and potential to capture these experiences and to include people without verbal language and with more advanced dementia. As a method it also enabled us to capture the more intangible aspects of hairdressing and hair care within care facilities and in care-giving roles. However, further to this, video also provides opportunities to connect in embodied and sensory ways to the data during analysis and to develop an approach that takes into account the multi-sensory dimensions of the care-based hair salon.

The study described in this chapter is our attempt to understand the process of 'doing appearance' (Ward and Campbell, 2013b) and explore the experience of delivering and receiving care related to a person living with dementia's appearance. The reason for considering hairdressing in the exploration of appearance was because of what might be learnt from, and useful for, practice in the spaces between the care sector and beauty industry (Ward *et al.*, 2016b). Care-based hairdressers provide an integral service to people who live with dementia and are a vital cog in the dementia care workforce in the activity of maintaining and supporting appearance in these settings. Normally positioned outside of the health and social care sector, hairdressers exist as part of a workforce that provides a service within 'pampering and body pleasing' industries (Cohen, 2011). As such, they bring a different approach to bodywork than health and social care workers whose jobs are often in relation to maintenance and managing the clients that they work with (Ward *et al.*, 2016b). Hairdressers provide opportunities for transformation and beautification, their work provides important opportunities for 'feel good' interactions (Cohen, 2010). There had been no previous research exploring this section of the dementia care workforce, and care-based hairdressers can be understood as 'hidden labour' within the health and social care field. (Ward *et al.*, 2016b).

There were a number of challenges to consider in devising methods for the Hair and Care Project in order to, first, represent and interpret the work of care-based hairdressers and second, create understandings of the experience of using their services. As previously shared, in this chapter we wish to focus on the method of 'videography' which we used in our work. We will present a discussion of the challenges of undertaking videography including the methodological challenges and practical challenges that we have encountered through using this method.

The study

The primary aim of the Hair and Care Project was to understand the value of care-based hairdressing in people's lives and to describe, and explore, the care-based hair salon and the role of care-based hairdressers. To achieve this, we pursued three more specific objectives: (i) contextualising appearance through drawing on the perspectives of diverse stakeholders; (ii) exploring the embodied histories of people living with dementia by conducting what we called 'appearance biographies' (see Ward *et al.*, 2014 for further discussion of this method); and (iii) engaging with the immediacy of the body in the salon environment using 'in-situ' and visual methods (Ward and Campbell, 2013b; Ward *et al.*, 2016a, 2016b).

To translate these aims and objectives into a research study, we set out to implement social research methods that would enable us to understand the experiences of using the salon beyond what people might tell us. This was important because we planned to include people living with dementia in the study who may not be able to tell us verbally about what the salon or the hairdresser meant to them.

The study took place in the North West of England and collected information from a number of stakeholders including people living with dementia, family carers, care workers, nursing assistants, nurses, occupational therapists, senior managers and care-based hairdressers. In total we worked in eight different settings which included two NHS hospital wards, three care homes, one day centre and two homes in the community where mobile hairdressers visited. We did this work over a period of 10 months from between three and eight hours each day and observed 23 people living with dementia on a number of occasions during visits to seven different hairdressers. We also observed in the communal spaces of the care settings where they lived. This amounted to 48 hours of video data and more than 300 hours of unstructured observations in the private (where permitted) and communal settings of the care facilities. We also carried out semi-structured interviews with nursing and care staff (n=17), care-based hairdressers (n=10), family carers (n=13) and we carried out 13 unstructured 'appearance biographies' (see Ward and Campbell, 2013b) with people living with dementia, sometimes alongside their family carers.

The project used a multi-site ethnographic methodology (Falzon, 2016) which was influenced by sensory ethnographic approaches (Pink, 2009) which we will discuss further as we unpack the specifics of using videography as a method. Ethnographies are particularly valuable in exploring everyday practices and the processes of cultural groups and the methodology encourages researchers to employ a range of methods through which to capture the multi-dimensional nature of everyday life (Mason and Dale, 2011). Through using a number of different data collection tools as part of the ethnographic approach, we were able to have a suite of methods that complemented – and augmented – each other to support the rigour and reliability of the study findings. Through using a mixed methods approach we have also been able to open-up areas of experience that we would normally not have been able to access.

The focus of this chapter is on our use of video within the care-based hair salon and we will consider what this method contributed towards the study. In preparation for this aspect of the study both authors undertook an intensive summer school training at The University of Manchester in using film as a resource for fieldwork (a link to this course is provided in the key resources). This intensive training helped us to consider particular approaches to film-making in the field and provided us with key insights that underpinned our project such as the role film plays in constructing knowledge in the field (Pink, 2006; 2013). In total, 48 hours of film was gathered over the study duration using four ways of conducting film making in the care-based hair salon and in the homes of people living with dementia:

1   'Real-time' filming. For this type of filming the camera was placed on the tripod in one position in the salon. We let the camera roll with a wide lens to capture the comings and goings of the care-based hair salon as it unfolded during the salon sessions. We would do this for the first one or two visits before adding in to the film sessions a series of 'process' filming.

2   'Process' filming. These films were where the researcher and the camera followed the participant around the salon space as they went through each aspect of the hairdressing experience, from the initial consultation, hair

wash, and dryer and to the final reveal, these sessions led us to undertake the next type of filming, 'in-situ' interviews.

3   'In-situ' interviewing. We recorded on film interviews undertaken with both hairdressers and clients to capture 'in the moment' narratives of the hairdressing experience.

4   Participating in the salon process. We undertook a filmed episode of the researcher (first author: Sarah Campbell) acting as a 'sensory apprentice' (Pink, 2009, p. 69; Jackson, 1983) whereby she underwent the same hairdressing experience as participants having a shampoo and set with one of the hairdressers.

We will move on to present considerations of these different filming methods as tools for data collection before critiquing the knowledge that is produced by them. As researchers using video as a tool for representing and interpreting participants experiences there are number of important issues to be considered as the data collection was an on-going, iterative process.

Video as data collection in the care-based salon

Using video to capture different aspects of the care-based hair salon we can show how using 'real time video data collection' allows us to see the experience of the salon for the people using it from the point of arrival to leaving the salon 'transformed' (see Ward *et al.*, 2016a). The real time video enables important insights into experiences from beginning to end, and captures not only verbal but embodied responses that could not be easily captured through other means. In this extract depicting the experience of the salon for 'Dulcie' we can see that during the process of the hairdressing experience, the work of the hairdresser and the experience of the salon unfold. Through this film work we gain insight into aspects of the salon practice that help to relieve anxiety and distress such as the warmth of the dryer and the gentle touch of the hairbrush soothing and restoring momentary peace to this participant. Equally, we see that being placed under the dryer can be strange as the hood is lowered and the engine sound of the dryer experienced in the enclosed space of the dryer hood which can be startling initially:

> Dulcie arrived at the salon feeling cold and anxious. Whilst the hairdresser attended to other participants she sat shivering in her wheelchair, huddled under her blanket, the hairdresser approaches her and provides her with a towel which she also wraps herself in and asks 'isn't it cold'?
>
>   We can see from the video that Dulcie appears worried (see Figure 6.1). It is the view of her facial expression of a frown, and a particular look in her eyes and hunched body captured on film that show her bodily response to her anxiety. The video has captured a full-bodied response from Dulcie on her arrival at the salon. During her time in the salon she is guided by the hairdresser through each process of the hairdressing experience from having

her hair washed to the dryer and back into the hairdressers chair, during the experience she sometimes relaxes, such as when she is captured falling asleep under the dryer, but on each waking moment, worry appears on her face again as she looks around the salon as if to make sense of her whereabouts. In the final part of the hairdressing process Dulcie appears to have had enough, she frowns and shifts in her seat; it is her bodily movements that signal her distress which is captured on film. However, when the hairdresser begins to brush her curls through, she sighs and says to the hairdresser 'that feels nice'.

For Dulcie as the experience of the salon ensues we see how the experience of the living with dementia and the experience of the salon show the opportunity for moments of relaxation from the sense of anxiety and uncertainty that Dulcie lives with. It is through capturing this as data in real time that we are able to see how Dulcie moves between these moments, back and forth and we can note the particular sensory experiences that contribute to her ease. The warmth of the dryer, the touch of the hairdresser brushing through her hair to ease her worry and to help her make sense of the here and now.

(Fieldsite 5, 20 March 2012)

This example enables us to see how the method helps to construct knowledge, as videography here creates moments on film that enable detailed analysis which provides valuable insight into the lived experience of dementia. It also shows how people move in and out of moments of anxiety and reassurance in the experience of living with dementia. Using video to record these lengthy salon visits in real time provides film that is unique in the ability to capture the interwoven experiences of the multi-sensory salon experience.

Figure 6.1 Film still with artistic impression. Fieldsite 5, 20 March 2012. Participant 5.

A great benefit of using film to capture data was in how it enabled us to include participants who were more advanced in their dementia and no longer used verbal language to communicate. For Audrey, who no longer spoke many words but would mainly make sounds and songs, as we observed her in the hairdressing salon she would sit upright in her chair during the hairdressing experience and look directly at herself in the mirror sometimes sitting more upright as the experience went on (see Figure 6.2). She would make sounds that appeared to signify her enjoyment or not as the process unfolded; for example, on one occasion she is captured on video as she is pinched by a hairpin and she lets out an 'ow' sound and her face contorts (Fieldsite 4, 25 January 2012, film sequence: 00012).

This seems a perfect illustration of the kind of pre-reflective embodied responses that dementia scholar Pia Kontos describes in her work which provides important evidence of an 'embodied selfhood' for Audrey as she experiences the world through her body (Kontos, 2005).

The second type of filming that we carried out were 'process films' where we followed each aspect of the salon experience in closer shots moving around the salon with our participants, filming the different detailed aspects of the hairdressing process from the initial chat or consultation in the hairdressers chair to the sink for hair washing, and back to the chair to have rollers and setting lotion assembled. Before moving to the hooded dryer and finally returning to the hairdressers chair for the 'dressing' of the hair and 'reveal' of the finished hairdo (Ward *et al.*, 2016a). This gave us the opportunity to view each element of the process in micro detail, filming the hairdresser's hands at work speedily taking rollers from her tray of tools and pinning them into the hair, or using the scissors for cutting, and we would see how the hairdresser would massage the heads of clients during a shampoo wash, and in the final dressing how each hairdresser would create the finishing of the hair with their own personal style. The hair salon is one of the few places in dementia care where bodily touch is experienced directly on the body

Figure 6.2 Film still with artistic impression. Fieldsite 4, 25 January 2012, film sequence 00012. Participant 1.

and does not involve the worker wearing blue latex gloves, so there would be body to body touch, unlike in other grooming activities where gloves were worn. It is during the process films where the haptic experience is captured in close frames and the skill of the hairdresser's touch is striking to observe. Hairdressers' hands massage firmly and gently as they lather the shampoo and rinse hair clean in long sweeps pushing the soap out of the hair. Care-based hairdressers see this as a very important part of their work, partly because working with clean hair was valued highly as it made their job easier, and they described their frustrations at hair not being washed properly in the care settings where there were no salon facilities. One hairdresser told us that they also saw this as a health giving process, massaging the scalp and as one hairdresser put it:

> my first twelve months at college it was all about massaging the scalp. Forget about the hair or the lengths, it's the scalp, massaging the scalp.... Stimulating the oils and just keeping it healthy ... the blood flowing. And rinsing it properly, not leaving soap on, which forms residue and you get scaly scalp, dryness from that.
>
> (Hairdresser 10)

The film allows us to capture the skilled touch of the hairdresser applying pressure and using their hands to get the blood circulating.

During one process film over the sink we see how the hairdresser moves her hands back and forth speedily lathering the shampoo; on film we can see closely the firmness of the hairdressers touch. This is illustrated in Figure 6.3.

The hairdressing process is extremely tactile and there is a high degree of trust as the client gives themselves over to the hairdresser's hands because of the vulnerable position of being over the basin covered in soap, eyes closed with sounds going on around them, without their glasses or hearing aids. As the films continue we see hairdressers putting in rollers, and how the skin can be pulled

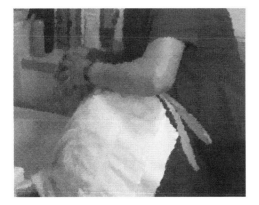

Figure 6.3 Film still with artistic impression. Fieldsite 5, 17 March 2012, film sequence 17. Participant 6.

by the tension in the roller; the films show the close texture of hair and the clients responses to prodding by the roller pins.

This detail captured via film gives us a micro insight into the haptic world of hairdressing and the intercorporeality of the hairdressing process. The process films allow us to see in close quarters how the hairdresser is not simply working on the body of the client but working with them. The hairdresser requires the clients' body to move with them and they direct their body not using words, but with their own hands and body putting pressure onto the bodies of their clients as they lean them towards the basin or as they move with speed around their body and head filling their hair with rollers (Ward *et al.*, 2016b).

A further type of filming that we undertook was to record 'in-situ' interviews with both the hairdresser and the client. For the person living with dementia these interviews meant that we were asking for an 'in the moment' response to how something felt for them. From those who were able to respond to the interview questions, we gained important insight into the sensory experience of the hair salon, the discomfort of setting lotion as it was sprayed onto the hair due to its cold feel, which we were able to ask about as we saw people start a little as the spray went onto the head; the dislike of the water rushing over faces and down necks at the sink but followed by the pleasure of the hairdressers hands massaging the scalp. Through asking participants to tell us how the experience 'felt' as it happened we were able to capture insights into the multi-sensory experience of hairdressing.

Interviewing hairdressers during these 'in-situ' interviews meant that we learnt things about the salon and the salon equipment that we may not have known to ask about in the interview sessions; for example, seeing how the hairdresser struggled to get wheelchairs close to the sink led us to have discussions with the hairdresser about how they manage this aspect of salon work. For instance, hairdressers often had to use their own bodies to push clients closer to the sink, or find creative ways to layer towels, even putting bin bags over clients to protect them from getting soaked during the hair washing. Asking the hairdresser why they did a particular action during the hairdressing process – as they were actually performing it – meant that the hairdresser answered the question in relation to the task or activity in hand. In contrast, asking hairdressers about their role in the interview sessions away from the salon told us something else about 'remembering back to the task' and this would not always equate as to how events unfolded in practice and in real time. For example in one such interview the following discussion takes place:

RESEARCHER: How do you choose which rollers to use?
HAIRDRESSER: Erm, depending on the length of the hair or whose hair is straighter or curlier, erm probably the plastic roller gives the better curl, but sometimes on the crown or in different places, erm, you can't get them in, so I use Velcro because it's just a bit more … it sticks to it better.

During this discussion, the hairdresser uses her hands to show as well as tell me, one hand holds the comb and the hairdresser points and shows on the hair of the client as she explains about using rollers, which type and where on the head is difficult (Fieldsite 8, 26 April 2012, film sequence: 0004).

During these 'in-situ' interviews it is possible to learn more about the embodied labour of the hairdresser, something that would not have happened without being in-situ and observing the work. This is because, as researchers, we would not have known enough about the work itself. Moreover, when participants reflected back on a process, they were, more often than not, unable to give the same detailed or visual response. Through the time spent creating the films and watching the hairdressing sessions we are able to ask detailed questions about the hairdressers practice.

For us, this specific approach addressed the particular challenge of understanding the experience of undertaking embodied labour, such as the work of the care-based hairdresser. Often in-situ hairdressers were juggling many tasks at once. In one of the participating salons the hairdresser had worked at the salon for more than 20 years. This hairdresser was very skilled and adept at her role and can be seen on film multi-tasking, such as undertaking work with her hands whilst watching someone else under the dryer through the salon mirrors and talking to someone else in the salon space (Ward *et al.*, 2016b). Hairdressers, when describing processes, would not be able to necessarily put into words 'how they do the task with their bodies', or even needing to see what they were doing, because they were so used to their roles and their skills were deeply embodied and embedded.

Another type of film work we undertook was to record the researcher (Sarah Campbell) undergoing a shampoo and set in order to experience the salon and work of the care-based hairdresser. In taking on the role of the 'sensory apprentice' (Pink, 2009, p. 69), Sarah was able to use her own body to get closer to how it felt to be manoeuvred around the salon space, to have rollers put into her hair and to face forward into a sink. Through this experience it was possible for the researcher to become more attuned to the salon space and to ask in-situ questions during interview that she may not have otherwise known to ask. It also gave insights into the feel of particular aspects of the practice such as the pinch of the roller, the cold of the setting lotion and the darkness of the front facing sink hair wash.

A particular benefit of using film to capture the salon happenings and the work of the care-based hairdresser is its ability to capture the multi-dimensionality and multi-faceted nature of the work. This would not be impossible, but far more difficult, to capture in field notes, particularly to the level of detail gained through video work. We move on to discuss this in the next section and to show how this is brought out through the analysis of the film because of the opportunity for layered understandings of the captured scenes (Pink, 2007). Through the ability to reflect on the sensory, the verbal and the embodied and to see how these are interwoven in nature of the work in the salon.

Analysis of video data

Pink (2009; 2013) suggests that video allows the researcher to return to the scene of data collection during the analysis process in a way that goes beyond other kinds of data, including even field notes in participant observation data. Pink argues that during analysis the researcher can 're-encounter the sensorial and emotional reality of the research situation' (Pink, 2009, p. 121). She suggests that in this moment the researcher who 'feels their way back' can remember the experience and their body can engage with the sensory in a bodily way, but it also produces new knowledge and insight into the research encounter. The researcher is now able to view and remember what happened in the field but with the knowledge of context, space and time that has gone by where ideas have developed and fermented. This process of watching back video is for the researcher a 'full-bodied' experience and one that can allow observations not made in the field to be experienced also. In the analysis of our data we have been able to continue to construct knowledge, and develop our understandings through our sensory and embodied engagement with the video captured in the field whilst watching back and re-experiencing the salon spaces and the feelings.

In our work the opportunity to view and review the video data and be reminded of the 'sensescape' of the salon was an extremely important part of the analysis process. Watching the film recreates the researchers sensory and embodied experiences of the space. Through watching the film we were able to remember the smell of the salon, and experience of noise in the different salon spaces. For example, in two of the particularly busy salons, there was a constant hustle and bustle with the background noise of the hooded dryers engines whirring in the background merging with the chatter of the hairdresser focused on the client now in the hairdresser's chair. Feld argues that 'the experience of place potentially can always be grounded in an acoustic dimension' (Feld and Basso, 1996, p. 97) and in the salon the sound of the dryers, the constant buzz of the chat or the television above the salon noises could be isolated and their visceral impact noted on the faces of those entering and using the salon space.

In analysis this allows us to focus in on aspects of the salon and to also watch as a whole to see how particular events in the salon unfold and impact on the people using the space. The video also allows us to watch particular incidents again and again so that we can explore in detail and look for particular movements, gestures, sounds and nuanced expressions on the faces of our participants and other clients showing responses to the events of the salon. Analysis of film allows a level of scrutiny that can pick out particular bodily movements, gestures, sounds that could be otherwise missed, a slight frown going under the dryer, a flinch at a pin catching on the head, the sound of a groan as the first splash of water is felt. The movement of the hairdressers body moves with the person living with dementia is also significant as captured on film as their bodies become one as they take part in the 'salon dance' (Ward *et al.*, 2016b). This level of analysis gives insights and the opportunity to produce knowledge that is highly detailed and can gain new understandings of the embodied experience of everyday life of the care-based hairdresser and client. It has enabled us to reposition the notion of people living with dementia as passive and unable to participate in these activities. Instead the work shows how people, even those living with advanced dementia can enter into the familiar setting of the salon and become part of the 'salon dance' with the help of the hairdresser who can guide their bodies through the hairdressing process (Ward *et al.*, 2016b).

These sections have illustrated the ways in which the use of film for data collection and analysis can bring a level of detail and insight that is hard to equal with other forms of data collection. However, there are challenges and limitations to undertaking research using video and the following sections of the chapter will move on to discuss these concerns before concluding what the overall benefits have been to this particular research study.

Challenges of using video: ethical governance

Whilst as described here there are many benefits to using video work in these settings and film can give deep insight into the bodily and sensory experiences of people living with dementia, there are also some important issues that need to be considered for the researcher entering into using video in care settings. First, there are many ethical considerations to take into account. There are issues relating to research governance, with regard the security of data management and storage. Video data takes a lot of room on a computer storage system. There is often the need to arrange for more space to be purchased or owned within an institution to manage the storage amounts. This took some time for us to organise and had cost implications for the project. In addition, we wanted to be able to back the film up and to also have it stored on a hard drive so that it could be transported due to the researchers not working at the same institution but both needing to watch the film or to be able to watch film together. Any mobile hard drive will also have cost implications and will need to have encryption software to ensure the security of the data and it is always worth discussing implications for moving data around with the research and governance department of the institution that is custodian of the data. For our study the process of having our study approved by a flagged[1] NHS research ethics committee, and then receiving research governance approvals took around nine months and longer if including the time to develop the materials and documentations for the study.

A further ethical consideration in using video to capture and observe everyday life is capturing people on film who are not participants in the study. The Hair and Care Project had ethical approval to film the day to day comings and goings of the care-based hair salon. We sought site specific research governance in each of the areas we were working in and the care settings where we were situated were asked to write to families in the care home to tell them about the research study. We also had posters in the salon spaces showing visually that filming was taking place and we would tell clients that filming was taking place and ask if they were ok; in fact, often the hairdresser would take on the role of being responsible for what was happening in their salon space and explain to visiting clients about the filming. In this instance we were mainly recording film for analysis rather than to show during presentations; however, if we did intend to show any film we would need to be aware that those visible individuals who were not participant in the project and had not consented to be shown would need to be blurred if the film was shown beyond the research team.

In fact, the consent process for being filmed and for film being shown outside of the research team was not one process. If any film was to be used outside of the study, for example in a presentation or training workshop, then consent had to be gained to show the specific part of the film from both the participant (or personal consultee) and the hairdresser or care worker in the film. Gaining ethical approval was a long and complex process because of the use of video and the outcome of having people on film raises concerns about data protection and how the imaging is stored securely. Therefore, any researcher intending using video in particular with what might be deemed a vulnerable client group must consider the time implications in seeking consent. As a study we supported our ethical application with an ethics protocol which considered the kinds of issues that may possibly occur in the process of carrying out the research and had a section on filming and there are a number of useful resources for researchers to access when considering using video in research that detail the kinds of ethical considerations to be taken into account (these are listed as suggested resources at the end of this chapter).

Ethics in video practice: representations

Capturing people on film creates a lasting record of that individual, and sometimes perhaps in ways that may not promote dignity; for example, wearing rollers or being shown sat with water dripping down their faces, slightly disorientated after having been returned to the light of the salon after the darkness of the hair wash. Researchers need to consider who will see the film and how these representations might be considered, particularly when working with people who have not consented themselves to taking part in the process but when the consent has been gained by proxy.[2] It may help to show film back to participants to gain their view on how they are represented in the films. This was something we had hoped to do within our study but did not fully realise and this would be a good move for future research. We were able to do this with one family carer and one hairdresser. In this film, undertaken in the home of a participant with a mobile hairdresser, we see a person with advanced dementia who is constantly being manoeuvred by the hairdresser because they are slipping down in their chair. The film displays the person through the process of hairdressing and although consent has been given by the person's spouse to show the film (and by the hairdresser) it has gained differing responses when it has been viewed by people outside of the study. For example, the hairdresser has, on occasion, been criticised by people watching the film as viewers suggest that the hairdresser isn't treating the participant with enough respect and dignity during the making of the film, and that she is treating the participant as an object or as a 'body without personhood'. However, when the hairdresser was shown the film they were pleased with how they felt it represented their working practice. They felt they were very professional in their role and the skills they showed in managing what they stated was 'a difficult situation'.

This insight reveals how film creates a lasting representation of someone but it is not the whole story. It does not capture a true story or something more objective than any other type of data collection method, although this can be an idea that is presumed from video (Wiles *et al.*, 2008; Karaman *et al.*, 2010; Clark and Morriss, 2015). As shown here film captures a partial story, and one that can be understood in different ways by different viewers. This possibility of film being open to different readings means that it can create different judgements that as researchers we cannot always predict. Hence, there is often concern about lasting images and the dignity of those involved in the films from ethics committees particularly for those no longer able to comment themselves on the images or even on taking part.

Ethics in video practice: the research encounter

Related to this is the notion that video data captures a 'natural scene'; however, this would not be an accurate interpretation. The environment is altered by the research process and by the video camera (Silverman, 2015). The camera can play an interesting role in either bringing the researcher closer to participants or it can act to put a barrier between the researcher and those being filmed. Silverman describes an awkward, intimate scene in her research which led her to turn away from the camera, though she left the camera running. It enabled her to keep looking without looking using the lens of the camera as her eye.

It can also be seen in our films how participants or clients in the salon perform for the camera, looking directly to the lens of the camera and playing the part of being on film. Sometimes participants were clearly aware and conscious of the camera presence. On other occasions participants look at the camera with a look of surprise, or inquisitively, wondering and not remembering what is happening. It is helpful to think about this in the staging of the research. The researcher is clearly positioned in the scene as part of the experience and the camera acts as an important reminder of the impact of the researcher on the everyday and how they are altering the scene. For example, some people would say 'oh I don't want to be on film' or others would ask of our participants 'are they going to Hollywood?'; the camera and the research would become a subject for discussion in the salon and therefore the normal everyday conversation of the salon was being altered by the presence of the camera and researcher. Sometimes the film captures me (Sarah) in the film data in a mirror, whilst I film, so when looking back in analysis I am part of the data too. The films capture data for the research but they also capture the research encounter, the films themselves become ethnographic events (Pink, 2009; Mason and Muir, 2013).

Clark and Morriss (2015) note that the idea that video captures 'real life' makes it appear more authentic. However, it is vital to recognise that the data is constructed by the researcher in the filming moment and again during analysis as it is used to illustrate particular themes. In reality, film captures a slice of experience within the boundaries of the video camera, a snapshot without context. Clark and Morriss (2015) argue the need for greater 'situated transparency' in order to deal with this issue. The researcher must work reflexively to consider their role in the production of the film and the scene that they capture and this transparency needs to be reflected throughout the analysis process (Clark, 2012; Emmel and Clark, 2011).

Using video as a data collection tool it is vital to consider the limitations of videography. The camera does not capture 'everything, indeed the lens only reaches so far' (Luff and Heath, 2012). For example, if something happens off camera to cause a shift in the salon dynamic then this is not there in the analysis, the researcher might remember what happened but it is in a sense 'missing data'. Silverman (2015) talks about this and the power dynamic with regard to what the film-maker captures or chooses not to capture. In the salon there was often little choice about where to situate the camera; the spaces didn't allow us to consider what might be the best shot rather this was dictated by the room layout, other uses of the room or using the angle of the camera to avoid capturing people who were not participant in the project. In one salon almost all the real time filming was carried out from behind the hairdresser so as not to film the faces of non-participants but to capture the hairdresser at work. Also due to the layout of the room there were very few spaces in which to place the camera on the tripod for the on-going film work. The room was a sitting and dining space, there were chairs located around the edges of the room with a television taking up a position near the door, the other side of the room were wide bay windows with a large dining table situated in the bay alcove which people would use to eat at or sit at whilst waiting for a client. The camera and tripod were positioned in a corner close to the back of the room behind the spot where the hairdresser worked. The camera would be held on the tripod capturing the day to day comings and goings, sometimes for a period of up to four hours. During this time the battery would require changing, the tripod would need to be moved to help allow people in and out of the space. A chair would have to be moved to situate the camera.

The camera would move with the researcher during process filming of project participants sometimes moving the tripod to be positioned in front of the dryer during particular routines. All of this needs to be considered when thinking about what is being captured from that angle and what is being lost to the film.

For example, the multi-use of the room including people eating at the table during hairdressing routines and this is not on any of the film, although sounds of these conversations are captured. The angle of the camera did mean that sometimes happenings in the corridor ended up on film because one wall was a window, so we saw beyond the salon room. In another salon, the waiting room and the corridor used as a waiting room are in the main not captured on film because the camera faces inwards to capture what is happening in the salon. Therefore the practical considerations of the placement of the camera have methodological implications. The camera has limits, and therefore it was often useful to write observation notes to accompany the filming. We also took photographs of the locations and spaces around the salon in addition to note taking.

Conclusion

As social research continues to develop to try and gain further insights into the lived experience of dementia it becomes all the more important to find ways to involve diverse voices and to find creative ways to get closer to people's experiences. There is a growing discourse that argues for research that involves people rather than researching on them as subjects (Swarbrick, 2015; and see Chapter 1 in this book). Participatory methods like filming, particularly when engaging with the participants, either through some kind of 'video tour' or as in our research in moving with a participant through the salon and asking questions 'in situ', can be empowering for participants in a number of ways. It enables the participant to be actively involved in the research; the researcher moves with them in their everyday life rather than asking them to remember or think back to an experience. As using video does not rely on the verbal then people who do not use verbal language can be involved on a much more equal footing because film can focus on embodied and sensory communication and experience. A significant number of the participants in our research had more advanced dementia and were not able to contribute verbally to the research; however, they were able to participate and their experiences have been vital in understanding the continued role that appearance and hairdressing play in people's lives.

Using video data collection and analysis in our study also enabled us to consider the spatial elements and atmospheric aspects of the 'salon spaces'. The care-based salon can be understood as an embodied and sensory space. It is important to consider what knowledge video data can produce, what using film brings to bear for a research study. Film does not provide a more authentic data set and it is important to keep an awareness that the lens through which the camera is viewing the world holds a particular framing of a scene and has limitations. It also changes the everyday scene by possibly even creating a performance at times through its presence as we saw in the salon as participants look directly into the camera. However, video as a data collection tool offers some opportunities to dementia studies. It can capture rich data, which allows the researcher the opportunity to explore layers of experience, and it provides opportunities for understanding the multi-dimensionality of experiences and their interconnections. In our study we were able to hear the sounds of the salon, the rhythmic snipping of scissors alongside the engine of the dryer and banter of the salon. It brings the researcher closer to the smells of the salon, remembering the smell of shampoo and the smell of setting lotion or hairspray whilst watching video footage of the hairdresser using these products. Film allows us as researchers to watch the bodily interactions and responses of the clients and hairdressers and listen to the stories being performed during the hairdressing encounter.

Certainly, as we have presented in this chapter, there are many opportunities for dementia studies through use of this method because of its ability to capture experience that is not reliant on verbal language and personal reflections on experience. It allows dementia studies to move away from involving people at the more early stages of their condition. The multi-sensorial experience of film brings a unique quality to its contribution to social research and to dementia studies.

Highlighted learning points from the method

- Using video for data collection in a dementia context allows for a more full-bodied approach to data collection.
- Video has the potential to include participants in research who are more advanced in their dementia and/or who no longer use verbal language.
- Video allows the researcher the opportunity to return to the scene of the data collection during analysis and can give new insights and context to the research process through also making analysis a more full-bodied event.
- Video data collection can create a large dataset and having the time to analyse all the data can be a challenge for a time-limited research study. Because of the nature of video data and the layers of experience included in the data consideration must be given to how much data is collected and how it will be analysed.
- It is essential to consider the complex ethics of using video as a data collection tool and ensuring enough time for gaining the correct approvals for using film.

Key references and recommended future reading

Videography training:
The University of Manchester, Granada Centre for Visual Methods: Film-making for fieldwork summer school: www.allritesreversed.co.uk/short-courses.html

National Centre for Research Methods: The Mode Project: University College London. Institute of Education: https://mode.ioe.ac.uk/about-us/

Books:
Back, L. (2012). 'Live sociology: social research and its futures', in *Live methods*. Oxford: Blackwell.

Heath, C. Hindmarch, J. and Luff, P. (2010). Video in qualitative research. *Introducing qualitative methods series*. London. Sage publications.
Margolis, E. and Pauwels, L. (2011). *The SAGE handbook of visual research methods*. London: Sage Publications.

Various texts by Sarah Pink:
Doing sensory ethnography, 2nd edition (2015). London: Sage Publications.
Doing visual ethnography, 3rd edition (2013). London: Sage Publications.
Situating everyday life: practices and places (2012). London: Sage Publications.
Advances in visual methodology (2012). London: Sage Publications.

Reports:
Cox, S., Drew, S., Guillemin, M., Howell, C., Warr, D. and Waycott, J. (2014). *Guidelines for ethical visual research methods*. The University of Melbourne, Melbourne.

Journal articles:
Clark, A. (2012). Visual ethics in a contemporary landscape. In Pink, S. (ed.) *Advances in visual methodology* (pp. 17–35). London: Sage Publications.
Emmel, N. and Clark, A. (2011). Learning to use visual methodologies in our research: a dialogue between two researchers. *Forum: Qualitative Social Research*, 12(1) Article 36.

Notes

1 A committee that has been established to deal with particular kinds of research project, this one was flagged to deal with studies that required mental capacity to be considered in the consenting process.
2 Informed consent via proxy is when a person who does not have mental capacity to give informed consent themselves has a person who acts as a 'personal consultee' and gives informed consent that assumes the person living with dementia would have wanted to be a part of such a research project and it would be in their best interest to take part.

References

Bartlett, R. (2012). Modifying the diary interview method to research the lives of people living with dementia. *Qualitative Health Research*, 22(12): 1717–1726.
Bartlett, R. (2014). Citizenship in action: the lived experiences of citizens with dementia who campaign for social change. *Disability and Society*, 29(8): 1291–1304.
Buse, C.E. and Twigg, J. (2015). Clothing, embodied identity and dementia: maintaining the self through dress. *Age, Culture, Humanities*, 2: 71–96.
Buse, C. and Twigg, J. (2016). Materialising memories: exploring the stories of people living with dementia through dress. *Ageing and Society*, 36(6): 1115–1135.
Capstick, A. (2011). Travels with a Flipcam: bringing the community to people living with dementia in a day care setting through visual technology. *Visual Studies*, 26(2): 142–147.
Capstick, A. (2012). Participatory video and situated ethics: avoiding disablism. In Milne, E-J., Mitchell, C. and de Lange, N., *The handbook of participatory video*. Lanham, MD: AltaMira Press.
Capstick, A. and Ludwin, K. (2015). Place memory and dementia: findings from participatory film-making in long-term social care. *Health and Place*, 34: 157–163.
Capstick, A., Ludwin, K., Chatwin, J. and Walters, E.R. (2016). Participatory video and well-being in long-term care. *Journal of Dementia Care*, 24(1): 26–29.
Clark, A. (2012). Visual ethics in a contemporary landscape. In Pink, S. (ed.), *Advances in visual methodology* (pp. 17–35). London: Sage Publications.
Clark, A. and Morriss, L. (2015). The use of visual methodologies in social work research over the last decade: a narrative review and some questions for the future. *Qualitative Social Work*, 16(1): 29–43.
Cohen, R.L. (2010). When it pays to be friendly: employment relationships and emotional labour in hairstyling. *The Sociological Review*, 58(2): 197–218.
Cohen, R.L. (2011). Time, space and touch at work: body work and labour process (re)organisation. *Sociology of health and illness*, 33(2): 189–205.
Cook, A. (2003). Using video to include the experience of people with dementia in research. *Research Policy and Planning*, 21(2): 23–32.

de Medeiros, K., Saunders, P.A., Doyle, P.J., Mosby, A. and Van Haitsma, K. (2011). Friendships among people living with dementia in long-term care. *Dementia: The International Journal of Social Research and Practice*, 11(3): 363–381.

Emmel, N. and Clark, A. (2011). Learning to use visual methodologies in our research: a dialogue between two researchers. *Forum: Qualitative Social Research*, 12(1) Article 36.

Erickson, F. (2011). Uses of video in social research: a brief history. *International Journal of Social Research Methodology*, 14(3): 179–189.

Falzon, M.A. (ed.) (2016). *Multi-sited ethnography: theory, praxis and locality in contemporary research*. London: Routledge.

Feld, S. and Basso, K.H. (1996). *Senses of place.* Santa Fe, New Mexico: School of American Research Press.

Gallagher-Thompson, D., Canto, P.D., Darnley, S., Basilio, L.A., Whelan, L. and Jacob, T. (1997). A feasibility study of videotaping to assess the relationship between distress in Alzheimer's disease caregivers and their interaction style. *Aging and Mental Health*, 1(4): 346–355.

Goffman, E. (1978). *The presentation of self in everyday life*. Harmondsworth: Penguin Books.

Heath, C., Hindmarsh, J., and Luff, P. (2010). *Video in qualitative research: analysing social interaction in everyday life.* London: Sage Publications.

Husebo, B.S., Strand, L.I., Moe-Nilssen, R., Husebo, S.B. and Ljunggren, A.E. (2009). Pain behaviour and pain intensity in older persons with severe dementia: reliability of the MOBID Pain Scale by video uptake. *Scandinavian Journal of Caring Sciences*, 23(1): 180–189.

Jackson, M. (1983). Knowledge of the body. *Man (n.s.) – now known as the Journal of the Royal Anthropological Institute*, 18, 327–345.

Karaman, S., Benois-Pineau, J., Megret, R., Dovgalecs, V., Dartigues, J.F. and Gaestel, Y. (2010). Human daily activities indexing in videos from wearable cameras for monitoring of patients with dementia diseases. In *Pattern Recognition (ICPR), 2010 20th International Conference on* (pp. 4113–4116).

Kindell, J., Sage, K., Keady, J. and Wilkinson, R. (2013). Adapting to conversation with semantic dementia: using enactment as a compensatory strategy in everyday social interaction. *International Journal of Language and Communication Disorders*, 48(5): 497–507.

Kontos, P.C. (2005). Embodied selfhood in Alzheimer's disease: rethinking person-centred care. *Dementia: The International Journal of Social Research and Practice*, 4(4) 553–570.

Lee-Treweek, G. (1994). Bedroom abuse: the hidden work in a nursing home. *Generations Review*, 4(1): 2–4.

Ludwin, K. and Capstick, A. (2015). Using participatory video to understand diversity among people living with dementia in long-term care. *Journal of Psychological Issues in Organizational Culture*, 5(4): 30–38.

Luff, P. and Heath, C. (2012). Some 'technical challenges' of video analysis: social actions, objects, material realities and the problems of perspective. *Qualitative Research*, 12(3): 255–279.

Mason, J. and Dale, A. (2011). *Understanding social research: thinking creatively about method*. London: Sage Publications.

Mason, J. and Muir, S. (2013). Conjuring up traditions: atmospheres, eras and family Christmases. *The Sociological Review*, 61(3): 607–629.

Offord, R.E., Hardy, G., Lamers, C. and Bergin, L. (2006). Teaching, teasing, flirting and fighting: a study of interactions between participants in a psychotherapeutic group for people with a dementia syndrome. *Dementia: The International Journal of Social Research and Practice*, 5(2): 167–195.

Örulv, L. and Nikku, N. (2007). Dignity work in dementia care: sketching a microethical analysis. *Dementia: The International Journal of Social Research and Practice*, 6(4): 507–525.

Pink, S. (2006). *The future of visual anthropology: engaging the senses*. London: Taylor and Francis.

Pink, S. (2007). Applied visual anthropology: social intervention, visual methodologies and anthropological theory. In Pink, S. (ed.), *Visual interventions: applied visual anthropology* (pp. 3–28). Oxford: Berghahn Books.

Pink, S. (2009). *Doing sensory ethnography*. London: Sage Publications.

Pink, S. (2012). *Situating everyday life: practices and places*. London: Sage Publications.

Pink, S. (2013). *Doing visual ethnography*. London: Sage Publications.

Silverman, M. (2015). Filming in the home: a reflexive account of microethnographic data collection with family caregivers of older adults. *Qualitative Social Work*, 15(4): 570–584.

Snow, A.L., Weber, J.B., O'Malley, K.J., Cody, M., Beck, C., Bruera, E., Ashton, C. and Kunik, M.E. (2004). NOPPAIN: a nursing assistant-administered pain assessment instrument for use in dementia. *Dementia and geriatric cognitive disorders*, 17(3): 240–246.

Swarbrick, C. (2015). The quest for a new methodology for dementia care research. *Dementia: The International Journal of Social Research and Practice*, 14(6): 713–715.

Ward, R. and Campbell, S. (2013a). An ethics journey: ethical governance of social research with vulnerable adults and the implications for practice. In Carey, M. and Green, L. (eds), *Practical social work ethics: complex dilemmas within applied social care* (pp. 151–167). Farnham, UK: Ashgate Publishing.

Ward, R. and Campbell, S. (2013b). Mixing methods to explore appearance in dementia care. *Dementia: The International Journal of Social Research and Practice*, 12(3): 337–347.

Ward, R., Campbell, S. and Keady, J. (2014). 'Once I had money in my pocket, I was every colour under the sun': using 'appearance biographies' to explore the meanings of appearance for people living with dementia. *Journal of Aging Studies*, 30: 64–72.

Ward, R., Campbell, S. and Keady, J. (2016a). 'Gonna make yer gorgeous': everyday transformation, resistance and belonging in the care-based hair salon. *Dementia: The International Journal of Social Research and Practice*, 15(3): 395–413.

Ward, R., Campbell, S. and Keady, J. (2016b). Assembling the salon: learning from alternative forms of body work in dementia care. *Sociology of Health and Illness*, 38(8) 1287–1302.

Ward, R., Vass, A.A., Aggarwal, N., Garfield, C. and Cybyk, B. (2005). A kiss is still a kiss? The construction of sexuality in dementia care. *Dementia: The International Journal of Social Research and Practice*, 4(1): 49–72.

Ward, R., Vass, A.A., Aggarwal, N., Garfield, C. and Cybyk, B. (2008). A different story: exploring patterns of communication in residential dementia care. *Ageing and Society*, 28(5): 629–651.

Wiles, R., Prosser, J., Bagnoli, A., Clark, A., Davies, K., Holland, S. and Renold, E. (2008). Visual ethics: ethical issues in visual research. *ESRC National Centre for Research Methods*, No. 11.

Yokokawa, K. (2012). Usefulness of video for observing lifestyle impairments in dementia patients. *Psychogeriatrics*, 12(2): 137–141.

Part II

Social research methods – application and innovation

7 Ethnographic methods for understanding practices around dementia among culturally and linguistically diverse people

Eleonor Antelius, Mahin Kiwi and Lisa Strandroos

Outline

This chapter introduces some general concepts and methods concerning ethnographic methods such as participant observations, the writing of field notes, video-ethnography and in-depth interviews. A general discussion is provided at first, which then progresses into a more detail analysis of such methods with regard to dementia studies, revolving around people of varied cultural and linguistic backgrounds. The chapter will discuss both how understandings of cultural practices concerning dementia among people from culturally and linguistically diverse backgrounds can be illuminated as well as a discussion concerning the influence the researchers own cultural/linguistic background could have. The three authors' own experience – and pitfalls – will be provided as examples in order to be able to discuss issues such as closeness/distance to one's informants; cultural competence vs. intercultural empathy; embodiment and ethical considerations. It will conclude with some gained insights and critical learning points.

Introduction

Movements of people across borders have shaped societies since time immemorial but what is distinctive of what has become known as 'the age of migration' (i.e. the post-Cold War period) is the global scope of such movements and the emergence of international migration and transnationalism as a force for social transformation. More and more people from different social and cultural backgrounds will be born in one country, but grow old, live their elderly days and last part of their lives in another. This fact, in combination with the expected increase in longevity resulting in more people developing age-related dementia diseases, poses a great challenge not only in economic terms but also in terms of coping with complex and varied responses to dementia that could be grounded in culture. Due to this, dementia needs to be understood not just as a biological fact caused by plaques and tangles in the brain, but also as lived experience. Because one thing we *do* know is that people's lived experiences vary tremendously, often due to ethnocultural differences: how one perceives, experience and responds to illnesses such as the dementias will always be rooted in culture no matter how biological the cause of the dementias is (Antelius, 2017; Antelius and Plejert, 2016).

A main authority in studies such as these is American anthropologist Arthur Kleinman and his approach to understanding illnesses, where he argues that in order to understand peoples experiences we need to understand that there are always normal ways of being ill (Kleinman, 1988). This implies that people might experience the same (biological) symptoms, but how these symptoms might be explained, understood and responded to will vary tremendously due to the cultural context (see, for instance, Antelius, 2017; Antelius and Traphagan, 2015). Just to give a short example, concerning dementia it has for instance been reported that a symptom such as hallucinations will not only be viewed and experienced differently depending on ethnocultural context but also how this will come to affect social interactions and how a person is perceived and treated. Researchers such as Neil Henderson (2002; Henderson and Traphagan, 2005) and Kristen Jacklin (Jacklin and Warry, 2012; Jacklin *et al.*, 2013; Jacklin *et al.*, 2015) have shown how members of Native American and First Nation tribes regard 'hallucinations' as a state of mind, body and soul where one is able to communicate with those dead or not yet born. In other words, one is able to be in contact with the spiritual world, something regarded as valuable and praiseworthy. Hence, the 'symptom' of hallucination is not considered pathological or disturbing, as it is in so many other cultural contexts; rather it gives way to an understanding of the person as a highly respected and valuable member of that society.

Hence, in order to be able to properly research issues related to dementia among people of culturally and linguistically diverse backgrounds, methods that are sensitive towards such complex and varied responses to illnesses ought to be used, an issue also picked up in the next two chapters of the book. One of the methods that has proven to be most fruitful in succeeding in such complex, yet every day, environments is the ethnographic. Ethnographic methods, such as participant observation, the writing of field notes and informal interviewing, lets the researcher learn about the people and contexts of those studied from an insider perspective. In short, if one wishes to say something about everyday life, one needs to observe it and try to understand it by living it and being a part of it (Antelius, 2009, p. 29ff.; Goode, 1994). Drawing on examples from on-going research programme, *Ethnocultural diversity and dementia* (URL1) we wish to show how a combination of participant observations, video-ethnography and informal interviewing were used in order to elucidate understandings of cultural practices around dementia among people from culturally and linguistically diverse backgrounds. We will also discuss insights on how the researchers own cultural background can be of importance – or an obstacle – in terms of access.

An ethnographic approach

If one wants to study how people live with illnesses such as the dementias, one needs to understand how people construct their social activities of their everyday lives. Everyday phenomena are constructed by those who live them and mechanistic descriptions, based upon medical models will capture very little (if anything) of the actual experience of living with (bodily and cognitive) disorders (Toombs, 2001). One of the key methods to use when studying everyday phenomena is ethnographic (e.g. Agar, 1996; Goode, 1994). According to Brewer (2000), ethnography is not one particular method of data collection, but rather a style of research that is distinguished by its objectives; to understand the social meaning and activities of people in a given setting, or field as it is often called. The goal of ethnographic research is thus to formulate a pattern of analysis, making (reasonable) sense out of human interactions in certain contexts, in a certain time (Fife, 2005). What is distinctive of ethnographic methods is thus that studies take place in naturally occurring settings, often for an extensive period of time as the goal of the study is to be able to interpret phenomena from the actors (participants) own point-of-view (Kovarsky and Crago, 1990–1991). Hence, in order to be able to understand a phenomenon such as dementia, how people experience, live and respond to such diseases, one needs to be able to learn to see the world from another person's perspective and, as far as possible, experience what they are experiencing and understand what different activities and concepts *mean*. This is no easy task and requires not only time but also a delicate craftsmanship and the ability to learn to use oneself as the prime research tool in data gathering because rather than being 'just' a method among others, ethnography is quite dependent upon forming social relations with informants. As such, ethnography could perhaps better be described as a research *process*, where the researcher experience the field and turn data into results by closely observing, recording and engaging in daily life (Marcus and Fischer, 1986). Thus, it goes beyond data collection to also include local experience, where the researcher, as much as s/he can, 'goes native' and tries to obtain an insider perspective (Geertz, 1973; 1994, p. 2f.).

Participant observations

Participant observations are a commitment to adopt the perspective of those studied by sharing in on their everyday day-to-day experiences (Denzin, 1970). It is, without question, very hard work as the concept of participant observations signifies: it is not only about data gathering but also about the ability to strike good, trusting relations with those observed (Blumer, 1969). It is almost as if living a double life is required (Denzin, 1970, pp. 78–79).

There are many different approaches, and opinions, concerning just how close you as a researcher should get with your informants, i.e. the people that you study. In its early days, in the beginning of the twentieth century, one of ethnography's founding fathers, Bronislaw Malinowski, strongly argued for the fact that you, as researcher, should set up boundaries between yourself and the people you study in order to keep a 'scientific ideal' (Malinowski, [1922] 2000). However, ethnography has evolved and adapted for the 100 years that has passed since the days of Malinowski, and today ethnography is being used in settings that would have been unimaginable when the method was developed (for a thorough read upon this subject, please see Agar, 1996 – it provides a comprehensive overview of how the method of ethnography has evolved).

Drawing from our own experiences, we have learnt that keeping one's distance, in order to keep some sort of 'scientific ideal' (as Malinowski pleaded for) is almost undoable. Rather than being someone who 'just hangs around' and observes as a bystander, being a *participant* observer has proven to be most necessary. Only by being there, day and night, helping with the washing, the feeding, participating in the excursions, the lunches, the dinners, the coffees, the just sitting on the sofa and watching TV together, have we been able to form trustworthy relations with the informants of our studies. And, if you wish to understand dementia from another person's perspective, how they perceive it and live it and deal with it, you need to gain their trust in order for them to let you into their lives and learn exactly that. Without gaining trust, one cannot follow people more closely and detect the stories they tell, often in their own ways as the dementias might have altered their way of being in the world as well as their ability to use verbal language.

However, through our own experiences, we have also learnt that as the ethnographer uses her body and senses to try to learn about other peoples' everyday life, this engagement makes it important to continuously reflect upon *how* one participates, what the own pre-understanding looks like, and how the way of participating matters for the knowledge we retrieve. Jackson – inspired by Merleau-Ponty's phenomenology which points out that we are our body and it is through the body we understand the world – argues that we learn from others by using our bodies the same way they do, to do the same activities in the same environment gives possibility to insights about their conditions and experiences. The idea is that participation leads to a 'deep' form of knowledge (Jackson, 1989). But there is not necessarily only one obvious way to participate. For instance, all of the authors of this chapter have conducted participant observation in different residential care homes for people living with dementia and one thing that we have learnt is that there are so many different ways to participate, and that the different ways lead to different knowledge and different perspectives. For instance, one of the authors of this chapter, Lisa Strandroos, realised that when she first came to the care home she observed, one issue became quite urgent; she didn't know where to place herself in the room, or for that matter, what to actually do. Lisa found it difficult that there were few common activities; different people sat dispersed and did different things or, more often, nothing at all. In the beginning, Lisa therefore asked different staff members if she could accompany them. She didn't do their work tasks but could function as an 'extra pair of hands'. This turned out well for several reasons: first Lisa quickly learned the rules and routines of the institution; second it was a way that made sense to the staff members to introduce her in, as it is how new staff members are often introduced; and third, Lisa demonstrated that being useful and 'good at working', as it was expressed amongst the staff members, gave her an easier start to being accepted and getting to know them.

Accompanying staff members doing their tasks was also useful in that Lisa got access to *their* perspective. But through participating in the way staff members did, Lisa also realised that she missed a lot of the residents' perspectives and their daily routines, and it was really them, and their perspective of living with dementia, that she was more interested in. It was easier to participate as staff member as, to Lisa, it often was more obvious what staff did. What the residents did was less obvious; they often sat, alone or together, without doing anything in particular. Some walked aimlessly. What Lisa then started to do was to sit there too, to chitchat with some of the residents, trying to find ways to interact that suited the environment and their competencies. So, Lisa started to watch a lot of television with the residents and was occasionally invited to sit in somebody's apartment. When there was a common activity, such as exercise or a movie in the assembly hall, and some of the residents were going, she went with those who attended. Hence, during the fieldwork as a whole, it proved vital for Lisa to try to participate both as resident and as staff member, as this, as already pointed out, gave different perspectives and different understandings. This is something that all three of us authors have experienced and learnt the usefulness of.

Writing of field notes

As the main ethnographic method is fieldwork, conducting participant observation, the main ethnographic data consist of written field notes. Emerson, Fretz and Shaw (1998) points out that there is not one right way to write field notes, but that it matters for the data *how* it is done, and that it is therefore important to reflect upon how what notes one writes and where and how they are written. The ethnographer needs to take into account what suits the field, the situation and the questions. For example, for the three authors of this chapter, the writing in their respective fieldworks varied between sometimes writing full notes while in the field, to scribbling down short sentences and bullet points in order to be able to flesh them out later on. There are pros and cons to both ways; for instance, writing in full, while in the field has its advantages as to make it clearer why one is there and what one is doing – i.e. to show that one is not a 'natural' participant in the setting – and, if it was not for the study, one would not be present. Of course, there is also an advantage to writing things down as soon as possible after something has happened, or even while it is happening. However, writing whilst in field could also detach the researcher from engaging in the pace of everyday life and thus be seen as an obstacle in obtaining data.

Regardless of how one finds time to write one's field notes, it is crucial to remember that field notes are the core-essence of the data gathered and as such it is imperative to also remember that the researcher works with his/herself as the prime research tool; *what* an ethnographer find out is thus inherently connected to *how* s/he find it out. Through participating, one's own feelings become central and such feelings can help understand what the participants are experiencing, or to discover subtle patterns. It thus becomes critical to document also one's own doings, conditions and emotional responses as these factors will shape the process of observing and recording others' lives (Emerson *et al.*, 1998). That there is not only a relation between method and data, but also between researcher and data, is true for all research, but perhaps it is more visible in ethnographic research because of the time spent in the field, the close relations to informants, and that the researcher he/herself is the prime research tool. This does *not* imply that the researcher should be at the centre of the research; after all we are not studying ourselves. We should write personally not confessionally (Antelius, 2009, p. 41). However, it *does* require us to be attentive to issues such as who we, the researchers are, in relation to our informants.

Another reason that there is no one-way of writing field notes is that description involves perception and interpretation. Whilst writing, the researcher: (a) transforms an event to written text; (b) makes a selection of what is written down and what is left out; and (c) chooses a particular frame of presentation. Albeit the diversity of data this process can give, there is some general advice: (1) write field notes contemporaneously – to write as soon as possible after an event has happened is necessary to see the process of doing fieldwork; (2) pursue indigenous meanings – what does the social activities mean to people in the field? (3) describe interaction in detail (Emerson *et al.*, 1995). The process of transformation, selection and presentation does, of course, not only take place when writing field notes, it is a general feature of turning social activity into text. An important point that Geertz (1973) makes is that the researcher must always focus on social action, rather than abstractions. He emphasises that things are 'about' what people are doing when they are doing something; that is, what meaning they ascribe their social action. It is further emphasised that culture is articulated through social actions. Thus, the researcher has to stay close and true to the empirical material, rather than favour elegance and coherence in theoretical abstractions. Hence, what defines ethnography is to look closely at what people are doing and search for the meaning of that doing. This is what Geertz (1973) refer to as 'thick description' – to carefully describe details and context, but also to interpret and find meaning in stratified hierarchies of meaningful structures (Antelius, 2009, pp. 40ff.; Geertz, 1973, p. 7). As such, conducting ethnographic fieldwork, and choosing what to write down as important data, is an ever-changing endeavour where the analysis is never ever conducted solely after the data gathering has been completed. To participate in everyday situations implies spending a lot of time together. This not only matters for their own experience, but also because the ethnographer gets to take part of small talk that says a lot about the worldview of the person involved. Participating thus give access to everyday talk and details of everyday practices. These small things, which Geertz (1973) refers to as *small facts*, are essential to understand greater connections. As the small facts are not generally something that the participants themselves pay much attention to, they can be hard to get a grip on without participation. As the ethnographer is often not aware of these small facts before the fieldwork starts, the issues studied might change as the study unfolds. As such, analysis is a continuous process; a process that has been described as an oscillation between induction and deduction, and as necessary to find patterns and a strati-fied hierarchy of meaningful structures, not simply ending up with providing a reporting or description of everything that is done and said (Hylland-Eriksen, 2015).

Video-ethnography

In addition to observations and the writing of field notes, it has become more and more common to use video-recordings in ethnography. Visual anthropolo-gists started to use video for its convenience and utility in the 1980s, and from the 1990s onwards researchers from different disciplines began using video-ethnography not simply as a way to capture, and store, data, but also as a medium in its own, a new way of creating knowledge (Pink, 2007). In one way videos could be perceived as a 'safety precaution', since it is impossible for any observer to capture all that is happening in social interactions. Videos thus allows for a greater coverage of activities as all the expressive dimensions that are fundamental to human interaction (body language, facial expressions, the flick of a hand, the blink of an eye etc.) could be almost impossible to capture by observation alone. The recordings could thus provide a sense of security in being able to return, and refer, to recorded data, as to 'guarantee' that the analysis does not only exist in the eye of the ethnographer. The complexity of interactions in natural settings could thus be somewhat 'double-checked' over and over again, as it is caught on tape (for an elaborated discussion concerning the use of video, please see Schaeffer, 1995).

It is, however, important to remember that video-recorded data also needs interpretation and the semantics captured do not necessarily provide the semi-otics, hence the two different sets of data, field notes and video-recordings, should not be mistaken for 'subjective' vs. 'objective' data. Video-ethnography can also be of great advantage while preparing for informal interviews (see section below), especially so if one interviews people with cognitive and/or com-municational disabilities. By having the possibility to watch recorded sequences over and over again, one can learn to detect (logical) communication patterns and structures that might be hard to detect 'in real life' and on-going interactions.

However, in regard to dementia studies there is one key element as to why video-ethnography could prove extra valuable, namely to be able to study non-verbal communication on a much deeper level than normal observations could provide. As we argue above, conducting fieldwork is a way to elicit data con-cerning everyday life and the *small matters* that people themselves might not be aware of: it is mainly a method that lets you get an insider perspective of other peoples' life-worlds. However, as also discussed above, *how* one is able to apprehend such perspective varies depending on contexts and the people studied. When studying people living with dementia diseases, one is most probably studying people who experience not only memory loss but also the loss of abilities such as thinking and planning, to be able to orient one's self, to take initiatives, to control one's feelings – all such abilities will most likely also be altered throughout the degenerating disease. Further, what has been reported to be of most significance to people living with dementia and their relatives/next of kin is how the ability to communicate will be affected and altered throughout the disease (see for instance, Murray *et al.*, 1999; Rosa *et al.*, 2010). Hence, when trying to study the life-worlds of people living with dementia, and to listen to their narratives, and their ways of engaging with the world, one necessarily needs to adapt to methods that allow for these altered ways of communicating. Participant observation, as described above, is one form of trying to embody the lives of others, to feel what they feel, and to try to understand their lives by living and thus experience the world as they do – to such extent that it is possible at least. But video-ethnography could then also provide another perspective, offering a much more detailed dataset when studying the embodied and non-verbal interactions between people. In order to not exclude important aspects of people living with communicative disabilities, one needs to use methods that are sensitive to those people who do not necessarily conform to conventional expectations of communication and storytelling. As earlier research has shown how inventive people with communicative disabilities are in finding ways of presenting themselves as competent interactors and communicators (e.g. Hydén and Antelius, 2011), it thus proves vital to use methods adapted to such endeavours. Video-ethnography is one such method.

Informal in-depth interviews, or reflective interviewing

Between the three of us authors we have conducted nearly 120 interviews during the research programme 'Ethnocultural diversity and dementia diseases'. These interviews have been conducted in different settings including interviews with people living with dementia living at home, people living with dementia living at residential care facilities, their close kin and family, different staff members at care homes, daily activities and home help carers. Author Eleonor Antelius has also, in other projects, interviewed people with acquired brain damage and with quite substantial experience; all three of us have learnt that posing simple questions is the easiest way to elucidate the most intriguing answers. By posing a question such as 'can you tell me about your day?' you get people to talk about familiar matters, the *small matters* and when they do, they will talk about what matters to *them*. Although an in-depth interview is more of an informal conversation rather than a strict interview, it is still a conversation with a purpose (Silverman, 2013). The purpose, however, is not so much to attain representativeness or generalisability, but rather to attain a deeper knowledge of different processes and social phenomena. In order to achieve this, there are some basic learning points concerning in-depth interviewing one needs to aware of which we will outline below.

First, one needs to understand that all interviewing is a *collaborative accomplishment*, meaning that an interviewer is never neutral and thus cannot just give some sort of stimuli to the interviewee in order to elucidate some sort of knowledge that s/he possesses on her/his own. Thus, as the respondents are never a repository of knowledge (or a treasury of information awaiting excavation), the knowledge and meaning constructed within the interview is always *co-constructed* between interviewer and interviewee (Holstein and Gubrium, 2004). As such, there is no 'pipe-line' transporting knowledge between interviewer and interviewees; interviews are interactional and co-constructed and as such, there is always an interpretation of the shared knowledge going on in the space between the interactors (Mishler, 1986; Riessman, 2008; Salmon and Riessman, 2008). As part of this process, researchers thus need to examine their subject positions in relation to participants, and examine their interview interactions systematically to inform research design, something that is often referred to as reflective interviewing (Roulston, 2011). As this way of understanding what an interview is also presupposes that the interview is a social situation – where the place, and the people who participate/interact have their preconceived ideas of said situation and context matters for the meanings given to it – it becomes crucial to acknowledge that the interviewees understand and respond to questions within the interview in relation to their (different) preconditions. This is the case in any interview but perhaps even more relevant to consider whilst interviewing people living with dementia who might not share an understanding of the preconceived situation (i.e. an interview-situation with a specific purpose) with the interviewer. Even more so, this situation needs to be handled with extra care if the respondent and the interviewer do not share the same (verbal) language. To use an interpreter is an option; however, this is not always a beneficial one as the small matters often seem to go under the radar.

Instead, a second learning point in conducting interviews with people living with dementia is that the interviewer benefits greatly from having very good knowledge of the person interviewed. In combination with participant observations it is therefore highly recommended that interviewing takes place at the end of the fieldwork once one has got to know the people within it quite well. Besides, not only has one got to know the people well but also one's own knowledge of the field in question is much deeper and as such one has a better sense of the meaning created within the interview, making it easier to pose relevant follow-up questions. Apart from gaining more knowledge of the field and its people, the people will also have got to know you, the researcher, better. In relation to people living with dementia who might have difficulty remembering who you are and what purpose you have, there is at least a better chance of them having got to know you and got accustomed and comfortable around you. The possibility of creating a relationship, based on mutual trust, is imperative, we would argue, when conducting interviews like these. As researcher Margareta Hydén so skilfully explained it: 'a person's speech cannot be driven, it must grow bit by bit. It cannot grow except in a situation of peace and security. This is where mutual trust can be developed' (Hydén, 1995). As such, interviewing could also be understood as a process, evolving over time, and the data gathered during an interview is quite dependent upon the setting of the interview.

Cultural equivalents of dementia?

All of the methods discussed above are of course 'general' in the sense that they are applicable in almost all ethnographic research. They are, however, extra valuable when researching issues such as the dementias among people with culturally and linguistically diverse backgrounds. First and foremost, it is imperative to never lose track of the fact that people of different cultural (and linguistic) backgrounds might have very different views of what dementia is, or could be, and thus how they respond to it. As mentioned in the introduction to this chapter, the lived experience of dementia varies tremendously and how one perceives of it, and responds to it, will always be rooted in culture, no matter how biological the causes of the dementias might be. In fact, whilst studying the dementias we should always keep in mind that we, the researchers, most likely have our own set of ideas concerning what dementia is, or is not. Most of us will most likely believe it to be a diagnosis for several different symptoms depending on different diseases and injuries to the brain. Most of us will probably also believe that these conditions are *not* natural to old age, that they are caused by abnormal degradation of cerebral neurons, caused by plaques and tangles in the brain. And although we might be fully aware of this, that this is our own perception and that other people might view the dementias quite differently, there is still a great chance that we might fall into what Arthur Kleinmann (1977) has called the category fallacy, meaning that we all too often make a hasty reification of historically and cultural specific concepts such as for instance 'dementia'. Researcher Lawrence Cohen has explained it delicately in his *No ageing in India* where he explains that:

> I wasn't supposed to look for an 'it' [dementia] at all. I was trained to avoid what Arthur Kleinmann has called a category fallacy.... I did not wish to presume the existence of a cultural equivalent of dementia in Varanasi, merely to change the labels.... But inherent in my imagined project was my belief that lurking somewhere in the pre-linguistic realm of bodily stuff was something enough like dementia that I could use a 'culturally appropriate' mental status examination (MSE) to create a sample of old persons who elsewhere might be termed demented. If I went to enough households and talked with enough old people, I would be sure to find a few who were enough 'like' demented persons that I could then ask their families if I could interview the elders and others in the household more extensively over the subsequent year. In this way I could learn what *would* be the relevant questions to ask of such families and such people, so as not to presume the language and logic of biomedicine and so as to avoid the category fallacy. Armed with a set of better categories, I could then return and construct a larger sample of people to interview and generate some better quantitative data. I could not see that the search for the better category was not a way out of category fallacy. Nor did I have a sense of why any categories, fallacious or not, should *matter* in these neighbourhoods.
>
> (Cohen, 1998, pp. 34–35)

Despite these well-intended plans, no older person Cohen initially meets appeared to be 'clinically demented' (as he puts it back then). And although he writes that, eventually, he does meet many older people who would have been labelled 'demented' by most physicians, his initial dilemma had pushed him into a direction he could never had anticipated beforehand, had he contended himself to work in metropolitan middle-class areas among people he knew were labelled 'demented'. By staying in the countryside, he slowly learned to practice what he had already learned in theory: *to listen to how old age mattered to those that he studied.* This example shows quite vividly a major insight that needs to be considered whilst researching dementia among people of diverse backgrounds: namely, the fact that although most of us researching dementia among people of culturally and linguistically diverse backgrounds most likely will end up trying to study 'cultural equivalents' of what we usually label as 'dementia' we should always be aware of this 'category fallacy trap' and be as open towards other worldviews as we can possibly be. We should never let go of the insight that although we might try to design our studies as 'open' as possible, just like Cohen, we might find ourselves with lurking beliefs that somewhere in all of that we study, there must be something equivalent of 'dementia', when in fact, there might not.

Cross-cultural competence vs. intercultural empathy

However, in many cases there do exist equivalents to dementia both linguistically and as socially and culturally constructed notions of the symptoms we mostly assign to the dementias. And whilst researching 'dementia' among people of diverse backgrounds it becomes vital to understand the difference between having (cross-)cultural competence and showing cultural empathy. Having cross-cultural competence means that you have knowledge of other people and their cultures, customs, traditions and are aware of how this might differ from your own set of ideas and understandings of the world. However, having this competence – of knowing lots about the culture of the people whom you study – is not sufficient in order to be able to create sustainable relationships, which have already been established above as crucial in all ethnographic fieldwork. Instead, the ability to communicate appropriately (and effectively) with people from cultures other than your own is based upon cultural empathy (Pedersen *et al.*, 2008), where one is able to develop understandings on an emotional level and true relationships can emerge. Intellectual understandings of a person's culture is thus often not enough, another quality is needed, the ability to participate in an emotional experience with the informant (Tseng and Streltzer, 2008).

Nearness and distance

In relation to studying dementia among culturally and linguistically diverse people, it thus becomes important to also reflect upon the insider/outsider-perspective. A main goal of all ethnographic work is – as discussed above – to become as close to your informants as possible, to feel what they feel, to experience the world from their perspective, and hence try to become an *insider*. However, it also seems to matter how you enter the particular field if you are perceived as an out- or insider already from start. Access to the field might be dependent upon this.

Drawing from our own experiences of researching dementia amongst people with immigrant backgrounds we have learnt that sharing a cultural (and sometimes linguistic) background of the ones you intend to study is sometimes almost a prerequisite; several fields that author Eleonor Antelius approached appeared shut to her (a native-born Swede) when she tried to enter them on her own. But, when accompanied by author Mahin Kiwi, whom has an Iranian background (and speaks several languages including Farsi and Azerbaijani) and who has lived in Sweden for almost 30 years, access to the field was much more attainable. People were always friendly, and agreed to meet and perhaps do a short interview also when Eleonor Antelius approached them alone, but the access to being able to do participant observations and thus to build those crucial close relationships seemed to be closed to her if not first 'properly introduced' by someone with a similar background which the informants seemed to trust more. However, one should not dismiss the advantage that being (perceived as) an outsider can also offer; many of the people with Middle Eastern background that author Eleonor Antelius interviewed explained themselves to be some sort of bridge-builders, i.e. people that saw themselves as bridges between the 'old culture' of their home country and the new (Swedish) society and its culture. They often described themselves as having a role to fill in that they understood the cultural background of residents/patients/day care participants and hence why they might experience – and respond – to the symptoms of dementia in the way that they did, at the same time as they, as bridge-builders, had a better understanding of how the (Swedish) healthcare system worked, and how people from 'their' culture viewed such systems. Thus, being perceived as an outsider sometimes actually helped in gaining access, as the bridge-builders often consisted of staff working in ethnoculturally profiled dementia care and thus also functioned as gate-keepers (i.e. a person/s who control research access to the field) and they were keen on helping build as many bridges between different cultural understandings of dementia as possible.

If trying to summarise our experiences concerning being an insider/outsider then, we believe that the fact that we have been working together in multicultural and multilingual research teams has been of immense importance in getting access to most of the fields in the first place. We have been able to meet all sorts of issues dealing with being perceived as both insiders and outsiders and all that comes with that in terms of getting access to data. Not only has it helped in retrieving access to different fields and data, but also in how we have been able to comprehend and analyse such data. How this is so, will be explained below.

Embodiment

As argued above, one of the key elements in all dementia studies is to also be able to study the non-verbal, but still salient, expressions of people living with dementia. As the dementia progresses this becomes more and more important in order to also be able to attend to those voices that are still expressed, even though the ways of communicating may have been altered due to the dementia. In regard to studying people living with dementia that might not share the same linguistic background, we the authors discovered that *not* sharing such actually prepared us better for some instances in the research. In 2014, for instance, author Eleonor Antelius got to travel to Japan with a Swedish colleague who was not only fluent in Japanese but also born in Japan (by Swedish parents) and lived the first 16 years of her life there. On top of that, she was now a researcher specialised in old age and dementia among both Swedes and Japanese, having worked, ethnographically, in both countries for several years. On this particular trip, Eleonor got to accompany her colleague to the Japanese care home for older people living with dementia the colleague had studied in her previous years in Japan. It was just a one-day visit and could not be described as an ethnographic fieldwork at all, but, nevertheless, it was an opportunity to get a glimpse of how life for these elders with dementia could manifest itself. And what became apparent after the visit had come to an end, and Eleonor and her colleague discussed their impressions of the day on the bus back to the house, was that Eleonor, not understanding a word of Japanese, had almost entirely focused upon how the elderly ladies and gentlemen had occupied the room, how they had moved their bodies in order to make their voices heard. The colleague, on the other hand, who did understand Japanese, had primarily focused upon how staff and residents seemed to have trouble understanding each other when verbal communication failed, and what strategies were used in such instances. What was *particularly* interesting, though, was that when comparing and discussing notes Eleonor and her colleague realised that by combining their two (somewhat different) approaches to studying the field they reached an *enhanced* understanding of a certain episode that had occurred during their visit and what sense of meaning an action such as the throwing of one's blanket could have. Eleonor had initially interpreted the action as if the old woman had difficulties holding on to it (due to bodily weakness), however Eleonor had started to question this as the woman seemed to throw it of more and more on purpose at the same time as she constantly uttered the same word コールド which Eleonor could not understand. At the same time, Eleonor noticed that the elderly lady did so whenever she was left alone. The colleague on the other hand had paid attention to the same situation but as she understood the Japanese word コールド as meaning 'cold' she assumed it to be related to the losing of the blanket. So, once discussing these different perceptions of the old lady's situation and the staff's respondents we realised that it had not so much to do with being actually cold, but rather being alone. As soon as the staff came back and placed their hands upon her shoulder, or knee, she would go silent and look very content, no matter if the blanket was put back on her or not. The ability to have both an insider and an outsider understanding of the situation thus seemed to increase the understanding of the occasion, as attention was paid to different aspects of the same situation.

Experiences such as these, in relation to the discussion above concerning the necessity of creating close relationships with one's informant within ethnographic lines, are thus imperative to have in mind in regard to studying dementia among people of culturally and linguistically diverse backgrounds. Because, what can sometimes feel like a frightening lack of understanding of the field one is taking part of (and which your research is dependent upon that you understand) could actually be turned into a great reminder that although you do not understand the language, you might understand so much more:

> What really struck me was how easy it is for researchers and research commissioners to take for granted the simple act of having a conversation with a respondent. It reminded me of the need for an ethnographer to put a great deal of effort into adapting themselves to those that they study. Working with people living with dementia was not just about asking the right questions, or having the right ethical procedures in place; it was about patience and empathy and a willingness to challenge myself to find new ways of communicating.
>
> (Holland, 2012)

Ethical considerations

Ethical principles are often quite straightforward in stating what one as a researcher can and cannot do. However, turning ethical principles into everyday practices is a less straightforward issue, especially so when conducting research among people living with dementia diseases, as the quote above by Holland suggests. First, the idea of 'informed consent' turns out to be complicated. First of all, for the obvious reason that the person living with dementia, due to cognitive and linguistic difficulties, could not always consent in the way we usually use the term. Many of our participants forgot what they had consented to, who we as researcher were and what we were doing there. Other residents may not have understood or related to the information at all.

We consider it reasonable, though, that to the extent possible one should ask for informed consent. Explain to the informants who you are, why you are there and what the project concerns, as well as asking them to participate while particularly emphasising that it is a voluntary thing to do, and that if they decline nothing in their ordinary lives will be changed or cancelled due to their saying no. This needs to be done repeatedly during the fieldwork as the informants, without exception but to a varying degree, might forget about it. If one is uncertain if they have understood, ask a relative of theirs to explain it to them, either in another language or in a way that could perhaps help that person to make sense of it. However, there will also be informant residents who will not understand the information and therefore could not consent to it. Hence, it is also imperative that the study is properly vetted, and approved, by an ethical board.

Rather than seeing informed consent as one occasion before fieldwork starts we have tried to view and handle it as a *process*, which means to be continuously informing and consenting. This means that sometimes we might have informed more often than the participants had been interested in listening to. This, however, raises another problem, namely that it can be quite intrusive to insist on informing about something that the participants might not be very interested in listening to. To do so and constantly remind the participants in what role one is there, disrupts the social interaction in a way the participants may find disturbing. Instead of constantly doing so we found it more fruitful to try to find ways to inform and remind of what we were doing that better worked in the social context. For example, one could quite frequently use the notebook, or the camera, as a reminder of what it is one is doing: for an extended discussion about ethics and the use of a camera among people with limited cognitive and communicative abilities please see Örulv (2008) and Antelius (2009).

Conclusion: gained insights

All of the above has thus provided us with some general insights that could be of guidance when conducting research among people living with dementia that are from culturally and linguistically diverse backgrounds. First and foremost, we must never lose track of the fact that we are all cultural beings, and as such we enter our fields of research not only with certain theory-shaped lenses on but also as human beings who have been raised in a certain place, at a certain time and in a certain context. And, as such, we all have certain lenses on that will make us understand – and respond to – the world from different perspectives. Understanding a phenomenon such as dementia is no exception, and whilst conducting research among people of diverse backgrounds it is even more important to remember this when one outlines the study design.

Second, understanding people living with dementia requires us to (try to) understand the person from their own perspective, how they might look upon the world and their take on it. Ethnographic methods have proven quite successful when researching people's everyday lives and the meanings people co-create together. However, these are methods that require the researcher to be reflective and in constant awareness of the fact that data, and the meaning of data, is not an objective existing on its own 'out there somewhere' but, rather, a joint accomplishment. As the main methods in ethnography are participant observation and in-depth interviewing, which are both contingent on building successful, trusting relationships, it becomes crucial to not only have cultural competence, but also to have/create cultural empathy with one's informants: access to meaningful data is dependent upon this. However, as we have tried to show, it is not that straightforward as being an insider is always unparalleled in circumstances like this; being perceived as a (cultural) outsider can actually, in some instances, be beneficial both in terms of accessing data but also in how one perceives and interprets such events.

Third, we thus argue that these prerequisites – of needing to be a reflexive ethnographer at the same time as one must be culturally competent and possess cultural empathy – make working in multicultural/multilingual dementia research teams particularly beneficial. This is not only helpful in gaining access to the field of study but to providing a deeper sense of meanings and understanding of data collected in such diverse settings.

Highlighted learning points from the method

- A key feature when conducting research among people with culturally and linguistically diverse backgrounds is to be constantly aware of the fact that you, the researcher, might inhabit quite different perceptions of what 'dementia' is – or could be – than the ones you aim to study.
- With such insight comes also the awareness that although you might strive for, for example, interviews to be open-ended and observations to be 'theory-free'; in order to capture 'the other's perspective' one must at the same time be constantly aware of not falling into the category-fallacy-trap; i.e. not to assume an existence of a cultural equivalent to dementia where there might be none to find.
- There are both pros and cons concerning sharing, or not sharing, cultural and linguistic backgrounds with those you aim to study. Not sharing such mutual background could, in fact, make people more open to you, wishing to explain how things work 'in their culture', often taking on the role of bridge-builders. However, others might work as gatekeepers, locking you out if you are perceived as an outsider. Working in multicultural/multilingual research-teams could thus prove helpful both in terms of getting access to data, but also whilst interpreting them, as the insider/outsider-position could provide different understandings of the data.
- In dementia studies, the ability to study non-verbal interactions is quite often a necessity and methods such as participant observations and video-ethnography ensures that also those who do not conform to conventional expectations of communication and storytelling gets heard.
- As such, studying embodiment becomes of crucial importance and there could be insights to gain from *not* sharing a mutual verbal language as one could be more tuned in to non-verbal interactions when not understanding the verbal ones.

Key references

- Agar, M. (1996). *The professional stranger: an informal introduction to ethnography*. San Diego: Academic Press, Inc.
- Cohen, L. (1998). *No aging in India. Alzheimer's, the bad family, and other modern things*. Oxford: University of California Press.
- Geertz, C. (1994). Thick description: toward an interpretive theory of culture. In Martin, M. and McIntyre, L.C. (eds), *Readings in the philosophy of social science* (pp. 213–231). Cambridge, MA: MIT Press.

• Henderson, N. and Traphagan, J. (2005). Cultural factors in dementia: perspectives from the anthropology of aging. *Alzheimer Disease and Associated Disorders*, 19: 272–274.

Recommended future reading

• Chatterji, R. (1998). An ethnography of dementia. *Culture, Medicine and Psychiatry*, 22: 355–382.
• Hydén, L.C. and Antelius, E. (2017). *Living with dementia: relations, responses and agency in everyday life*. London: Palgrave Macmillan.
• Hydén, L.C. and Antelius, E. (2011). Communicative disability and stories: towards an embodied conception of narratives. *Health: an Interdisciplinary Journal for the Social Study of Health, Illness and Medicine*, 15: 588–603.
• Innes, A. (2009). *Dementia studies: a social science perspective*. London: Sage Publications.
• Roulston, K. (2011). *Reflective interviewing. A guide to theory and practice*. London: Sage Publications.
• Sharp, T.J. (2008). *An ethnography of dementia care in an assisted living facility*. (Doctoral dissertation). San Francisco: University of California, Nursing Division.

References

Agar, M. (1996). *The professional stranger: an informal introduction to ethnography*. San Diego: Academic Press, Inc.
Antelius, E. (2009). *Different voices – different stories. Communication, identity and meaning among people with acquired brain damage* (Doctoral dissertation). Linköping: LiU-Tryck.
Antelius, E. (2017). Dementia in the age of migration: cross-cultural perspectives. In L.C. Hydén and E. Antelius (eds), *Living with dementia: relations, responses and agency in everyday life*. London: Palgrave Macmillan.
Antelius, E. and Plejert, C. (2016). Ethnoculturally profiled care: dementia caregiving targeted towards Middle Eastern people living in Sweden. *Anthropology and Aging*, 37(1): 9–26.
Antelius, E. and Traphagan, J. (2015). Ethnocultural contextualization of dementia care: cross-cultural perceptions on the notion on self. *Care Management Journals*, 16: 62–63.
Blumer, H. (1969). *Symbolic interactionism: perspective and method*. New Jersey: Prentice-Hall Inc.
Brewer, J. (2000). *Ethnography*. Buckingham: Open University Press.
Chatterji, R. (1998). An ethnography of dementia. *Culture, Medicine and Psychiatry*, 22: 355–382.
Cohen, L. (1998). *No aging in India. Alzheimer's, the bad family, and other modern things*. Oxford: University of California Press.
Denzin, N. (1970). *The research act: a theoretical introduction to sociological methods*. Chicago: Prentice Collage Hall Div.

Emerson, R., Fretz, R. and Shaw, L. (1998). *Writing ethnographic fieldnotes*. Chicago: The University of Chicago Press.

Fife, W. (2005). *Doing fieldwork: ethnographic methods for research in developing countries and beyond*. London: Palgrave Macmillan.

Geertz, C. (1973). *The interpretation of cultures: selected essays*. New York: Basic Books.

Geertz, C. (1994). Thick description: toward an interpretive theory of culture. In Martin, M. and McIntyre, L.C. (eds), *Readings in the philosophy of social science* (pp. 213–231). Cambridge, MA: MIT Press.

Goode, D. (1994). *A world without words. The social construction of children born deaf and blind*. Philadelphia: Temple University Press.

Henderson, N. (2002). The experience and interpretation of dementia: cross-cultural perspectives. *Journal of Cross-Cultural Gerontology*, 17: 195–196.

Henderson, N. and Carson Henderson, L. (2002). Cultural construction of a disease: a 'supernormal' construct of dementia in an American Indian tribe. *Journal of Cross-Cultural Gerontology*, 17: 197–212.

Henderson, N. and Traphagan, J. (2005). Cultural factors in dementia: perspectives from the anthropology of aging. *Alzheimer Disease and Associated Disorders*, 19: 272–274.

Holland, J. (2012). *Creating conversations: an ethnography of life with dementia*. Available from: www.esro.co.uk/field-notes/creating-conversations-an-ethnography-of-life-with-dementia.html (retrieved on 31 March 2017).

Holstein, J. and Gubrium, J. (2004). *The self we live by. Narrative identity in postmodern world*. New York: Oxford University Press.

Hydén, L.C. and Antelius, E. (2011). Communicative disability and stories: towards an embodied conception of narratives. *Health: An Interdisciplinary Journal for the Social Study of Health, Illness and Medicine*, 15: 588–603.

Hydén, M. (1995). Verbal aggression as prehistory of woman battering. *Journal of Family Violence*, 10: 55–71.

Hylland-Eriksen, T. (2015). *Small places, large issues. An introduction to social and cultural anthropology*. London: Pluto Press.

Innes, A. (2009). *Dementia studies: a social science perspective*. London: Sage Publications.

Jacklin, K. and Warry, W. (2012). Forgetting and forgotten: dementia in aboriginal seniors. *Anthropology and Aging Quarterly*, 33: 13.

Jacklin, K., Pace, J. and Warry, W. (2015). Informal dementia caregiving among indigenous communities in Ontario, Canada. *Care Management Journals*, 16: 106–120.

Jacklin, K., Walker, J. and Shawande, M. (2013). The emergence of dementia as a health concern among First Nations populations in Alberta, Canada. *Canadian Journal of Public Health*, 104: e39–e44.

Jackson, M. (1989). *Paths towards a clearing: radical empiricism and ethnographic inquiry*. Bloomington: Indiana University Press.

Kleinman, A. (1977). Lessons from a clinical approach to medical anthropological research. *Medical Anthropology Quarterly*, 8: 11–15.

Kleinman, A. (1988). *The illness narratives*. New York: Basic Books.

Kovarsky, D. and Crago, M. (1990–1991). Toward an ethnography of communication disorders. *National Student Speech Language Hearing Association Journal*, 18: 44–55.

Malinowski, B. (2000) [1922]. *Argonauts of the Western Pacific: an account of native enterprise and adventure in the archipelagos of Melanesian New Guinea*. London: Routledge.

Marcus, G. and Fischer, M. (1986). *Anthropology as cultural critiques. An experimental moment in the human sciences*. Chicago: University of Chicago Press.

Mishler, E. (1986). *Research interviewing. Context and narrative*. Cambridge: Harvard University Press.

Murray, J., Schneider, J., Banerjee, S. and Mann, A. (1999). Eurocare: a cross-national study of co-resident spouse carers for people with Alzheimer's disease. *International Journal of Geriatric Psychiatry*, 14: 662–667.

Örulv, L. (2008). *Fragile identities, patched-up worlds. Dementia and meaning-making in social interaction*. Linköping University: Linköping Studies in Arts and Science No. 428.

Pedersen, P.B., Crethar, H.C. and Carlson, J. (2008). *Inclusive cultural empathy: making relationships central in counselling and psychotherapy*. Washington DC: American Psychological Association.

Pink, S. (2007). *Doing visual ethnography*. London: Sage Publications.

Riessman, C. (2008). *Narrative methods for the human sciences*. Thousand Oaks: Sage Publications.

Rosa, E., Lussignoli, G., Sabbatini, F., Chiappa, A., Di Cesare, S., Lamana, L. and Zanetti, O. (2010). Needs of caregivers of the patients with dementia. *Archives of Gerontology and Geriatrics*, 51: 54–58.

Roulston, K. (2011). *Reflective interviewing. A guide to theory and practice*. London: Sage Publications.

Salmon, P. and Riessman, C. (2008). Looking back on narrative research: an exchange. In M. Andrews, C. Squire and M. Tamboukou (eds), *Doing narrative research* (pp. 78–85). London: Sage Publications.

Schaeffer, J.H. (1995). Videotape: new techniques of observation and analysis in anthropology. In P. Hockings (ed.), *Principles of visual anthropology* (pp. 255–284). Berlin: Mouton de Gryter.

Sharp, T.J. (2008). *An ethnography of dementia care in an assisted living facility*. (Doctoral dissertation) San Francisco: University of California, Nursing Division.

Silverman, D. (2013). *Doing qualitative research*. London: Sage Publications.

Toombs, K. (2001). Reflections on bodily change: the lived experience of disability. In K. Toombs (ed.), *Handbook on phenomenology and medicine* (pp. 247–261). Dordrecht: Kluwer Academic Publishers.

Tseng, W.S., and Streltzer, J. (eds) (2008). *Cultural competence in health care*. New York: Springer. URL1: *Ethnocultural diversity and dementia diseases*. Available from: www.isv.liu.se/ceder/etnokulturell-mangfald-och-demenssjukdom?l=en&sc=true (retrieved 16 December 2016).

8 Photography and case study interviewing to document intergenerational family care in Singapore-Chinese families where one member is living with dementia

May Yeok Koo and Helen Pusey

Outline

This chapter will outline the importance of genograms and ecomaps in the longit-udinal contact with people living with dementia who live in an intergenerational family context at home. The chapter draws on one case study to illustrate the dynamic nature of interaction with the family and the importance of understanding different positions within family systems. Some of the ethical issues from the data collection are discussed especially when people living with dementia were excluded from being part of the data collection, not by choice of the researchers, or family as it turned out, but because of organisational uncertainty about such engagement practices.

Introduction

This chapter will focus on the use and development of photographs, genograms, ecomaps and family interviews with Singapore-Chinese families who live together and provide care at-home to a family member who is living with dementia.[1] The study was conducted in Singapore between 2015 and 2016 and is one of the few that has focused on mapping intergenerational family care for a person living with dementia from a number of perspectives, although external ethical restrictions placed on the study meant that people living with dementia were unable to participate. The main social research methods used in the study were a combination of family interviews, photographs, drawings, walking inter-views and co-created genograms and ecomaps with the photographs taken by either the family member(s) or the main researcher. Clustered together under the umbrella of longitudinal case study design, these social research methods tell a story about intergenerational family care where the internal descriptive narrative of the photographs helped to shape and direct future data collection and family storytelling. Whilst the study as a whole involved five inter-generational Singapore-Chinese families over the study time frame, this chapter will focus on only one recruited intergenerational family to help illustrate this prolonged period of engagement and the points of method development. The main research-er's (May Yeok Koo) reflexivity will also be reported as part of the methods appraisal. However, we will commence the chapter by describing the importance of intergenerational family care and the culture and context of Singapore and Singapore-Chinese families who acted as the focal point for the study.

Singapore: culture and context

In terms of land mass, Singapore is a relatively small country in the Asia-Pacific region with a population of 5.1 million people, and growing. To cope with land-scarcity and the ever-present housing demands, it has been estimated that around 85 per cent of all Singaporeans live in high rise accommodation, mainly flats, thus restricting immediate access to outside space. Such towering living struc-tures frame the natural landscape for Singaporeans (Thang and Mehta, 2009) with the built environment intersecting with one of the most rapidly ageing pop-ulations in the Asia-Pacific region (Department of Statistics, 2012). For example, by 2030, it is projected that 18.7 per cent of Singapore's current population will be aged 65 years and over (Department of Statistics, 2012) with those aged 75 years and over projected to increase six-fold from 48,000 in 2000 to 291,000 in the year 2030 (United Nations, 2004). This means that by 2050 Singapore's population could be the world's fourth oldest, with a projected median of 54 years of age (United Nations, 2006). Against this backdrop, the Asia Pacific members of Alzheimer's Disease International have predicted the prevalence of dementia in Singapore to double every 20 years to 80,000 in 2030 and 186,900 in 2050 (Access Economics Pty Limited, 2006). Moreover, the Parents' Mainte-nance Act in Singapore ensures continued financial support of older people (including those living with dementia) from adult children (Mehta, 2006).

The impact of such policy and demographic trends is significant as the Chinese population form the largest ethnic group in Singapore (Singapore Department of Statistics, 2012) with Vascular dementia being the most common type of dementia affecting the Singapore-Chinese community (Ampil *et al.*, 2005; Sahadevan *et al.*, 2008). Indeed, an epidemiological survey on the Singaporean-Chinese community population (aged 60 years and over) found the prevalence of cognitive impairment and dementia to be 15.2 per cent (Depart-ment of Statistics, 2012; N = 1,538) which is similar to the prevalence of demen-tia as reported in Caucasian and other Asian populations (Hilal *et al.*, 2013). This is important as in parts of Asia and Singapore the person living with dementia is cared for at-home by their spouse and/or their adult children rather than being admitted into a residential care facility (Huang *et al.*, 2008). The primary reason for such home-based care is culturally determined in that Chinese children are socially mandated by the tradition of filial piety to care for their 'disabled' older family member(s) (Patterson *et al.*, 1998). To explain further, Hsueh (2001) linked filial piety to four key domains: (i) concern for parental health; (ii) financially supporting parents; (iii) fulfilling the housing needs of parents; and (iv) providing respect for parental authority. Filial piety is also a cultural touchstone that acts to bind together several generations of Singapore-Chinese families who may, or may not, co-habit together (Thang and Mehta, 2009).

The main caring role in a typical intergenerational Chinese family is hierarchical, relational and gender determined. Previously, the main responsibilities for care started with the spouse and then passed downwards to the daughter, daughter-in-law, son and, finally, to other next-of-kin (Kua and Tan, 1997). However, these long-held and accepted social norms are changing. The extended Chinese family, once a common sight in Singapore, has started to fragment. There are many reasons for this fragmentation that go beyond the scope of this chapter, but the changes can be distilled down to three main factors: first, the financial pressures placed on 'average' Chinese families to meet the high costs of living and accommodation expenses; second, changing gender expectations where women (predominantly) are expressing the need for greater independence and career fulfilment in the workplace; and third, grandchildren on the cusp of adulthood now plan to embark upon a career, or further education, that takes them away from the family home, including finding University and/or work positions overseas (The National Family Council and the Ministry of Community Development, Youth and Sports, 2009).

Indeed, nowadays, the family caregiving hierarchy of a typical Singapore-Chinese intergenerational family starts with middle-aged children (usually married women with part-time work responsibilities), then passes to spouses, then to the unmarried daughter (or son) with grandchildren largely removed from the demands of filial piety (Yap and Seng, 2009; Seow and Yap, 2011). This revisionist caring hierarchy was seen in the present study. However, these quite radical changes in Singapore-Chinese family caregiving structures has led to some unexpected, and unanticipated, social consequences. For instance, a common solution to filling the domestic 'care gap' created by the new caring hierarchy is for families to employ a 'live-in maid' who is usually female and from the Philippines, Indonesia or Myanmar (Seow and Yap, 2011). As the name suggests, the live-in maid will reside in the same house as the person living with dementia and their main duties are to attend to the 'hands-on' care of a family member living with dementia and perform the family's household chores. The live-in maid is also expected to adapt to the existing relational and living structures of the intergenerational family. For example, should the intergenerational family not co-habit together then the live-in maid – and the person living with dementia – will move between homes in order to stay in the domestic addresses of the appropriate family member(s) (Seow and Yap, 2011). For smaller families, the live-in maid may also be the only person staying with, and caring for, the person living with dementia in a one or two room high rise flat (Seow and Yap, 2011). Indeed, a study in Singapore revealed that around 50 per cent of families of people living with dementia have a live-in maid (Tew *et al.*, 2010). This organisational and domestic arrangement was seen in the present study.

Conducting intergenerational research

Research setting and research question

The choice of families living 'under one roof' was pragmatic in the sense that: the Chinese community made up the largest ethnic group in Singapore and therefore the prospect of obtaining a sample was greater; Chinese families had a long-held tradition of co-habiting together in one intergenerational space; the main researcher could act as a 'cultural insider' in the sense that she was familiar with the cultural traditions, beliefs, language and dialects of the Chinese speaking community likely to be recruited; and it was more financially economical for the main researcher to access and observe family support over time and in one location. Moreover, mapping such home-based intergenerational care was also a significant gap in the literature that the study set out to address.

However, as intimated earlier, the authors were not permitted to include the person living with dementia within the sampling frame. This was mainly due to current diagnostic and post-diagnostic practices in Singapore where neuropsychological assessments are conducted on the (undiagnosed) person presenting with memory complaints, for example, but once the formal diagnosis of dementia is made, its disclosure is channelled solely through the main carer and not the newly diagnosed person him or herself. This practice is mainly fuelled by a professional and practice belief that the person living with dementia – if informed of the diagnosis – would react negatively to the news and be unable to cope with their new-found situation. The powerful constructs of shame and stigma are also present in the mix of non-disclosure to the person living with dementia him or herself. Whilst there are some cultural variations in the current Singapore context, this is a situation that was a common occurrence in the UK in the early to mid-1990s and which took a number of years to challenge so that today (2017), post-diagnostic and peer support for people with a new diagnosis of dementia is seen standard (and good) practice and part of the Prime Minister's Challenge on Dementia (Department of Health, 2015). However, this is a journey that Singaporeans are presently engaged upon and the research team can only report, and reflect, current policy and practice realities that exist, however challenging this may be from a personally-situated ethical or citizenship standpoint.

Research aims and objectives

With the above caveat and limitation in mind, the primary aim of this study was to better understand the positioning and relational dynamics of intergenerational Singapore-Chinese families who co-habit together and care at home for a person living with dementia. The objectives of the study were fourfold, namely:

i   What system of beliefs and values underpin the intergenerational Singapore-Chinese families' caring actions?

ii   What is the specific role and responsibility of each member in an intergenerational Singapore-Chinese family?

iii   How does the hierarchical order of care and filial piety in intergenerational Singapore-Chinese families play out over time and in real time?

iv   What formal and informal support services and systems do intergenerational Singapore-Chinese families rely upon?

The study inclusion criteria were:

a   'traditional' family which may include the spouse, children, children in-law, step children, step-children in-law, sibling, nephew, niece, grandchildren or others who are related by blood, marriage or adoption;

b   Singapore-Chinese intergenerational family; at least two intergenerational family carers residing with a person living with dementia in a single household;

c   literate in English, Mandarin or dialects;

d   be able to complete a survey questionnaire or be interviewed;

e   aged 12 years and above;

f   providing care or assistance to a person living with dementia.

A decision was taken by the research team not to see the live-in maid as a member of the family and thereby to fall outside the scope of the study.

Study recruitment

The local Alzheimer's Disease Association in Singapore acted as the access gatekeeper to the family carers who met the study inclusion criteria. Following this initial organisational screening and approach, potential participants were then contacted by May Yeok and provided with further information about the study and given time to clarify any questions, or concerns, that they may have about the research process and taking part in the study. After a period of 48 hours, potential participants were contacted again by May Yeok to gain consent about entering the study, or otherwise. Should the family consent to take part, special arrangements were made in the recruitment of adolescents with parental/ guardian consent being necessary and a specially adapted consent form and information sheet developed for this purpose. Table 8.1 provides an overview of all participants recruited into the study.

Methodology and methods

Once consented into the study, each participating family (see Table 8.1) was viewed as a 'case' and Yin's (2009) multiple case study design was adopted to operationalise the aims and objectives of the study. Each family was then interviewed and visited at home over a period of around one year so that the study aims and objectives could be explored as fully as possible. To capture such dynamics, a number of data collection methods were available for use by the main researcher, including: interviews, photography and painting with the co-production of a family genogram and ecomap seen as an integral component in appraising the familial structure and nuanced intergenerational relationships. An opportunity for walking interviews was also available to be conducted as, and when, the occasion(s) arose. Photographs could be taken by either the family member(s) or researcher. All sole and co-produced data generated by May Yeok/ family carers was analysed through a narrative lens (Riessman, 2008) with the Computer Assisted Qualitative Data Analysis Software (CAQDAS) used to organise the various sources of data. The decision to use CAQDAS was based on the user-friendly features of the software programme. All data was stored in accordance with the data management plan attached to the study and was password-protected, encrypted and kept in the main researcher's locked office and locked filing cabinet at the Nanyang Polytechnic, May Yeok's place of work.

Ethical permission

As the main author was registered for a part-time PhD at The University of Manchester in the UK, whilst simultaneously being based in Singapore, ethical permission to conduct the study was required from both The University of Manchester, UK and the Nanyang Polytechnic, Singapore. Following submission of the necessary documentation and the research protocol, such approvals were granted by The University of Manchester Research Ethics Committee in August 2014 (ref: 14207) and then, several months later, by Nanyang Polytechnic Institutional Review Board in December 2014 (ref: SHS-2014–011). As this was one of the first longitudinal qualitative studies conducted in Singapore, and the first to recruit an entire family as a point of social research connection, the Institutional Review Board in Singapore was especially keen to ensure that an appropriate risk management procedure was in place. Adhering to such procedures took a little longer than expected to finalise and approve.

Creative social research methods in practice

Whilst Table 8.1 provides an overview of the entire study sample, henceforward we will focus solely on Family 2 to help illustrate how some of the data collection methods were used in practice. We have also chosen Family 2 for this purpose as the main family carer was an extremely artistic and creative person who immediately understood the ideas behind the study and he was keen to promote the loving and relational nature of care from within his own frame of reference and living arrangements. We will start this section of the chapter by giving Family 2 a dominant narrative storyline that summarised the individual case, a set of pseudonyms (as per the study protocol and ethical permissions) and a brief pencil sketch to provide a context for the methods that follow. The choice

Table 8.1 Overview of the five Singapore-Chinese intergenerational families

Name for the family	Family 1 – finding reconciliation	Family 2 – kindred spirits	Family 3 – overcoming crisis	Family 4 – valuing a diagnosis	Family 5 – care in transit
Description of the family	Filial love. Main caregiver filed for parents' maintenance against her elder and second brothers under the 'Parents' Maintenance Act'. Wishes for brothers to be more responsible, supportive and participative.	Kindred spirit. Reciprocity, solidarity and mutual respect for each other.	Baby boomer. Asset rich, cash strapped. Only son. Stoic and dutiful. Care of the 'Peranakan matriarch'.	Great faith and trust in the LORD. Sisterly bond and support from extended family. Filial love.	Took over the care of her mom whom for the past 40, 30 and 10 years has been staying on a rotational basis with her 2 other siblings and her in their homes. *7 August 2016 Sibling conflicts – 2 camps
Type of housing/ Floor of residence	3-room HDB apartment, 3rd floor	5-room HDB apartment, 12th floor	Double storey semi-detached house	5-room HDB apartment, 17th floor	Executive apartment, 10th floor
Island location	City area	North-east	Central	North-east	North-east
Household composition and age of caregiver NOTE: # = participants who can be accessed for interview	Main caregiver (#Olive (48) – Youngest daughter) Secondary caregiver (#Pete (50) – Second son) Care recipient (Angel – Mother of main caregiver) Foreign domestic worker (Myanmese) TOTAL No. in household = 4	Main caregiver (#Clive (53) – Son in-law) Secondary caregiver (#Joy (53) – Youngest daughter and #Kit (19) – only grandson) Care recipient (Dolly – Mother in-law of main caregiver) TOTAL No. in household = 4	Main caregiver (#Ben (65) – Only son) Secondary caregiver (Barbara – Daughter in-law) Care recipient (Pam – Mother of main caregiver – Passed away on Wed 6 Apr 2016) 2 foreign domestic workers (Filipinos) *Only grandson is working overseas (UK). Comes back for Christmas. Just got married in January 2016. Came back for funeral. TOTAL No. in household = 5	Main caregiver (#Ellie (64) – Eldest Daughter) Secondary caregiver (Ginny (63) – Daughter and C – grand-daughter) Care recipient (Elaine – Mother of main caregiver) – Passed away on Tues 3 May 2016) Foreign domestic worker (Indonesian) TOTAL No. in household = 5	Main caregiver (#Mindy (59) – Youngest Daughter) Secondary caregiver (Son in-law and #Shaun (23) – grandson) Care recipient (Margaret – Mother of main caregiver) TOTAL No. in household = 4
#Caregiver's educational level	#Olive and #Pete = Secondary School	#Clive = Secondary School #Joy = Diploma #Kit = Pre-U	#Ben = Masters Barbara = Degree	#Ellie = Diploma Ginny = Secondary School	#Mindy = Secondary School #Shaun = Diploma.

#Caregiver's occupation (F/T = Full time; P/T = Part-time)	#Olive = F/T Senior Accounts Officer #Pete = Self-employed Videographer	#Ben = P/T Lecturer	#Clive = P/T security guard #Joy = F/T HR administrative executive #Kit = National service; going to university at end of 2016	#Ellie = F/T General Administrative Officer Ginny = Retired; Retrenched legal secretary	#Mindy = P/T elder sitter at ADA #Shaun = F/T undergraduate in a university
Care recipient's gender, age, type of dementia and stage	• Female • 84 yrs old • Late moderate stage vascular dementia	• Female • 88 yrs old • Late stage Alzheimer's Disease	• Female • 88 yrs old • Early stage vascular dementia	• Female • 85 yrs old • Late stage dementia (Parkinson's Disease)	• Female • 90 yrs old • Moderate stage dementia (Parkinson's Disease)
Date of interviews, duration, who was interviewed	5 Apr 2015 (1600–1900hr) with #Olive 12 Apr 2015 (1530–1800hr) with #Olive – Audio recording from 1752–1814hr • 22 minutes 2 seconds 04 Oct 2015 (1540–1837hr). Interview with #Olive/Audio recording Interview with #Olive; Interview with #Pete • 50 mins 52 sec. 6 Dec 2015 @ 1530–1730hr – Interview with #Olive 17 Jan 2016 (1545–1815hr – Interview with #Olive; Audio recording (Duration): from 1615–1810hr (1:49:30 hours)	6 Jun 2015 (1505–1650hr) with #Ben 13 Jun 2015 (1516–1728hr) with #Ben. Audio recording – 2 hr 2 mins 26 secs 23 Jan 2016 @ 1530–1730hr with #Ben. Audio recording from 1637–1717hr – 39 mins 04 secs 30 April 2016 @ 1508–1700hr with #Ben. Audio recording from 1516–1617hr – 1hr 52 secs 14 May 2016 @ 1533–1725hr. Audio recording from 1552hr to 1650hr – 56 mins 45 secs 11 June 2016 @ 1505–1755hr. Audio recording from 1625 to 1638hr (12 mins 43 secs)	8 April 2015 (1600–1900hr) with #Clive 26 June 2015 (1500–1900hr) with #Clive 03 Jul 2015 (1528–1915hr) with #Clive (Audio recording – 1 hr 19 mins 54 secs) 12 Jul 2015 (1100–1300hr) with #Joy (Audio recording – 27 mins 22 secs) and #Kit (Audio recording – 7 mins 37 secs) 9 Dec 2015 @ 0900hr (Audio recording – 1:02:18) 20 Jan 2016 @ 0930–1230hr (Audio 1146hr to 1201 hr recording 45 mins 50 secs)	25 Jan 2016 (1220–1300hr) with #Ellie 26 Feb 2016 (1305hr to 1400hr); Interview with #Ellie. Audio recording from 1313 to 1358hr Duration: 45:11 minutes. 30 Mar 2016 (1220–1345hr) with #Ellie. 08 Apr 2016 (1230–1330hr); Interview with #Ellie. Audio recording from 1252–1332hr Duration: 37:13 minutes. 4 May 2016 (0845–0935hr) – Funeral wake. 3 June 2016 (1130–1315hr) with #Ellie. Audio recording from 1142–1256hr (53:29 minutes)	18 Feb 2016 (1000–1200hr) with #Mindy 17 Mar 2016 (1000hr to 1200hr) with #Mindy. 28 Apr 2016 (1545–1829hr) with #Mindy. 26 May 2016 (1010–1249hr) with #Mindy. Audio recording from 1105–1235hr Duration: 1 hr 28 minutes. 15 Jun 2016 @ 1009 to 1324hr; Interview #Shaun from 1054–1220hr (Duration: 1:07:22). Interview #Mindy from 1235–1324hr (Duration: 48:51 minutes). 21 Jul 2016 (1015–1318hr) with #Mindy. Audio recording (1 hr 38 minutes 22 seconds).

continued

Table 8.1 Continued

Name for the family	Family 1 – finding reconciliation	Family 2 – kindred spirits	Family 3 – overcoming crisis	Family 4 – valuing a diagnosis	Family 5 – care in transit
	3 Apr 2016 @ @ 1515–1815 hr – Interview with #Olive 19 June 2016 @ 1530–1800 hr – Interview with #Olive; Audio recording 1605–1711 hr (Duration: 1:06:42 hours)	14 Feb 2016 @ 1630–1835 hr – CNY (7th day of Lunar NY) visit. 24 Mar 2016 0902 to 1200 hr – Interview with #Clive; Audio recording (Duration): 1049–1200 hr (1:11:23 hours) 15 May 2016 @ 1520–1800 hr – Interview with #Joy; audio recording 1553–1641 hr (Duration: 47 minutes 12 seconds) 14 June 2016 – Hospital visit 5 July 2016 @ 1455–1825 hr; Interview #Kit from 1609–1701 hr (Duration: 51:48 minutes)		20 Jul 2016 (1215–1330 hr). Audio recording with GC: (1258–1316 hr) Length of recording: 18:23 minutes.	
Monthly to 2 monthly interview schedules	1 5 Apr 2015 2 12 Apr 2015 3 4 Oct 2015 4 6 Dec 2015 5 17 Jan 2016 6 3 Apr 2016 7 19 June 2016	1 8 Apr 2015 2 26 June 2015 3 3 Jul 2015 4 12 Jul 2015 5 9 Dec 2015 6 20 Jan 2016 7 14 Feb 2016 8 24 Mar 2016 9 15 May 2016 10 14 Jun 2016 11 5 July 2016	1 6 Jun 2015 2 13 Jun 2015 3 Dec 2015 – Nil 4 23 Jan 2016 5 Feb 2016 – Nil 6 Mar 2016 – Nil 7 9 Apr 2016 – Postponed. Mom passed away. 8 30 Apr 2016 9 14 May 2016 10 11 Jun 2016	1 25 Jan 2016 2 26 Feb 2016 3 30 Mar 2016 4 08 Apr 2016 5 4 May 2016 – wake 6 3 Jun 2016 7 20 Jul 2016	1 18 Feb 2016 2 17 Mar 2016 3 28 Apr 2016 4 26 May 2016 5 15 Jun 2016 6 21 Jul 2016

Types of data collected	Family genogram, ecomap, photographs, audio recording and field notes.	Family genogram, ecomap, photographs, audio recording and field notes. • Straits Time report on #Ben which he has shared with me: http://yourhealth.asiaone.com/content/singapore-caregivers-can-now-sleep-easy-thanks-new-service • Catholic Welfare Services – Annual 2014/2015: www.catholicwelfare.org.sg/aboutus/reports/cws_ar.pdf • www.lienfoundation.org/project-1?revision_id=318	Family genogram, ecomap, questionnaire, photographs, audio recording, field notes and *videos. . Shared an email with all the email exchanges between #Joy and her eldest brother on the care decision related to #Joy's mom.	Family genogram, ecomap, questionnaire, photographs, audio recording and field notes.	Family genogram, ecomap, questionnaire, photographs, audio recording and field notes.

of using Western pseudonyms for Family 2 was May Yeok's decision and was not an expectation of the authorship or the Editors.

Family 2: Clive, Joy and Kit – kindred spirits

Pencil sketch

Family 2 comprised Clive (son in-law, 53 years old), Joy (youngest daughter, 53 years old), Kit (grandson, 19 years old) and Dolly (person living with dementia, 88 years old). Once all ethical consent forms and procedures had been completed, May Yeok first met Clive as a participant on the study on Wednesday, 8 April 2015 and it was not until two months later that she met with Joy and Kit. The family were mainly Mandarin and dialect-speaking – Hokkien and Hainanese – with Taoism-Buddhism as the focal religion. Typical of most Singaporeans, the family resided in a five-room Housing Development Board high-rise apartment on the 12th floor with lift landing. The outside and inside of their apartment is shown in photographs 1, 2 and 3, all taken by May Yeok. The family had lived in this apartment for about 13 years but planned to move to their new home near to the sea towards the end of 2016. Planning and anticipating this transition was an important feature of the time May Yeok and the family spent together. Clive explained to May Yeok that the new home was to be 'more accessible' and 'elderly friendly' in preparation for Dolly's later stages of dementia. Both the old and new residences were located on the north-eastern part of Singapore. Dolly has been widowed since her 70s and is living with early-stage vascular dementia which was diagnosed in January 2011. She does not know she has dementia as the family have kept it from her. In May Yeok's experience and usual engagement with

Photograph 8.1 HDB apartment block where Family 2 lived.

Photograph 8.2 Lift lobby on the second floor of the apartment block.

Photograph 8.3 Living room and dining area on the right and left accordingly.

family members of elderly people in Singapore, very often, the younger members of the family would make the decision not to share the diagnosis with the older person for fear that the news would devastate them.

Dolly has another two children – an older son and daughter – who have migrated overseas with their families. She has been staying with Clive, Joy and Kit for 20 years. The family have been receiving support from available services and initially received information on how to cope with Dolly's condition from the general hospital nearest to them (Changi General Hospital) and the local Alzheimer's Disease Association, such as Chinese remedies (what medicine can and cannot be eaten) and music and medical therapies. From the time spent together, May Yeok observed that the family was loving, well-meaning, courteous, respectful and closely-knit: kindred spirits.

Overview of research encounters

A total of 11 face-to-face interviews were conducted in the home from April 2015 to July 2016. The contacts were lengthy lasting ranging from between 120 minutes (interview 4) to 265 minutes (interview 5) in duration. The time with May Yeok included the researcher and family construction of the genograms and ecomaps, which were completed over the year-long duration of involvement, audio recordings of interviews, the taking of digital photographs of the home and outside environment by May Yeok, drawings, outside walks and other activities conducted together. The family also contributed digital photographs of activities that the family did together outside of May Yeok's visits to the family apartment. A summary of the research contacts with all the members of Family 2 is presented in Table 8.2.

Establishing rapport

The interviews were held mainly in the dining area of the apartment and Clive, May Yeok and Dolly usually sat in the same places around the family dining table, as diagrammed below:

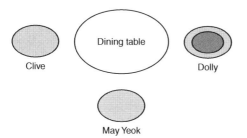

In the seating diagram, Dolly's chair is distinguishable by an inner circle which symbolically denotes a soft red coloured cushion that Clive had provided for Dolly. The purpose of the cushion was to prevent (any) pressure sores. Moreover, giving and exchanging gifts was an essential part of the cultural expectations in undertaking research with the Chinese community in Singapore. For example, on her first visit, May Yeok brought the family a bag of grapes to which Clive responded by offering refreshments for May Yeok. In the social roles, it was Dolly who often made May Yeok a Chinese tea. Such cultural etiquette and continuation of social roles was essential in enabling (any) research and relationships to develop.

Table 8.2 Research contacts with all members of Family 2

Contact	Day and date	Nature of contact	Duration
1	Wednesday, 8 April 2015	Brought a bag of purple grapes. Relationship building; gathered background information about family. In-depth interview with Clive. Face-to-face personal introduction and project explanation, informed consent taking, construction of the family genogram and ecomap, completion of questionnaire. Field notes. Arranged next visit.	1600 to1900 hr (3 hours = 180 minutes)
2	Friday, 26 June 2015	Brought a punnet of purple grapes. In-depth interview with Clive. Conducted at the dining table area. Today is generally taking digital photographs and chit chatting with Clive and Dolly. Taking digital photographs of the outside of the housing development board (HDB) apartment and inside, games created by Clive, paintings done by Clive, Clive and Dolly exercising together, Dolly preparing dinner, folding the laundry and feeding the pet tortoise, Dolly's walking stick and her organised medication. Dolly shared about her earlier days in Hainan and the Japanese occupation. Taking field notes.	1500 to 1900 hr (4 hours = 240 minutes)
3	Friday, 3 July 2015	Brought a bag of packet of Sunkist oranges. Clive offered 2 cups of cold guava juice. He offered a selection of digital photos which he had taken of Dolly since 2013. He showed me some of the videos which I may use if I deem them as useful.

In-depth interview with Clive; Audio recording from 1736 to 1856 hr – 1 hr 19 mins 54 secs. Digital photographs of HDB block/surrounding, view from living room window, void deck, lift lobby, Dolly's organised medication. Field notes. He also shared about why the family preferred stainless steel cooking pot over the electric rice cooker; Aluminium is not desirable for people living with dementia. He cited facts linking Aluminium to dementia. | 1528 to 1915 hr (3 hours 47 minutes = 227 minutes) |
| 4 | Sunday, 12 July 2015 | Brought a punnet of golden kiwis. In-depth interview with Joy and Kit. Face-to-face personal introduction and project explanation, informed consent, assent consent, family genogram, ecomap and questionnaire. Interview with Joy; Audio recording from 1246 hr to 1313 hr – 27 minutes 22 seconds. Interview with Kit; Audio recording from 1108 to 1115hrs – 7 minutes 37 seconds. Took digital photographs of – rice biscuits/titbits Clive bought for Dolly and stainless steel pots and pans for cooking to prevent dementia. Field notes. Completed demographic information | 1100 to 1300 hr (2 hours = 120 minutes) |
| 5 | Wednesday, 9 December 2015 | Brought Christmas cookies and sugar-free wafers. In-depth interview with Clive; Audio recording from 1218 to 1320 hr – 1 hour 2 minutes 18 seconds. Took digital photograph of Clive's fish painting for Kit. Field notes. | 0920 to 1345 hr (4 hours 25 minutes = 265 minutes) |

continued

Table 8.2 Continued

Contact	Day and date	Nature of contact	Duration
6	Wednesday, 20 January 2016	Brought a box of butter cookies. In-depth interview with Clive; Audio recording from 1146 to 1201 hr – 45 minutes 50 seconds. Digital photographs of – more sketches and paintings by Clive to aid Dolly's memory; handicrafts done by Dolly and Clive; Potted plant which 'emits ion which is beneficial for dementia'; Dolly watering the potted plants; Dolly playing the xylophone. Videos from Clive on Dolly doing daily/routine activities. Field notes.	0930 to 1230 hr (3 hours = 180 minutes)
7	Sunday, 14 February 2016	Brought Chinese New Year (CNY) cake (Sticky sweet rice cake or Nian Gao), Chinese mandarin oranges and a box of crispy, salty biscuit and red packets for the visit. Today is more of an observational visit to see how the family celebrates CNY. Chinese New Year (7th day of Lunar New Year) visit. Field notes.	1630 hr to 1835 hr (2 hours 5 minutes = 125 minutes)
8	Thursday, 24 March 2016	Brought a box of tea from Crabtree and Evelyn. In-depth interview with Clive; Audio recording from 1049 to 1200 hr – 1 hour 11 minutes 23 seconds. Digital photographs of – Dolly's chief complaints and medical history from her discharge memo; new bag, cardigan and sneakers. Floral accessories for bag and cardigan were added on by Clive. Field notes.	0902 to 1200 hr (2 hours 58 minutes = 178 minutes)
9	Sunday, 15 May 2016	Brought a box of 25 sachets organic Camomile tea from Waitrose and a bottle of healthy snack (Pumpkin seed, black bean, raisins and, wolfberries). In-depth interview with Joy; Audio recording from 1553 to 1641 hr – 47 minutes 12 seconds. Field notes.	1520 to 1800 hr (2 hours 40 minutes = 160 minutes)
10	Tuesday, 14 June 2016	Went to the florist to buy a colourful "Get Well Soon" balloon for Dolly in addition to the pre-ordered S$50 gift hamper with tonics which was on the way to the ward. Hospital visit when Dolly was admitted. Field notes.	0902 to 1200 hr (2 hours 58 minutes = 178 minutes)
11	Tuesday, 5 July 2016	Brought a packet of Ceylonese tea which Clive does not mind accepting. Earlier on, he had forbidden me from buying a box of chicken essence tonic drink for Dolly; explaining that his mom in law normally does not drink them. In-depth interview with Kit; Audio recording from 1609 to 1701 hr – 51 minutes 48 seconds. Took digital photographs of Clive and Dolly. Field notes. Clive shared all the email exchanges between Joy and her eldest brother on the care decision related to Joy's mom.	1455 to 1825 hr (3 hours 30 minutes = 210 minutes)
TOTAL			1,948 minutes (34 hours 51 minutes)

Co-producing genograms and ecomaps with Family 2

Whilst the development and construction of a family genogram (or family tree in describing it in this context) is reasonably well understood, ecomaps are a little more complex in formulation and meaning. Turning to the literature to aid such understanding, ecomaps are a visual and graphical representation of interconnections and relationships of a family system as set within a larger social matrix or system (Bronfenbrenner 1979). Ecomaps were developed in 1970s by the sociologist, Hartman (1978), and usually illustrated two types of support: informal and formal. Informal supports are those provided by friends, extended family members and, in the cultural context of the presented research study, the live-in maid. Formal supports on the other hand document contacts, such as access to community services. An ecomap can also be used as a research methods tool to help establish rapport with families (Cox, 2003), learn more about the perceptions of the families (Hartman, 1978), and to organise information and facts about the family situation (Hanson and Boyd, 1996). These additional functions of an ecomap were an integral part of the study and will now be used to frame – and illustrate – some of the key encounters with Family 2.

For Family 2, production of the family genogram and ecomap took over a year to complete. For this family, May Yeok began with the construction of individual – or separate – genograms and ecomaps as based on the initial face-to-face interviews with each family member (see Table 8.2). During Clive's first interview in April 2015, the process began of co-producing a genogram and ecomap together. However, the first task was actually to apprise Clive about what a genogram and ecomap actually looks like and what form it could take and, perhaps more importantly, why it was a necessary task to start. To help guide this process, May Yeok used an anonymous and illustrative example of a completed genogram and ecomap that was included in the study ethics approval forms to demonstrate their typical flow and context. Clive was quick to catch on with what was being asked of him and enthusiastically shared some of the main elements of his family genogram and ecomap with May Yeok. Clive asked if May Yeok would document the early stages of this work together. The initial sketching of the genogram and ecomap were therefore done on May Yeok's mobile tablet with May Yeok later refining the contents with reference to her research notes and audio-taped interview transcripts. On 12 July 2015, May Yeok showed Clive the updated version of the genogram and ecomap to seek his clarification, input and confirmation that this illustration was moving in the right direction. This working diagram is shared in Figure 8.1.

Similarly, when May Yeok interviewed Kit and Joy on 12 July 2015, it was clear that these participants preferred to visualise and document their genogram and ecomap using 'pen and paper'. Keeping flexible and sensitive to the needs of the participants was key in helping to co-produce and diagram together. Similar to the previous situation, Kit and Joy required some help to initially understand

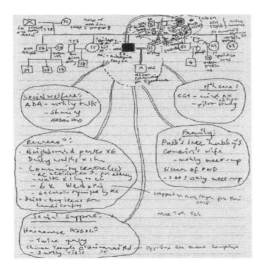

Figure 8.1 Version 1: genogram and ecomap with Clive on 8 April 2015.

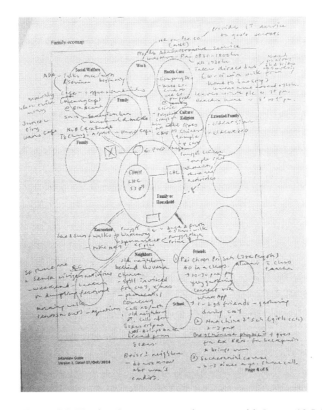

Figure 8.2 Version 1: genogram and ecomap with Joy on 12 July 2015.

what a genogram and ecomap looked like. However, this time, instead of an anonymous genogram and ecomap being shared, Clive gave permission for his initial map (in Figure 8.1) to be used for this purpose. The first (separate) sketchings of Kit and Joy's genograms and ecomaps are shared in Figures 8.2 and 8.3 respectively with their different stylings immediately apparent.

The genograms and ecomaps were used at the beginning of each interview by May Yeok to frame the time that was spent together and to give an opportunity to re-check the authenticity and representativeness of the diagrams as family relationships naturally move and change over time. Indeed, the final version of the family genogram and ecomap (a synthesis of all the ecomaps produced over the time together) was eventually agreed by Clive, Joy and Kit on the last interview and it is these final versions that are shared in Figures 8.4 and 8.5 respectively.

Coding guidance: G1 and CG2 indicate the case study participants (CG1 = Clive; CG2 = Joy and Kit) and CR (Dolly) indicates the person living with dementia.

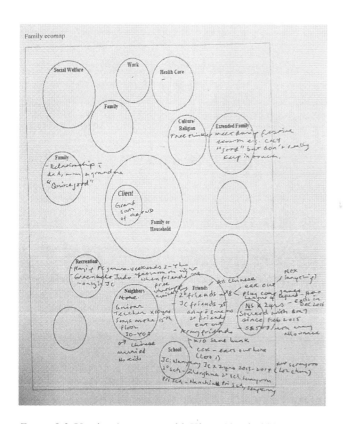

Figure 8.3 Version 1: ecomap with Kit on 12 July 2015.

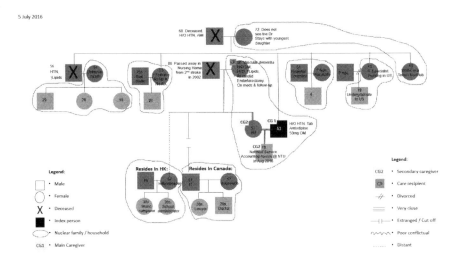

Figure 8.4 Final genogram of Family 2.

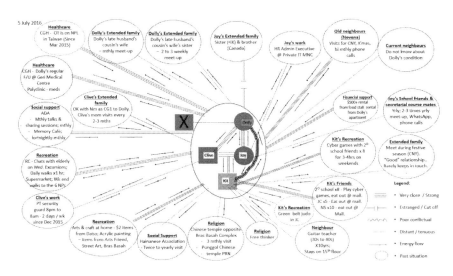

Figure 8.5 Final ecomap of Family 2.

Final ecomap: sharing stories

Story 1: everyday intergenerational representation

Developing a number of iterations of the genogram and ecomap with Clive, Joy and Kit opened up conversational pathways as to why caring was structured in the family in the way that it was and how events have unfolded to allow this to happen. As can be seen in the final ecomap, Dolly, Joy, Kit and Clive are 'safe' within an inner circle in the ecomap with strong lines linking the family together. As part of this safe space, and in developing the ecomap, Clive shared more about why he ended up staying at home to provide the care for Dolly.

> My wife and I have discussed this. It's better for her to work while I stay at home to look after mama. She works in Human Resource and the salary pays well. We are comfortable financially. Luckily, we don't have to worry about our son. He knows how to focus on his study. And, he is on a government scholarship.

As well as opening up such details, actually sitting down together around the kitchen table created its own intimate atmosphere and as Dolly was seated with May Yeok, it was simply impossible not to include her within the conversation. Indeed, Clive actively encouraged Dolly's participation and encouraged her to share about her life in Hainan during her younger days – life in the farm and during the Japanese occupation. It is a great shame that Dolly's conversations could not be shared in the context of the study (for the ethical constraints identified earlier) but such openness encouraged May Yeok to share about her own grandparent's life and actions in that most turbulent of historical times. As such, the ecomaps were a democratising process in relationship building.

The ecomaps also facilitated a discussion on household routines and how Dolly's role in the family was supported. For example, during one visit, Clive gently reminded Dolly that it was 'time to feed the pet'. May Yeok observed Dolly feeding the family's 12-year-old pet 'tortoise' which Clive claimed had a strong bond and affiliation with Dolly. He also engaged Dolly to take down the laundry and fold it while the interview was ongoing. Later, Clive excused himself intermittently from the activities to prepare dinner with Dolly in the kitchen and their camaraderie was obvious. May Yeok could see that he was also watching her discreetly from the dining area after he left her to continue with the food preparation and would provide instructions from the dining area, such as: 'Don't forget to fill up the water for the rice.' Then, he would remind her to take out the vegetables to wash them. At the same time, May Yeok could hear the active discussion on what menu to prepare for dinner.

During the time of May Yeok's involvement with the family, Kit, the only son of Clive and Joy, was undergoing his compulsory two and a half years of National Service and was only home for the weekends. Kit was due to commence an accounting degree under a scholarship scheme in August 2016. Kit did not provide any physical care for Dolly. According to Clive, however, he has a unique emotional bond with Dolly, as these two slices of data attest:

> Because at home, he regards Po Po [Maternal grandmother] as a very important member. In fact, he has very little interactions with his 'Ah Ma' [Paternal grandmother]. He has more interactions with Po Po. When he was very young, she really looked after him. Childcare, taking bus, looking after

him. Therefore, his meals, everything was cared for by Po Po. The relationship is very good. But, my son, in reality, is not a very expressive person.... Therefore, when mom was hospitalized, a few years ago ... when he returned home, the first thing he did was look around. When he realized something was amiss, he asked me. When he is worried, he does not openly express his emotions but when he takes notice and asks, we know he is worried. He is very attentive. He will ... after returning home from secondary school, ask, 'Is Po Po at home?' He will show concern. For instance, when Po Po was having fever.

(Interview 3 with Clive)

Po Po's fever situation.... When Po Po was having fever and rushing to go to the hospital, it so happened to be just before his book-in [National Service book-in]. Therefore, he happened to see Po Po in that state, having fever and having chills.... She was having high fever and having very bad chills. First time we saw her having chills like this. He was looking for her. Actually, he has already changed to his uniform for book-in [to camp], he went to look for a thick sweater to cover her.

(Interview 3 with Clive)

Intergenerational bonding was facilitated through the family doing routine things together. For instance, Joy and Kit's weekends would be spent accompanying Dolly for activities; Clive continued to do the grocery shopping with Dolly and supervised the payment at the cash register from afar. Walking and outside activities were important too, as Clive shared:

Along the way, we look at the houses, birds' nest. The one you saw just now. We look at it slowly. We look at fruit trees. There was one time, we even saw a squirrel. We will go examine. Sometimes when we walk pass and smell the aroma of curry, I will ask her, 'Ma ma, what do you smell?' I ask her to take note of everything around her. This is based on what we have learnt. We are not sure if it works or not but want to do, must do.

(Interview 3 with Clive)

All taken by Clive, the photographs below bring to life data on the ecomaps in a most vivid and necessary way – the commentary on each photograph is that provided by the family.

Going for walks (From Clive who took them in June 2015)

From left to right – Joy and Dolly

Going out for a meal at a cafe (From Clive who took them in March 2013)

Clockwise from the left – Kit, Joy and Dolly

Accompanying Kit to the army camp for his National Service enlistment

Clockwise from the left – Joy, Dolly and Kit

Accompanying Dolly for an activity organised by the Residents' Community Centre

Dolly, dressed in blue cardigan

Dolly examining a bird's nest during her morning walk

Dolly examining the papaya tree with fruits during her morning walk

Dolly Making payment at the cash register

Dolly buying groceries at NTUC

The family has ingeniously articulated and re-customised some of Dolly's routine to enable her to have continuity in family role, identity and status.

Story 2: painting pictures

The acrylic paintings in this section, all done by Clive, bring out the colour of life, outline the diversity of what defines a 'caregiving' role and provides a vivid illustration of the thinking – and meaning – inherent in using the environment as a canvas of care.

Paintings 1 and 2 were drawn around two years and one year ago and are hung in the living room and dining area respectively – painting 2 can be seen in photograph 3 in this chapter to show a sense of scale. Painting 1 is a presentation of two peonies with leaves drawn in a heart shape, accompanied by three Chinese carps and set against a golden peacock. Painting 2 of an Arowana fish, also called 'Kam Lung Yue' in Chinese-Cantonese, meaning Golden Dragon Fish. Clive believed that this fish brings good luck and prosperity. Painting 3 is a

Painting 1

Painting 2

Painting 4

Painting 3

symbolic painting of Chinese New Year oranges, the sunrise and Chinese Koi fishes. The oranges symbolised a happy occasion; the sunrise symbolised a new beginning every day; and the fishes symbolised prosperity and abundance. This particular painting was strategically hung on the wall facing Dolly's bed, so that she could see it every day when she wakes up. Painting 4, an acrylic painting of a Chinese Koi fish, was hung on the wall between the master bedroom (Clive and Joy's) and Dolly's bedroom. Kit has helped Clive to surf the internet for live pictures to aid his paintings. Clive did the composition himself though. He candidly shared his intent:

> Because when we were at ADA, we saw that some, towards the end, could not even recognise themselves. Therefore, paint big, big paintings for her to remember. Drawing big paintings became a natural progression. Exactly like this. [Laughs].

> (Interview 4 with Clive)

The description of the paintings and the assembling of the ecomaps are intrinsically linked. They were elaborate and laborious but Clive had taken great effort to paint them for an intended purpose – symbolic in nature and strategically hung on the wall in the apartment in different rooms of the house to create a familiar environment in preparation for Dolly when they move house at the end of 2016. The explanations bring out the value of relationships and the necessary 'fleshing out' of the ecomaps into a more explanatory and three dimensional theoretical and conceptual space.

Discussion – genograms, ecomaps and photographs

Genograms

When constructing the genogram for Family 2 as illustrated in Figure 8.4, May Yeok had to go with the flow when collecting information about the three generations of the family from Clive, Joy and Kit. She took advantage of 'natural' openings during her interactions with the family to obtain the information needed, linking questions to specific caregiving experiences each member underwent and which were clear to them. She noted that when sufficient levels of trust were established, it was easier to explore issues such as relationships that were relevant to the provision of care for Family 2. Also, it assisted in providing a visual representation of the family's connection and relationship with their extended family. In this case, the family's connection and relationship with Joy's other siblings which was initially unrevealed became more apparent with the help of the genogram. Relating to Figure 8.4, the use of the genogram had assisted May Yeok in drawing out sensitive information which the family was initially weary of sharing but eventually shared as they began to appreciate the visual representation of their family. They have even mentioned to May Yeok how amazed they were upon seeing the elaborate construction of the genogram. It had shown that Joy's eldest sister and brother had a distant and estranged/cut-off relationship with the family and Dolly which Clive and Dolly had confirmed upon seeing the constructed genogram. This has also provided the impetus for May Yeok to ask more detailed questions on why this was so and if this had any impact on Dolly's long term care which contributed to the ecomap.

Ecomaps

The ecomap for Family 2 as illustrated in Figure 8.5 is visualised with circles representing various systems in the family's ecology. There are lines connecting these circles to Family 2, representing May Yeok's assessments of the quality of the relationships between these systems with Family 2. This was co-constructed in close discussion and confirmation with the family. For example, three solid lines running in parallel represent a very close or strong relationship, such as the lines connecting Clive, Joy, Kit and Dolly, and Clive, Joy and Dolly with ADA and the recreational activities with Clive, Joy and Dolly. A dotted line represents a distant or tenuous relationship, such as Dolly's relationship with her own extended family – her eldest sister. Estranged or cut off relationship is depicted by hash marks drawn through the line. An estranged or cut relationship is depicted in Figure 8.5 between Family 2 and Joy's extended family, that is, her eldest brother as mentioned earlier on. An example of how the ecomap has facilitated further probing in accordance with the family's comfort level to share was when Clive eventually shared how contacts with Joy's eldest brother have been purposely kept to a minimal to avoid more negative outcomes that would create added stress to the family. Clive had even gone on to reveal that the family would be changing their email address and telephone number after they shift to their new house to cut off all ties and start life anew.

Arrows were used to indicate the flow of energy. Energy here would mean the amount of effort or investment put in by the family or its members and the support services. For example, the three solid parallel lines connecting Family 2 with ADA indicates a strong relationship. The line ends with arrows pointing from the family to ADA and from ADA to the family, indicating that the family invests a great deal of energy in ADA and receives a great deal of support from ADA. In fact, Clive and Joy had made it a point to accompany Dolly to the Dementia Café which is organised by ADA every weekend. The three solid lines connecting the recreational activities with Clive, Joy and Dolly have an arrow on one end, pointing from the recreational activities to Clive, Joy and Dolly. This indicates that the recreational activities invest a great deal of energy in Clive, Joy and Dolly but the relationship is not reciprocal. Clive, Joy and Dolly do not return the investment. May Yeok recalled Clive mentioning that the recreational activities were useful to the family for the fun part and they have simply made use of these as a free resource. Family 2 depicted in Figure 8.5 has a limited support system pertaining to the care of Dolly. In fact, the only strong reciprocal relationship they have was with ADA. For instance, they received strong support from the recreational activities but this support may not continue if Clive, Joy and Dolly remained non reciprocal.

May Yeok's co-construction of the genogram and ecomap with Clive, Joy and Kit facilitated a relational process that led to in-depth conversation and further disclosure of their experiences of supportive and non-supportive systems in their ecology. The use of the genogram and ecomap supported the ongoing and iterative question-posing which was integral to the generation of data for this case study. Furthermore, the process of genogram and ecomap construction paved the way for the generation of additional interview questions.

Photographs

May Yeok first started taking digital photographs of the inside and outside of the house and the specific objects as she believed that the digital photographs would represent the context of the family's caregiving experience. In order for this to succeed, she also made a conscious effort to co-produce the digital photographs with Clive. The effort has led to Clive's contribution of digital photographs of their family outings and doing things together. The intent was to meaningfully link these images with the ecomaps, interview field notes, audio-recording and transcripts to bring more meaning to her engagement with the family and give readers a visual lens to what she saw during her time with them. The interactional nature of the digital photographs with the ecomaps, interview field notes, audio-recording and transcripts was not merely just combining visual with graphical, textual and audio data but as a contribution to the methodology of photo elicitation. The inter-actional nature of the digital photographs as illustrated in the main texts of this chapter can be seen in, for example, Painting 4 which served to compliment the field observation of Clive's laborious effort and expressed purposeful intent in pro-viding and preparing care for Dolly. The many digital photographs provided a visual link to the other data which depicted a supportive and kindred family. The digital photographs as shared by Clive also provided May Yeok with an additional lens into the family's routine which she had no opportunity to experience and observe first hand.

Whilst highly individualised, this chapter reveals some of the complexity and rewards in working alongside families. There is a significant investment by the researcher, May Yeok, in time and trust in developing such work although the authentic representation of this family's lived reality could not be reported without it. We hope that some helpful pointers for future research, and researcher practice, can be taken from this chapter and applied to other contexts and situ-ations around the world.

Highlighted learning points from the method

- To co-produce genograms and ecomaps, the study design needs to allow for time to build trusting relationships.
- To generate additional interview questions, the researcher needs to utilise genograms and ecomaps as visual tools and guides.
- To incorporate digital photographs into the interview, the researcher should try to link the provided images with the other data such as genograms, ecomaps, audio recordings and field notes. This may well bring more meaning to the engagement with families and give readers a visual lens to what was seen in the field.
- Contributed digital photographs from the family provide an additional lens into the family's routine which the researcher may not have an opportunity to experience and observe first-hand. The provision of such artefacts requires time and trust between the researcher and the family.

Key references

- Hartman, A. (1978), Diagrammatic assessment of family relationships. *Social Casework*, 59(8): 465–476.
- The National Family Council and the Ministry of Community Development, Youth and Sports (2009). *Family first: state of the family report 2009*. Singapore.
- Tew, C.W., Tan, L.F., Luo, N., Ng, W.Y. and Yap, P. (2010) Why family caregivers choose to institutionalize a loved one with dementia: a Singapore perspective. *Dementia Geriatric Cognitive Disorder*, 30: 509–516.
- Yin, R.K. (2009) *Case study research: design and methods* (4th ed.). Thou-sand Oaks: SAGE Publications.

Recommended future reading

* Hinthorne, L.L. (2014). Using digital and instant film photography for research documentation: a research note. *Qualitative Research*, 14(4): 508–519.
* Rempel, G.R., Neufeld, A. and Kushner, K.E. (2007). Interactive use of genograms and ecomaps in family caregiving research. *Journal of Family Nursing*, 13(4): 403–419.
* Woodward, S. (2008) Digital photography and research relationships: capturing the fashion moment. *Sociology*, 42(5): 857–872.

Note

1 Author note: in this chapter 'family caregiver' or 'family carer' will be used to describe family members (spouse, children/children, in-law and other relatives) who provide regular at-home care, supervision and/or other support to a person living with dementia.

References

Access Economics Pty Ltd (2006). *Dementia in the Asia Pacific region: the epidemic is here*. Meeting of the Asia Pacific Members of Alzheimer's International, Singapore, May 2006.

Ampil, E.R., Fook-Chong, S., Sodagar, S.N., Chen, C.P. and Auchus, A.P. (2005). Ethnic variability in dementia: results from Singapore. *Alzheimer Disease Associated Disorder*, 19(4): 184–185.

Bronfenbrenner, U. (1979). Contexts of child rearing: problems and prospects. *American Psychologist*, 34: 844–850.

Cox, R.P. (2003). *Health related counselling with families of diverse cultures: family, health and cultural competencies*. Westport, CT: Greenwood Press.

Department of Health (ND) Policy: Dementia (online). Available from: www.gov.uk/government/policies/dementia (accessed 27 February 2017).

Department of Statistics, Singapore. (2012). Singapore in figures 2012 (online). Available from: www.singstat.gov.sg (accessed 11 April 2017).

Hanson, S. and Boyd, S. (1996). *Family health care nursing: theory, practice, and research*. Philadelphia: Davis.

Hartman, A. (1978), Diagrammatic assessment of family relationships. *Social Casework*, 59(8): 465–476.

Hilal, S., Ikram, M.K., Saini, M., Tan, C.S., Catindig, J.A., Dong, Y.H., Lim, L.B., Ting, E.Y., Koo, E.H., Cheung, C.Y., Qiu, A., Wong, T.Y., Chen, C.L. and Venketasubramanian, N. (2013). Prevalence of cognitive impairment in Chinese: epidemiology of dementia in Singapore study. *Journal of Neurology, Neurosurgery, and Psychiatry*, 84(6): 686–692.

Hsueh, K.H. (2001). *Family caregiving experience and health status among Chinese in the United States*. PhD dissertation. Ann Arbor, MI: UMI Dissertation Services, ProQuest Information and Learning.

Huang, X.Y., Sun, F.K., Yen, W.J. and Fu, C.M. (2008). The coping experiences of carers who live with someone who has schizophrenia. *Journal of Clinical Nursing*, 17(6): 817–826.

Kua, E.H. and Tan, S.L. (1997). Stress of caregivers of dementia patients in the Singapore Chinese family. *International Journal of Geriatric Psychiatry*, 12: 466–469.

Mehta, K.K. (2006). A critical review of Singapore's policies aimed at supporting families caring for older members. *Journal of Aging and Social Policy*, 18(3/4): 43–57.

Patterson, T.L., Semple, S.J., Shaw, W.S., Yu, E., Zhang, M.Y., Wu, W. and Grant, I. (1998). The cultural context of caregiving: a comparison of Alzheimer's caregivers in Shanghai, China and San Diego, California. *Psychological Medicine*, 28: 1071–1084.

Riessman C.K. (2008). *Narrative methods for the human sciences*. Thousand Oaks, CA: Sage Publications.

Sahadevan, S., Saw, S.M., Gao, W., Tan, L.C.S., Chin, J.J., Hong, C.Y. and Venketasubramanian, N. (2008). Ethnic differences in Singapore's dementia prevalence: the stroke, Parkinson's disease, epilepsy, and dementia in Singapore study. *Journal of the American Geriatrics Society*, 56(11): 2061–2068.

Seow, D. and Yap, P.L.K. (2011). Family caregivers and caregiving in dementia. *The Singapore Family Physician*, 137(3) (supplement1): 24–29.

Singapore Department of Statistics. (2012). Singapore in figures 2012 (online). Available from: www.singstat.gov.sg (accessed 9 April 2017).

Tew, C.W., Tan, L.F., Luo, N., Ng, W.Y. and Yap, P. (2010). Why family caregivers choose to institutionalize a loved one with dementia: a Singapore perspective. *Dementia Geriatric Cognitive Disorder*, 30: 509–516.

Thang L.L. and Mehta, K.K. (2009). *The dynamics of multigenerational care in Singapore*. Seminar on Family Support Networks and Population Ageing. Doha, Qatar, 3–4 June 2009.

The National Family Council and the Ministry of Community Development, Youth and Sports. (2009). *Family first: state of the family report 2009*. Singapore: The National Family Council and the Ministry of Community Development, Youth and Sports.

United Nations. (2004). *Population division of the department of economic and social affairs of the United Nations secretariat*, World Population Prospects: The 2004 Revision and World Urbanization Prospects

United Nations. (2006). *UN population division's world population prospects: the 2006 revision.* New York: United Nations Publications

Yap, P. and Seng, B.K. (2009). *Profiling the dementia family carer in Singapore* (online). Available from: www.alz.org.sg/about-dementia/publications (accessed 18 April 2017).

Yin, R.K. (2009). *Case study research: design and methods* (4th edition). Thousand Oaks: Sage Publications.

9 Storying stories to represent the lived experience of Deaf people living with dementia in research

Emma Ferguson-Coleman and Alys Young

Outline

This chapter will feature an in-depth exploration of Deaf British Sign Language (BSL) users who are living with dementia and how their stories were shared with a wider hearing audience using an approach to re-presentation of data based around cultural brokering for the reader. The visual methods employed to explore the lived experience of dementia for Deaf people through story telling will also be discussed.

Introduction

Deafness is most readily understood as the inability to hear and usually considered from the perspective of audiological levels of deafness, ranging from mild to profound. The most recent statistics via Action on Hearing Loss (2015) state that there are more than 11 million people in the UK with a hearing loss, which equates to one in six of the UK's population. The prevalence of hearing loss increases exponentially with age; Age UK (2015) states that 41.7 per cent of over 50-year-olds and 71.1 per cent of over 70-year-olds have some form of hearing loss. In post-industrial developed countries around the world, the prevalence is similar although much higher in the developing world with 70 per cent of the world's deaf children living in South Asia, Asia Pacific and Sub-Saharan Africa (World Health Organisation, 2012).

However, within this chapter, we are not writing about the vast majority of people with a hearing loss. Instead we focus on a separate group who differentiate themselves from the larger population by identifying themselves as members of a cultural-linguistic group (Ladd, 2003; Young and Hunt, 2011). To be Deaf is to use a distinct language, for example the UK British Sign Language (BSL), as a first or preferred language. BSL is a language with its own grammar, syntax and iconicity, separate from the spoken/written language(s) of the country (Sutton-Spence and Woll, 1999). Conventionally, the use of an upper case 'D' (Deaf) distinguishes culturally Deaf people from the wider population of deaf people with a lower case 'd' who are spoken language users, who may have lost their hearing later in life and who do not consider themselves as part of a linguistic and cultural community (Woodward, 1975; Padden and Humphries, 1988).

The legal and citizenship status of signed language users varies in different nation states (De Meulder, 2014) but BSL was formally recognised by the UK Government as an indigenous, natural language of the UK in 2003. More recently, the BSL (Scotland) Act 2015 (The Scottish Parliament, 2015) has taken this recognition one step further in guaranteeing protection and promotion of the rights of its users in Scotland. Like any other language-using group, Deaf people have a distinctive culture associated with language use and community (Padden and Humphries, 1988; Bauman and Murray, 2009) marked out by strong historical traditions, culturally distinct preferences, values and behaviours (Ladd, 2003) as well as a thriving artistic tradition (for example, Deafinitely Theatre in London; Pollitt, 2014). The same identification of Deaf peoples' cultural linguistic identity is apparent throughout the world and is endorsed in the United Nations Convention on the Rights of Persons with Disabilities (De Meulder, 2014).

There are varying estimates of how many BSL users there are resident in the UK. Furthermore, there are no concrete figures confirming how many Deaf people are aged over 65. While considering the possible prevalence of an older Deaf population, Young, Ferguson-Coleman and Keady state:

> Conservative estimates suggest a population of Deaf BSL users of between 50,000 and 100,000. Extrapolating from general population estimates (Office for National Statistics, 2012) of over 65s constituting 17 per cent of the population, rising to 23 per cent by 2035, this suggests a population of Deaf over 65s of between 8500 and 17,000 rising to 11,500 and 23,000 by 2035.
>
> (2016, p. 40)

Moreover, according to the Alzheimer's Society (2014), there are 850,000 people in the UK living with dementia, with only 44 per cent receiving a formal diagnosis. The overall number of people being diagnosed with dementia increases each year, because (a) the UK has an ageing population, due to people living longer, and (b) there is an increasing awareness about dementia via the mainstream and social media (Craig and Strivens, 2016). However, there are currently no confirmed statistics on how many Deaf BSL users are living with dementia, mostly because of the difficulty in determining accurate numbers of Deaf BSL users currently residing in the UK (see above). Nevertheless, Young, Ferguson-Coleman and Keady (2016) do offer a conservative estimate that 5 per cent of the 8,500–17,000 Deaf BSL users aged over 65 in the UK may have a diagnosis of dementia (in other words between 450 and 850 people). This clearly identifies a minority group in need of support, but also one about whom little is known; this is true within the UK context and internationally.

The Deaf with Dementia Project, funded by the Alzheimer's Society, ran from 2010 to 2013 at The University of Manchester in collaboration with other partners[1] and this chapter draws from some elements of that project (Alzheimer's

Society, 2013[2]), later published work (Ferguson-Coleman *et al.*, 2014; Young *et al.*, 2014; Young *et al.*, 2016) and further research (Ferguson-Coleman, 2016). The overarching aim of the initial project was to address the evidential gap in understanding the barriers to the earlier identification of dementia in the signing Deaf community. The highly limited literature and published evidence on an international basis prior to this project was confined to a small number of case reports of diagnostic challenges (Allan *et al.*, 2005; Dean *et al.*, 2009) and two first person autobiographical pieces from the perspectives of carers of Deaf people living with dementia (Conrad, 2004; Parker *et al.*, 2010). There was no pre-existing literature from the perspective of Deaf people who were *living* with dementia and who had been engaged in a research project, nor had the experiences and priorities of the Deaf community in general been sought about understanding, knowledge and awareness of dementia as well as available service provision. This chapter specifically focuses on the narrative work we carried out with Deaf people living with dementia and their care partners; publications relating to other aspects of the overall study are also available (see Atkinson *et al.*, 2015; Denmark *et al.*, 2016).

Why is personal evidence of lived experience important in the case of Deaf people living with dementia?

The recording of lived experiences of people living with dementia started in the late 1980s, as medical and health professionals realised that their client group were actually able to express themselves and that their views and opinions should be valued. Their personal testimonies reinforced the significance of a sense of self and being in their everyday worlds while living with dementia. It influenced professionals to prioritise their research and care approaches to become more person-centred. Kitwood's (1997) initial theory about identifying, engaging and respecting personhood evolved further to encompass, engage and elicit the direct lived experiences and the stories of people living with dementia and their care partners (Pearce *et al.*, 2002; Keady *et al.*, 2007; Kindell *et al.*, 2014).

Bartlett and O'Connor (2010) crucially challenged the concept of embracing personhood that was largely focused on the individual and their interactive self in context. Instead, they recognised the structural and societal elements and influences on the self living with dementia in opening up the perspective of citizenship. This has bolstered the argument that people living with dementia are and can be political citizens discussing their condition, how they should be treated and supported, and what the wider obligations of the society in which they live should be towards them, including a rights based perspective. This has empowered a movement where people living with dementia are now more visible and no longer unheard or under-represented (Bartlett and O'Connor, 2010; Bartlett, 2016; Brannelly, 2016).

Deaf people in general have experienced, historically, a similar evolution in citizenship claims and status throughout the decades. Instruction in sign language was removed from the educational system for deaf children in a sweeping

European-wide political reform in the late nineteenth century (Lane, 1984; Davies, 1995). In effect, this has meant that the Deaf community's visibility was removed from the mainstream until the late 1970s and recognition of citizenship on basis of language use and associated culture denied (Ladd 2003). Emancipation from this has only occurred in recent years after activism from the National Union of the Deaf (Ladd, 1982) and the Federation of Deaf People (Beschizza *et al.*, 2015) that led eventually to the recognition of BSL as a community language in the UK in 2003. Since then, there has been much improved public representation of sign language in the media and via social media. In Scotland in 2015, recognition in law was finally passed on the status of BSL (The Scottish Parliament, 2015) and enforcement of legal and citizenship rights on this basis with obligations placed firmly on social structures and organisations to meet those rights (Reid, 2016). The revolution in personhood and citizenship for Deaf people living with dementia, however, is still a very long way off, a fact not unconnected with systemic failures to recognise the linguistic and cultural status of Deaf users of BSL and therefore failure to identify needs, requirements and rights on that basis.

Deaf citizens with dementia telling their stories

Parker, Young and Rogers (2010) published the first first-person narrative of a Deaf carer discussing her experiences of caring for her Deaf mother while she was living with dementia. This paper (written in English, not presented in BSL) evidenced how Deaf people living with dementia do not have a say about their care and how the significance of their language use and cultural history to their personhood is largely unrecognised. At one point in the paper, Parker remarks that 'the lack of structured activity in her (mother's) life, and the lack of company and conversational stimulation, led to a shrinking of her ability to communicate and interact with people' (p. 19). Other evidence from carers' stories paints a similar picture and discusses everyday experiences throughout the diagnosis and aftercare support strategies offered (Conrad, 2004; Rantapää and Pekkala, 2014). However, these stories are solely published through the carers' personal narratives. Deaf people living with dementia have remained largely invisible until the inception of the Deaf with Dementia Project.

The Deaf with Dementia Project included individual in-depth interviews with four Deaf people with a confirmed diagnosis of dementia on at least two occasions (Young *et al.*, 2014). The project enabled and empowered Deaf BSL users living with dementia and their families to share their stories, for the first time, directly with a Deaf researcher (author Ferguson-Coleman). The impact and the significance of this sharing process are not to be under-estimated. This was the first time throughout their dementia journey that members of the signing community had been directly asked in their own language about their personal experiences of accessing mainstream services, which, in their view, did not effectively or sufficiently cater for their cultural or linguistic requirements. By sharing their stories with a Deaf researcher, in their language, BSL, their contributions to original knowledge was captured without the need for modification in their communication or use of interpreters. Participants who were living with dementia and their family members did not need to adjust their communication methods in order to fit in with a non-source language interviewer, i.e. a hearing person who does not use sign language, or a hearing person using an interpreter (Young and Ackerman, 2001).

Those who participated in the research also reflected on the significance of *being enabled* to tell their stories, as well as simply telling them. The significance consisted of several points from their perspective. First, they were visible (quite literally) for the first time. They were very aware of, and welcomed, the fact that Deaf people and their families who were living with dementia were going to be formally acknowledged and they, too, were going to be included. Sign language users are aware that they do not fit easily into the discourse of disability, sensory loss and dementia as this mostly deals with those who have been hearing and become deaf and of those who speak (Alzheimer's Society, 2016; All-Party Parliamentary Group, 2016). Nor do they fit into policy and practice documents about minority linguistic or cultural communities who experience dementia because Deaf people are rarely recognised as such (All-Party Parliamentary Group, 2013) despite BSL achieving formal recognition as an indigenous community language since 2003. Furthermore, within the Deaf community itself, there has been little acknowledgement or recognition about those in the community who live with dementia and their valued contribution. Therefore, significance lies first in the power of the stories to identify and recognise this group of people.

Second, Deaf participants told us that they wanted their stories and experiences to be recorded in order to make a difference to others who were Deaf and who may go on to develop dementia. The phrase '[this discussion we are having now], it's not for me, but for them' was a repeated sentiment. The 'them' was positioned in in the future aimed at the mainstream community and also their Deaf community because some of what we were told were bitter and sad accounts of how poorly their needs had been recognised and how they had suffered as a result. For example, Harold and Pearl[3] shared their experiences in having a lack of support from their local Deaf community. Despite having attended the same Deaf club(s) for 40 years, the onset of Harold's dementia meant that he was no longer welcome to participate in regular games (such as bridge and dominoes) as he had become 'too slow' and could not keep up. Moreover, Pearl was ostracised for being at the Deaf club having a cup of tea with her friends because she had left Harold at home despite this being his wish, as he acknowledged she needed some respite. Pearl's 'friends' could not appreciate the reciprocal relationship between Harold and Pearl, instead making the accusation that she was neglecting her husband. Yet mainstream dementia support groups were also not the answer for Pearl who was very anxious about accessing them because she felt she was going to be the 'stupid one' for not being able to follow what was being said between the other predominantly hearing carers (Ferguson-Coleman, 2016).

Third, participants had a strong feeling that it was not only their own lives which were being represented and recognised through the research but that they were also representing the whole community to which they belonged. To appreciate their personal stories was to appreciate the perspective and lives of the whole Deaf community. For example, Beryl wanted her local Deaf communities to know about her dementia, as it was important for them to understand what living with dementia was like, and to maintain her presence within the local Deaf club was, in her view, absolutely crucial to her wellbeing. However, she was frustrated at the Deaf club members' attitudes towards her presentation of self. They remarked that she 'looked' the same as before, she 'signed' the same as before, so really, there was nothing wrong with her (as if she were not living with dementia). There was no appreciation or bolstering of the fact that she was maintaining her *self* and therefore, her Deaf *identity*. Deaf cultures throughout the world are characteristically collective rather than individualistic cultures in their orientation (Bauman and Murray, 2014) and the sense of 'do it to one and you do it to all of us' is a very emotive response to challenging barriers (Young *et al.*, 2014).

Making visible the hidden experiences and lives of Deaf people living with dementia both to the mainstream services/general population and to the Deaf community was, in itself, a significant step towards better lives and services for those Deaf people living with dementia, but how exactly was this achieved?

Visual methods and approaches in data collection with Deaf people living with dementia

The story telling medium within Deaf culture

An important facet of Deaf culture is how stories are told and shared with one another (Bahan, 2008). In part, this is because Deaf communities are 'oral' cultures in the sense of passing on of heritage and history happens without a written form, because signed languages are entirely visual, not orthographic languages. Story telling is also commonly regarded as a method of fact-sharing, rather than seen as fiction or narrative. The sharing of information in a storied form is an effective way of retaining information and details for ongoing transmission. In a hearing, auditory and print based majority world, this alternative method of sharing and processing information has always been regarded as precious amongst Deaf people and communities because information can be so hard to obtain (Lane *et al.*, 2010). It is also something that is necessary to be shared. Finally, stories are an essential part of shared cultural identity from Deaf people's perspectives because they are often used to highlight the special and visual nature of Deaf people's orientation in the world. Bahan (2008) and Rutherford (1993), amongst others, have collected typical stories in Deaf communities around the world and showed how they are reproduced and connected across continents. Stories, therefore, are a crucial visual means to bolster the Deaf person's identity and their sense of belonging to a community with shared values and experiences as minority citizens. Given this socio-cultural context, it was crucial that Deaf people living with dementia were given a culturally recognisable means to participate in the research, one in which they felt comfortable within this same level of sanctuary that was familiar in mutual Deaf to Deaf storytelling. We therefore chose narrative based interviews in which Deaf people living with dementia were invited to tell their stories directly with another Deaf person who they knew would share a heritage of storytelling with them through their shared culture.

Cultural aspects of rapport building

Prior to the first interview taking place, there was an exchange of personal information between author Ferguson-Coleman and the participants present. Within Deaf culture, the positioning of the Deaf person is necessary to understand one another's backgrounds (for example, one's education, employment) as common ground can be quickly established and linguistic registers are also adjusted (Jones and Pullen 1992; Young and Ackerman, 2001). For instance, Ernest had been a BSL teacher for many years. At the commencement and through the interview, he took up this role in deliberately correcting Emma's signs to what he believed were the appropriate signs to be used. This correction was an exchange of linguistic and hierarchical positioning ('I am the teacher here') but also an activity that established a comfortable rapport with one another. If this exchange had taken place with a hearing non-fluent researcher, this deliberate positioning may have been perceived differently; instead of building rapport, the non-fluent person might have felt insulted by Ernest's correction. Moreover, Ernest used an inappropriate sign for a word (using it in the wrong context) as a nod to his extensive knowledge of BSL, but also as a nod to understanding that our rapport had been built securely enough for him to inject his humour at this point.

Languages can break and build trust

After this rapport had been established, Emma asked the participants' permission to video-record the interviews taking place. Informed consent was recorded by going through each item on the research ethics committee-approved consent form individually in BSL. The video camera additionally recorded this consent process as a visual back-up to the written initials and signature provided by each participant. The rapport built up prior to this stage was imperative to gaining consent in BSL; Emma then became, in the participant's view, a trustworthy person who communicated in the same language, which meant that the participant (a) felt able to clarify the information shared, (b) could check in with their spouse or primary carer that they were understanding what was taking place, and (c) affirmed their consent to taking part in the study in their own language. However, this rapport was threatened by the break in dialogue that occurred when the participant needed to physically sign each item with their initial and signature. As soon as they were faced with the English language, the preparation that had been undertaken and mutually understood in BSL by Emma then broke down and was lost, as this did not match their understanding of the written word. Ernest, in particular, directly sought clarification from Emma, and also from his spouse, as he became very anxious that he did not know what he was agreeing to on the paper version of the consent item as it was not in his first and preferred language, BSL. It did not matter to him that he had consented willingly in his own language seconds before – the sudden change in modality was unfamiliar to him and he responded accordingly. Ernest was given reassurance with Emma signing each consent item again, allowing him the time to look at the English version and build his trust in that Emma had signed in BSL what was there on paper.

Sightlines

The visual world is very important to Deaf people – you have to be able to see each other to communicate. It is also important for comfort – distractions in the sight line, whether from objects or patterns, are distractions to concentration. For example, if a person is wearing a multi-coloured top, it can be very difficult to distinguish signs against this backdrop, even more so if the person has issues with their eyesight or with the reception of signed communication over a long period of time. With this in mind, Emma wore plain colours that were as least visually distracting as possible. In conducting the interviews, it was therefore vital to ensure that everyone within the visual environment was non-distracting and that the physical environment was optimal for shared interactions. Emma then checked with the participants and their care partner(s) that they were sitting in their preferred positions (for example, Maggie was sitting on her usual place on the sofa near the window and, in another interview, Ernest was sitting in his chair in the conservatory) for their comfort and for their familiarity. Emma (and in some interviews, the carers) would locate themselves around the Deaf person living with dementia so that their faces and hands could be seen through the video camera lens for recording purposes. Deaf people generally do not sit directly next to each other when talking to one another, as this impedes the opportunity to access the other person's eye contact, facial expressions, body language, and their communication. Ensuring appropriate sightlines was vital to effective data generation.

Carer's scaffolding strategies

This awareness of the physical positioning of the participants was represented in the interviews, but there was another subtext in that the primary carers antici-pated the additional role of providing scaffolding to enable their family member to fully participate in our conversations. However, once again this was a visual requirement. It was a naturally assumed role, which was not directly discussed, but observed by Emma and recognised throughout the subsequent analysis of the data. For example, Beryl and Sheila (her daughter) were sitting slightly facing one another, where Beryl could watch Sheila's face intently for cues for when it was appropriate for her to join in with the conversation. In another situation, Harold would lift his forefinger in a clasped handshape and wave this from side to side (which is not a usual convention within BSL dialogue) to indicate that he wished to say something while watching his wife and daughter signing. His care partner(s) supported this unusual convention for joining a conversation as they recognised that Harold was maintaining his presence, and thus his autonomy, in our conversation the best way he knew how to. In some instances Harold did contribute a comment, in others he did not; the point was he was telling people he was part of this too.

Eye contact and managing flow

An imperative part of communicating in BSL is the use of eye contact. This reflects how one is taking part (or not) within a shared conversation. For the Deaf person living with dementia, this visual means of communicating reflected their inner feelings about the situation they found themselves within. For example, Beryl and Sheila were talking about future care options and about whether Beryl could move to a local residential home where the residents were hearing (or non-signing people). Beryl expressed her discomfort at this thread of dialogue taking place so she dropped eye contact with both Sheila and Emma, thus disengaging herself from the conversation. It was a non-verbal means of disengagement that is much more powerful for those who used a visual language because if you do not look, you are not part of a conversation, literally. It was a means also of expressing her feelings about the proposed support – not worth her engagement (eye contact). Attention to those aspects of conversational engagement that were visually meaningful, not just visually grammatically salient were also important in the narrative approach we took to data generation.

Signing space

BSL has a usual (invisible) frame of reference in which a person will sign while they are communicating. This is across the chest within arm's length within a 3D space (Sutton-Spence and Woll, 1999). However, this frame slightly changed for each Deaf person living with dementia who was interviewed. For example, Harold would sign across his stomach area and limited this space within a 6-inch square. Beryl signed from her lap, or would 'mouth' her words to Sheila and Emma as she knew that she would be understood by both parties present. These linguistic features were noted also in how the visual data we collected were ana-lysed and are akin to verbal changes such as getting words in the wrong order, or finding it difficult to construct a sentence. This aspect of how dementia affects Deaf people is only beginning to be recorded (Rantapää and Pekkala, 2014). In this study, we considered it from the perspective of continued but changed means of communicative involvement. For example, although from a linguistic perspective it was grammatically 'wrong', from Harold and others' perspectives it was an effective means of continued conversational engagement, which did not stop just because the signing space was altered.

Analysing visual data

The participants' interviews were video-recorded, as mentioned previously, and securely stored within a remote data server that was password-protected. These videos were then opened via the qualitative data analysis software, NVivo 9 (QSR, 2012), but not directly stored within the software for confidentiality purposes. NVIVO 9 and above has the facility to tag (add a thematic category) to visual data without the requirement to translate and transcribe it into written text first. The data were kept in the source language and each video was tagged with relevant themes as they developed throughout the dialogue. English notes were contemporaneously typed alongside each video as well while it was viewed. These themes were discussed within the research team to confirm that they were representative of the stories shared by the participants and a number of minor alterations made.

Through watching the videos, however, it became evident that the actual physical environment in itself held positive contributions to each participant's involvement in the interview for reasons such as those outlined above, linked with their visual environment, scaffolding strategies, means of joining and leaving conversations, and how Deaf people living with dementia asserted their presence and agency, regardless of whether a direct contribution to conversation was made. In other words, not just the content of what was said (signed) was important but also different aspects of the holistic environment. In spoken language qualitative studies of people living with dementia, a second layer of analysis is often referred to as analysing the 'non-verbal'. But given that Deaf people's language *is* non-verbal, this more holistic approach exceeds those usual considerations of the non-verbal. In the case of Deaf people, the non-verbal *is* linguistic. Therefore the non-verbal features observed often contained within them aspects of the linguistic, grammatical and common usage of how Deaf people communicate, be it transposed into a different form because of effects of dementia (Young *et al.*, 2014). Therefore this approach to data analysis sought to capture these multiple layers.

What follows is a tabular example of the first stage in data analysis working with the raw data in BSL. It concerns only two responses within an interview that lasted two hours that were being watched by the lead author. Whilst maintaining the original BSL on screen, she first translated alongside them the content of the utterance. She included also remarks on the location for the interview but also the location of the participants. This was important when the scaffolding strategies mentioned above were looked at in greater detail. Next, notes were added of visual observations that were a part of the exchanges and interactions and were regarded as data too. Finally, the researcher's own reflections arising from this process of watching and noting segments of the data were added. This painstaking process occurred for all the recorded material.

Interview 003 Part 1	Participant 1 (person living with dementia)	Participant 2 (Deaf or hearing carer)	Emma (Deaf researcher)	Location (whereabouts of interview)	Time on video (to visually support the written version of these notes)	Notes from researcher
				We are all sitting in the conservatory. Ernest is sitting in his preferred chair, while Libby (his wife) sits next to him on his right.	00:01	
Question			So … tell me about what was different for you, when did you notice there was a change?		13:38	I deliberately make eye contact with Ernest to show clearly I am asking him the question.
Response (1)	Well … erm … do you want to say something?				13:45–13:58	Ernest moves his eyes towards his wife, Libby, to indicate his wishes that she should respond to this initial question.
Response (2)		You, you started to be different. Our daughters, you know, they told me, they said Dad's not the same as he was … You have to understand having dementia is OK, you're not the only one, Margaret Thatcher, and, you know, the president of USA, they have it too, they are marvellously clever and you are too.			14:15–14:59	Libby is quite hesitant in being descriptive about the onset of Ernest's dementia. She tries to repair this with the following message in column 3. Libby is conveying this message with fervour while she signs with Ernest as she is so keen to reassure him that it's OK to talk about this sensitive subject with an external person to their tight family unit.
Contemporaneous notes			I was observing both parties while this dialogue was taking place. I wanted to ensure Ernest was comfortable with this shared information. I reiterated that this interview video would not be shown to anyone and that their names would be confidential.		14:23–14:59	Ernest has tapped Libby on her knee or on her elbow while she is signing with Emma to indicate his presence in our dialogue. Libby's body language is very animated, she is keenly leaning forward towards Ernest as she really wants him to appreciate her contribution without feeling demeaned.

The second stage of the analysis process involved considering where the points of similarity and difference were in the interviews, in other words, a process of abstraction into themes. However this was only applied to the 'content' of the interviews – i.e. recurring ideas and issues in what was 'said', for example, problems with interpreters, professionals who don't understand, things that happen too late. However, this did not capture other features of how the narratives were performed by and through those participants, such as those noted in the final column of the researcher's notes and which were essential to sustaining the narrative. These, too, contained overarching thematic considerations such as: 'scaffolding strategies'; 'processes that enable agency'; 'arriving at shared meanings'. Therefore these were coded separately. They were not present in the text if by that one means the translated words on the page, or the actual signed utterances. They were, nonetheless, there in the culturally embedded and embodied behaviours shared between participants and observed by the researcher. As an additional aid at this stage of the analysis, contextual drawings were also produced for each interview that showed the location and orientation of participants during the interviews. An example of how the original visual context was drawn up is demonstrated below.

Diagram 1

At each stage in this process, the lead author shared the development of these ideas and the thematic structures with the research team in order to verify how

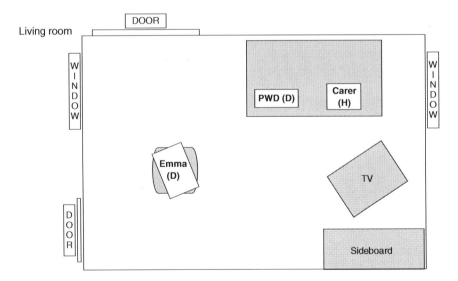

Diagram 9.1 Example of visual content drawing.

Note
There were no alternative seats in the room so the researcher borrowed a chair from the adjacent kitchen.

this data analysis was undertaken. One member of the research team could not sign fluently so a BSL interpreter was booked to facilitate communication. Authors Ferguson-Coleman and Young shared their cultural observations of what was happening throughout the video.

A case study approach (Yin, 1989) allowed for the participant's personal histories to be understood before their stories were presented. Second, a narrative analysis (Riessman, 2008) was used to explore the themes and the structures that afforded the opportunity for these stories to be shared. The final stage of data analysis was concerned with how this complex, multi-layered expression of living with dementia might be conveyed in a written form. For this stage we adopted an approach of storied stories (McCormack, 2004) that enabled the re-presentation of the participants' stories in order for them to be understood by the majority community (hearing, non-signing people). For the purpose of this chapter, we have chosen to focus on aspects of the narratives and the approach of storying stories.

Storied stories

We are aware that a traditional qualitative analysis and presentation of participants' data (whether thematically or in the form of narrative analyses) could potentially only give a partial view of their experiences of living with dementia. It could show important content and perspectives, perhaps, but it could not reproduce the feel of those narratives. In part, this is a problem of how one represents what might be characteristic of how dementia is affecting their communication, interaction and sense of self. Research can have a tendency, in how we write up data, to clean up and make formal that which is more textured and unorthodox. Additionally, there was a problem of conveying cultural significance and embedded cultural meanings that may not be apparent in what or how something is said or signed if those reading the interpretation and presentation of the data are cultural outsiders. An element of cultural brokering was required in the presentation of the data analysis. This was true both in the sense of the hearing communities who may understand little of Deaf people's language and culture and in the sense of the Deaf community who may understand little about dementia and its effects.

'Storying stories' (Mishler, 1999; McCormack, 2004) is a process of reconstructing someone's story that does not necessarily entail using the same words/signs but which conveys the same meanings through additions that contextualise and positioning someone within their own life history during the re-telling. This can take the form of commentary and interjection in which the author is both the teller and the commentator. It can take the form of judicious use of language and syntax that re-presents and conveys additional textures and layers of feeling through syntactical and lexical choices.

Within this specific socio-cultural context, it was important for the reader to understand, for example, features of Deaf heritage, culture and history that the original participant implied and assumed Emma would appreciate but that were not explicit. Nonetheless, they were cultural components of his/her experience of living with dementia that were conveyed through how the participants expressed themselves i.e. allusions within their expression itself. In other cases, explication was required about the meaningfulness of the non-verbal components of BSL – features of the language that have no direct translation but which have semantic intent. Finally, just as in spoken language, an influence of dementia might be changes in how something is expressed or how language is used; in a signed language this occurs in space through differences in shape, location and orientation of signed components. The conveying of meaning expressed differently would be particularly difficult in translation from signed original data to translated English/written presentation.

Storied stories, therefore, represented an appropriate means and opportunity. First, the researcher becomes a cultural broker through the in-depth explanation of Deaf cultural norms to the uninitiated hearing reader; second, the researcher illuminates understanding by re-presenting the Deaf person living with dementia as a narrator using their own language, BSL; and, third, the hearing reader becomes aware of the compromises, such as power and language imbalances, that exist through the ontological pre-assumptions that occur in everyday lives living as a minority group within a majority community. Furthermore, from the perspective of the Deaf community members who are not living with dementia, storying stories offers an alternative dimension to understanding one of their own. In this research study, the Deaf community informed us that role-play and story-telling were the most appropriate method in which to educate and understand what it might be like to live with dementia (Young *et al.*, 2016). We therefore also produced storied stories (representation of data) in BSL, not just in written English. These were undertaken by asking a well-known Deaf actor in BSL to represent first-hand narrative. It was important to choose a well-known actor as this offered linguistic and cultural validity of the story being told, as he was someone who was known, and therefore a knower of the shared experiences of the Deaf community. A story was filmed in four parts. Alongside his monologue, Emma also filmed four corresponding explanations in BSL as to why and how it was important that the participant represented has shared different elements of his personal experiences and the consequential impact of this sharing. Below, we have reproduced storied stories in English and to see the BSL version of these storied stories, these are available at: www.deafwithdementiahub.com

Harold's story: knowing

I met with Harold, a gentleman in his 80s, and his family to share his personal stories. We met at his family home where he had resided for over 40 years. He used BSL as his first language for all his life and had received his diagnosis of Alzheimer's within the last two years. Within our dialogue together, Harold shared a wealth of information around his everyday experiences; for example, what it was like for him to attend GP appointments without an interpreter, what it was like for him to cope with an overtly interfering paid Deaf carer who overruled Harold's communication with his GP and the memory clinic, and what it was like to be ostracised from his local Deaf community of which he had been a member all of his life.

While Harold was signing with me, he shared some personal stories about how his son was now supporting him with personal care; how his wife now had to support him by guiding him on where to sign his name on cheques and how he thoroughly enjoyed chatting with his daughter regularly via Skype on his iPad.

While we were sitting together, Harold was quietly confident that he, with his family's support, could contribute to our discussion with one another by maintaining eye contact, using his hands to indicate that he wished to sign something to us and asserting his views by fixing his gaze on his wife or towards me to share his comments. Harold commanded the conversation when it was his turn to contribute and the use of BSL, with its non-verbal components, meant that everything he signed held value and was structured with linguistic meaning.

In the midst of Harold's explanation of his understanding why things were changing around him, he signed evocatively, but minimally, his knowledge that his self and his identity were slowly eroding. He signed two words: 'me' and 'diminish'. However, the non-verbal elements and embodiment of this sentence elaborated far more the story he was telling than just those two signs. From the movement of his eyes, which had previously held me in his gaze, from breaking his eye contact and looking downwards (as if he were looking inwardly) to the facial movement he made to emphasise the loss of his identity, which was to blow out his cheeks with a moue shape on his lips (which demonstrated to me and meant to him the magnitude of this loss), Harold powerfully shared the knowledge that his language was slowly disappearing, and therefore his sole means of communication was being slowly taken away by dementia.

Maggie's story: refusal

I also met with Maggie, a lady in her late 80s, with her daughter in her supported living accommodation. This was a purpose-built block of residential flats, owned by a housing association, which had 15 floors. There was a manager and a team of support workers who visited each flat daily to offer care and support to the residents if this was needed. Maggie felt very isolated and lonely in this flat, as she was the only Deaf BSL user living there, and the people who she met on a daily basis were all hearing non-signers. Maggie's daughter, Teresa, visited her mother either every day or every other day.

While Maggie and I were talking about her current living arrangements, I asked Maggie questions about her flat. She was content to explain to me the layout and the purpose of each room. However, when I touched upon the subject of the care staff that visited Maggie each day, asking what they were like, it became very clear that this was a sensitive issue for her. I was already aware that this was because the care staff did not communicate in her first language. We were sitting in her living room facing one another, with Maggie maintaining her presence in the conversation by using eye contact with me, and nodding towards me in agreement when I asked her questions.

Within the living room, there was a red cord behind the sofa attached to the ceiling for Maggie to pull if she should need help. Maggie was sitting on the sofa and the red cord was out of her line of vision. I pointed to this red cord and asked what it was for. In BSL, eye contact and the lines of eye contact are really important, as previously highlighted when discussing Harold's story. First, if two people signing with one another are pointing at things that are external to the eye line, it is natural for one person to look at the actual item before the conversation is continued with the return and directness of the eye gaze. Additionally, if a Deaf person moves their eye gaze beyond your face while you are in conversation with them, this can be a clear indicator of intention; for example, this can mean that the person is demonstrating that they want to show you something, that they might be thinking about their response to what you've just said or that they have refused to continue the conversation. Within this scenario, Maggie was making it very clear to me that she wished to cease this line of questioning and did not wish to contribute further. This was her way of clearly saying 'No, I do not wish to discuss that red cord (that I know you've just pointed at) because I know that pulling it means those hearing carers will come to the door, and what is the point in that because I cannot communicate with them (or rather, they cannot communicate with me)'. By Maggie using her embodiment to deliberately break her eye contact with me, this message could not have been any more explicitly meant. If a hearing person who did not use sign language or who was not familiar with Deaf cultural norms, they may have pressed this issue further as they may have assumed that Maggie had not understood the question.

Summary

The way in which Harold and Maggie's stories have been shared is a method of cultural narrativity that supports the relaying information within their socio-cultural context. By explaining the multiple layers of BSL as a visual language and all its components, the stories of Deaf BSL users can then be understood and valued by the mainstream hearing community, as well as directly empathised with and owned by Deaf community members who will immediately understand the impact of what has been shared. These layers of cultural narrativity bolster the understanding of the needs of Deaf BSL users when accessing healthcare services; to simply say Maggie does not have access to interpreters for her healthcare needs does not offer an insight into what this means for her as a citizen and for her existence in a hearing environment. Her emotive response to the question posed about the red cord contributes a significant understanding of her frustration and loneliness in the flat where no one uses her language. For Harold, the emotive way in which he embodied his feelings about losing his identity were not about the formal structure of BSL being followed; his ownership and life-long use of the language enmeshed with the emotions and knowledge that he was diminishing. These stories have been captured through Deaf eyes and re-presented with Deaf eyes, so that the impact of these experiences has not been lessened.

Ethical considerations in this study

The Deaf community is geographically diverse within the UK; however, it is very small in number (British Deaf Association, 2016). It was therefore imperative that names and any other identifying characteristics were removed from the data. This issue was discussed with all of the participants who were reassured that their anonymity would be maintained throughout.

Informed consent was of priority in this study. Author Ferguson-Coleman used a method called process consent (Dewing, 2007) whereby she would check in with all parties at different stages throughout the information sharing and subsequent interviews that they were satisfied that they were happy to continue our dialogue. This process of taking consent at different times ensured that their permission to continue remained timely appropriate, rather than agreeing consent once and assuming that this remained the same without checking again. This was at times a lengthy process due to the necessary translation of the supporting statements in English to BSL. The fact that these interviews took place between Deaf people (author Ferguson-Coleman and the participants) was vital to the method of process consent.

Ethical approval for this study was granted by the National Research Ethics Service Committee North West – Greater Manchester South Research Ethics Committee (reference number 11/NW/0669).

Conclusion and reflections

Within the last decade, there has been an emergent philosophy within the dementia movement that asks researchers and care professionals to consider and value the impact of the non-verbal aspects of communication and embodiment when supporting a hearing person living with dementia (Kontos, 2005; Kontos and Martin, 2013; Ward *et al.*, 2014). It is acutely evident that non-verbal cues can impart valuable layers of information in a person's narrative, with undoubtedly demonstrable evidence of embodiment; for example, Kontos (2005) discusses how a woman is sitting in her chair in the dining hall (in the residential unit where she lives) lifting her hand to ensure that her pearl necklace is still at her neck, as this is an important part of her identity and life-long experience of wearing jewellery.

While considering embodiment and its meaningfulness for the signing Deaf population, there was soon the realisation that Deaf people are actually embodied, by being visual beings as a lifelong experience. As earlier explained, BSL is a visual language, which encapsulates the use of facial expressions, body language, the use of the chest as a linear concept amongst other components. Furthermore, in addition to considering how embodiment might be reflected while using a visual language, it became evident that the structure of the Deaf person's story was not just based on what was signed, but *how* it was signed; how their feelings and emotions might be placed on the non-verbal continuum, in space and place, such as on or around their body, underpinned by lifelong use of visual grammar and syntax. In BSL, non-verbal cues are not positioned within the non-linguistic cues; they are actually part of BSL as a structure, and are therefore holistically meaningful.

Within a face-to-face conversation between two people, there can be elements of non-verbal communication that may not be considered as meaningful if they cannot be interpreted within the frame of embodiment. For example, if a hearing person called Anna, living with dementia in a residential unit, moved her eyes away from her hearing care worker, Susie, while they were talking together in the lounge, Susie might not consider this as a noticeable adjustment in their communication.

However, if Anna was Deaf and Susie was Deaf, then Susie would notice this change in eye movement and would check in with Anna as to why she moved her eyes in that particular direction: maybe someone else has entered the room; or maybe Anna is using her eyes to 'point' at the person or object that she is talking about; or Anna might be saying she does not wish to continue her dialogue with Susie. There are many layers of meaning to the eye movement that can only be observed by another fluent BSL user, or through 'Deaf eyes', who is present in that dialogue, to interpret and value that deliberate non-verbal modification in the conversation. This is one representation of how Deaf citizens are non-verbal beings.

Storying stories has enabled the mainstream hearing non-signing community to value and appreciate the different elements of the cultural and linguistic representation of the Deaf person living with dementia and their carers. If their stories were just written in a 2D format, the impact of their personal experiences would not be as powerful. It has also provided a culturally relevant means of the Deaf community engaging with the sensitive and largely unknown topic of dementia through engaging with stories in BSL about people living with dementia that act as a trigger for exploration and knowledge acquisition.

As discussed earlier, those who took part were firmly of the view that this was not about them, it was about 'us' and that 'us' reached into a future where it might be possible that the understanding of Deaf people living with dementia, their lives, contributions and needs could be better attended to. Since this study took place, three of the participants have passed away but their stories shared in this chapter are part of their legacy to this community.

Highlighted learning points from the method

- Visual methods of generating data with Deaf people living with dementia are culturally effective. However, these methods are also transferable to the mainstream community for those who wish to capture a non-verbal representation of people living with dementia.
- The Deaf community is a hidden population within the mainstream community; using narratives and storying stories enables the opening up of an otherwise invisible cultural and linguistic minority group and facilitates a better understanding of this population.
- Empowering and enabling opportunities for citizenship holds parallels for the mainstream dementia community and the Deaf community, particularly for Deaf people living with dementia.
- The non-verbal is not a differentiation from the majority dementia population; Deaf people are fundamentally non-verbal in their language, culture and values. Exploring the non-verbal is a new concept for the majority population, while for Deaf people, and for Deaf people living with dementia, this is an ontological way of being in the world.

Key references

- Ferguson-Coleman, E., Keady, J. and Young, A. (2014). Dementia and the Deaf community: knowledge and service access. *Aging and Mental Health*, 18(6): 674–682.
- Parker, J., Young, A. and Rogers, K. (2010). 'My mum's story': a Deaf daughter discusses her Deaf mother's experience of dementia. *Dementia: The International Journal of Social Research and Practice*, 9(1): 5–20.
- Young, A.M., Ferguson-Coleman E. and Keady J. (2014) Understanding the personhood of Deaf people living with dementia: methodological issues. *Journal of Aging Studies*, 31: 62–69.
- Young, A., Ferguson-Coleman, E. and Keady, J. (2016). Understanding dementia: effective information access from the Deaf community's perspective. *Health and Social Care in the Community*, 24(1): 39–47.
- Young, A. and Hunt, R. (2011). *Research with d/Deaf people* (vol. 9). London: NIHR School for Social Care Research Methods Review.

Recommended future reading

- McCormack, C. (2004). Storying stories: a narrative approach to in-depth interview conversations. *International Journal of Social Research Methodology*, 7(3): 219–236.
- Mishler, E.G. (1999). *Storylines: craftartists' narratives of identity.* Cambridge: Harvard University Press.

Notes

1 The Deaf with Dementia Project partners were The University of Manchester, Deafness, Cognition and Language Centre within University College London, City University London and Royal Association for Deaf people. More information can be found here: www.manchester.ac.uk/deafwithdementia
2 Details can be found here: http://research.bmh.manchester.ac.uk/deafwithdementia/PublicationsDissemination/laysummarydwdBSL.pdf
3 All the names of the research participants in this chapter have been changed to preserve anonymity.

References

Action on Hearing Loss. (2015). *Facts and figures on hearing loss, deafness and tinnitus* (online). Available at: www.actiononhearingloss.org.uk/your-hearing/about-deafness-and-hearing-loss/statistics.aspx
Age UK. (2015). *Hearing loss* (online). Available at: www.ageuk.org.uk/health wellbeing/conditions-illnesses/hearing/causes-of-hearing-loss/
All-Party Parliamentary Group on Dementia (2013). *Dementia does not discriminate.* London: All-Party Parliamentary Group on Dementia.
All-Party Parliamentary Group on Dementia (2016). *Dementia rarely travels alone.* London: All-Party Parliamentary Group on Dementia.
Allan, K., Stapleton, K. and McLean, F. (2005). *Dementia and deafness: an exploratory study.* Stirling: University of Stirling.
Alzheimer's Society. (2014). *Factsheet: what is dementia?* (online). Available at: www.alzheimers.org.uk/site/scripts/download_info.php?fileID=1754 (accessed 2 February 2017).
Alzheimer's Society. (2016). *Factsheet: communicating* (online). Available at: www.alzheimers.org.uk/download/downloads/id/1789/factsheet_communicating.pdf (accessed 2 February 2017).
Atkinson, J., Denmark, T., Marshall, J., Mummery, C. and Woll, B. (2015). Detecting cognitive impairment and dementia in deaf people: the British Sign Language cognitive screening test. *Archives of Clinical Neuropsychology*, 30: 694–711.
Bahan, B.I. (2008). Upon the formation of a visual variety of the human race. In Bauman, H.-D. (ed.), *Open your eyes: deaf studies talking.* Minneapolis: University of Minnesota Press.
Bartlett, R. (2016). Scanning the conceptual horizons of citizenship. *Dementia: The International Journal of Social Research and Practice*, 15(3): 453–461.
Bartlett, R. and O'Connor, D. (2010). *Broadening the dementia debate: toward social citizenship.* Bristol: The Policy Press.
Bauman, H.-D.L. and Murray J.J. (2009). Reframing: from hearing loss to Deaf gain. *Deaf Studies Digital Journal* 1 (Fall 2009).
Bauman, H.-D.L. and Murray J.J. (2014). *Deaf gain: raising the stakes of human diversity.* Minneapolis: University of Minnesota Press.
Beschizza, P., Dodds, J. and Don, A. (2015). Campaigning for a better life. *British Deaf News.* August 2015, London.
Brannelly, T. (2016). Citizenship and people living with dementia: a case for the ethics of care. *Dementia: The International Journal of Social Research and Practice*, 15(3), 304–314.
British Deaf Association (2016) *What is BSL?* (online). Available at: www.bda.org.uk/what-is-bsl (accessed 2 February 2017).

Conrad, P. (2004). *Gentle into the darkness: a deaf mother's journey into Alzheimer's.* Edmonton, Alberta: Spotted Cow Press.

Craig, D. and Strivens, E. (2016). Facing the times: a young onset dementia support group: Facebook(TM) style. *Australasian Journal on Ageing*, 35(1): 48–53.

Davis, L. (1995). *Enforcing normalcy: disability, deafness and the body.* London: Verso.

De Meulder, M. (2014). The UNCRPD and SIGN LANGUAGE PEOPLES. In Pabsch, A. (ed.), *UNCRPD implementation in Europe – a deaf perspective. Article 29: participation in political and public life* (pp. 12–28). Brussels: European Union of the Deaf.

Dean, P.M., Feldman, D.M., Morere, D., and Morton, D. (2009). Clinical evaluation of the mini-mental state exam with culturally deaf senior citizens. *Arch Clin Neuropsychol*, 24(8): 753–760.

Denmark, T., Marshall, J., Mummery, C., Roy, P., Woll, B. and Atkinson, J. (2016). Detecting memory impairment in Deaf people: a new test of verbal learning and memory in British Sign Language. *Archives of Clinical Neuropsychology: the official Journal of the National Academy of Neuropsychologists.* PMID 27353430.

Dewing, J. (2007). Participatory research: a method for process consent with persons who have dementia. *Dementia: The International Journal of Social Research and Practice*, 6(1): 11–25.

Ferguson-Coleman, E. (2016). *Deaf with dementia: a narrative.* PhD thesis, University of Manchester.

Ferguson-Coleman, E., Keady, J. and Young, A. (2014). Dementia and the Deaf community: knowledge and service access. *Aging and Mental Health*, 18(6): 674–682.

Jones, L. and Pullen, G. (1992). Cultural differences: Deaf and hearing researchers working together. *Disability, Handicap and Society*, 7(2): 189–196.

Keady, J., Williams, S. and Hughes-Roberts, J. (2007). 'Making mistakes'. Using Co-Constructed Inquiry to illuminate meaning and relationships in the early adjustment to Alzheimer's disease – a single case study approach. *Dementia: The International Journal of Social Research and Practice* (Special Issue), 6: 343–364.

Kindell, J., Sage, K., Wilkinson, R. and Keady, J. (2014). Living with semantic dementia: a case study of one family's experience. *Qualitative Health Research*, 24(3): 401–411.

Kitwood, T. (1997). *Dementia reconsidered: the person comes first.* Buckingham: Open University Press.

Kontos, P.C. (2005). Embodied selfhood in Alzheimer's disease: rethinking person-centred care. *Dementia: The International Journal of Social Research and Practice*, 4(4): 553–570.

Kontos, P. and Martin, W. (2013). Embodiment and dementia: exploring critical narratives of selfhood, surveillance, and dementia care. *Dementia: The International Journal of Social Research and Practice*, 12(3): 288–302.

Ladd, P. (1982). *The national union of the deaf Gallaudet encyclopedia of deaf people and deafness,* edited by John V. Van Cleve. New York: McGraw-Hill, 1987.

Ladd, P. (2003). *Understanding deaf culture: in search of deafhood.* Clevedon: Multilingual Matters Ltd.

Lane, H. (1984). *When the mind hears: a history of the deaf.* New York: Random House.

Lane, H., Pillard, R.C. and Hedberg, U. (2010). *People of the eye: deaf ethnicity and ancestry.* New York: Oxford University Press.

McCormack, C. (2004). Storying stories: a narrative approach to in-depth interview conversations. *International Journal of Social Research Methodology*, 7(3): 219–236.

Mishler, E.G. (1999). *Storylines: craftartists' narratives of identity.* Cambridge: Harvard University Press.

Office of National Statistics (2012). Population ageing in the United Kingdom, its constituent countries and the European Union. Available at: http://webarchive.nationalarchives. gov.uk/20160105160709/www.ons.gov.uk/ons/rel/mortality-ageing/focus-on-older-people/population-ageing-in-the-united-kingdom-and-europe/rpt-age-uk-eu.html (accessed 2 February 2017).

Padden, C. and Humphries, T. (1988). *Deaf in America: voices from a culture.* Cambridge: Harvard University Press.

Parker, J., Young, A. and Rogers, K. (2010). 'My mum's story': a Deaf daughter discusses her Deaf mother's experience of dementia. *Dementia: The International Journal of Social Research and Practice*, 9(1): 5–20.

Pearce, A., Clare, L. and Pistrang, N. (2002). Managing sense of self: coping in the early stages of Alzheimer's disease. *Dementia: The International Journal of Social Research and Practice*, 1(2): 173–192.

Pollitt, K. (2014). *Signart: (British) sign language poetry as Gesamtkunstwerk.* PhD thesis University of Bristol.

QSR. (2012). NVivo (Software) Version 9. www.qsrinternational.com/support/downloads/nvivo-9 QSR International Pty Ltd.

Rantapää, M. and Pekkala, S. (2014). Changes in communication of Deaf people living with dementia: a thematic interview with a close family member. *Dementia: The International Journal of Social Research and Practice*, 15(5): 1205–1218.

Reid, M. (2016). Deaf sector partnership – BSL (Scotland) Act 2015 annual report April 2015 to June 2016 (online). Available at: http://deafsectorpartnership.net/dsp2/wp content/uploads/2016/10/DSP-Annual-Report-2015_2016.pdf (accessed 2 February 2017).

Riessman, C.K. (2008). *Narrative methods for the human sciences.* Thousand Oaks, United States: Sage Publications.

Rutherford, S.D. (1993). *A study of American deaf folklore.* Washington DC: Linstok Press.

Sutton-Spence, R. and Woll, B. (1999). *The linguistics of British Sign Language: an introduction.* Cambridge: Cambridge University Press.

The Scottish Parliament: British Sign Language (Scotland) Act (2015) (online). Available at: www.scottish.parliament.uk/parliamentarybusiness/Bills/82853.aspx (accessed 2 February 2017).

Ward, R., Campbell, S. and Keady, J. (2014). 'Once I had money in my pocket, I was every colour under the sun': using 'appearance biographies' to explore the meanings of appearance for people living with dementia. *Journal of Aging Studies*, 30, 64–72.

Woodward, J. (1975). How you gonna get to heaven if you can't talk with Jesus: the Educational Establishment vs. The Deaf Community. *International Meeting of the Society for Applied Anthropology*, 1975, Amsterdam.

World Health Organisation (2012). *Global estimates on prevalence of hearing loss* (online). WHO. Available at: www.who.int/pbd/deafness/WHO_GE_HL.pdf?ua=1 (accessed 2 February 2017).

Yin, R.K. (1989). *Case study research: design and methods.* London: Sage Publications.

Young, A. and Ackerman, J. (2001). Reflections on validity and epistemology in a study of working relations between Deaf and hearing professionals. *Qualitative Health Research*, 11(2): 179–189.

Young, A.M., Ferguson-Coleman E. and Keady J. (2014). Understanding the personhood of Deaf people living with dementia: methodological issues. *Journal of Aging Studies*, 31: 62–69.

Young, A., Ferguson-Coleman, E. and Keady, J. (2016). Understanding dementia: effective information access from the Deaf community's perspective. *Health and Social Care in the Community*, 24(1): 39–47.

Young, A. and Hunt, R. (2011). *Research with d/Deaf people* (vol. 9). London, UK: NIHR School for Social Care Research Methods Review.

10 Critical discourse and policy analysis as a method to understand dementia policies

Ann-Charlotte Nedlund and Jonas Nordh

Outline

This chapter outlines the use of critical and interpretive policy and discourse analysis as an approach to explore dementia policies including its political and institutional practices, i.e. the process where policies are enacted by the actors, including citizens living with dementia. This chapter gives examples on the relevance of studying policy and its practices by presenting a study on how citizens with dementia have been constructed as a policy target group, as a social problem, its solutions and which knowledge it is based upon as well as its underlying meanings and rationales that are in play. It also presents a study on how to critically study policy practice, in the case of how policies are being enacted by public officials that encounter citizens living people living with dementia. By using a critical and interpretive policy and discourse analysis one can reveal the underlying accounts and power relations that influence the citizenship practice and its content.

Introduction

In this chapter, we will present how a critical and interpretive approach on policy processes can be used to develop our understanding of dementia policies, including its practices. Policy is a concept in the social sciences that can be critically important. Many actors in our public life use it when attempting to shape the organisation of public life. So, policy is not 'a thing' but rather an idea that gives actors a way of handling a specific situation – a social problem – and a way of making sense of how problems should be handled in a complex process (Nedlund, 2012). Hence, policy does not have a single meaning; instead the meaning of a policy differs for different policy actors. By that, it is easier to think of policy as a dynamic process that can take different forms that can be articulated in policy documents, such as legislations and written guidelines, and in work, such as routines created by actors involved in policy process, and in practices, such as the way of enacting policies and handling the different situations at hand (Nedlund, 2012; Colebatch, 2009). These different forms of polices are intertwined and interrelated to each other.

Using an interpretive and critical approach when analysing policies implies that one seeks to uncover or discern what actors believe they are doing in their policy work and policy practice, i.e. when they are making sense of what they should do in a specific situation. We are thus interested in the construction of meanings and normative assumptions underlying these ways of acting and further aiming to critically explore and contest taken-for-granted institutional-ised structures and practices. By that, we are interested in shedding light on the power relations involved in the formation and shaping of policies. Commonly, the policy process is comprised of several interests that aim to influence the for-mation of policies. These interests are not value-neutral and are based on assumptions about knowledge and what is considered true knowledge. Policy is thus not only instrumental and rationalistic, studying inputs and outputs and technocratic knowledge, but rather of why certain knowledge has the power to influence specific policy areas, how they construct problems and solutions as well as policy targets. It is thus important to disentangle which actors are involved, what type of knowledge, what rationales and logics are present but also the underlying accounts as to why these, particularly, have the power to influence policies.

In this chapter, we will first give a brief overview on the relevance of studying policies, the research methods used, and give example of insights from the methods as well as implications for dementia research and dementia care and practice. In our illustrations, we will draw on examples from two different studies that aimed to explore the discourse in which people living with dementia have been constructed as a policy target group, people living with dementia as a social problem as well as its immanent solutions and also on which rationales and knowledge these are based. The practices in which policies are enacted, when public officials encounter the citizens and make use of policies, will also be explored.

Policies and how we can understand them

The definition and construction of dementia and the category of citizens living with dementia are seldom explicit, but often embedded in policies. Policies are not mirrors of reality; rather they create meaning and give a specific question a particular value. The policy process relates to the construction of political prob-lems where the construction of policy areas, targeted groups, goals and appropri-ate solutions do not come into being until they are recognised as political problems. Public policies are dynamic instruments where authorities, at national and/or at local level, give signals and legitimise how citizen groups are valued and regarded by other citizens, which attitudes and courses of action are regarded as appropriate and what services they can expect from welfare organisations. They are also instruments to change the social constructions of citizens. The policy process is a struggle over ideas, stories and interests where various actors compete. Policies and the construction of policy targets is dependent on which actors are involved in the policy process and, to be more specific, have the power to get involved or to be considered, which actors claim, or are claimed to have knowledge.

Policies in the form of documents

The activities within welfare institutions are highly governed by, and based on, texts. They can be found at macro level in the form of top-down government policies or at a meso and micro level in the form of policy work where actors, such as occupational therapists or care-managers, are trying to find a mutually acceptable outcome related to the broader framework of meaning in which they are located (Nedlund, 2012). By that, recommendations (including inherent values and norms) are articulated into policies that commonly are assembled into a document. These documents are important and powerful tools for governments. They are also important in the way they give signals and generate how matters should be understood and handled, also by whom and further together with whom. We will come back to this later in the chapter.

Policy documents can be understood narratively and as discourses (Baldwin, 2013; Nedlund and Nordh, 2015, 2017). Policy narrative constructs a view of social reality, selecting different features and relations through a policy process. These narratives determine what facts are 'true' and what arguments are relevant. Policy narratives are a way of presenting reality as a coherent whole, drawing on a simplified causality and as something deriving from facts even though this might not be the case, and by that simplifying a phenomenon they are seeking to steer. Policy narratives encompass various persuasive arguments and elements of discourse but are held together by a similar conceptualisation of the world. Thus, narratives portraying problems and solutions as comprehensive, convincing and acceptable and accordingly legitimise a certain course of action.

Policies in form of policy work and policy practice

Policies also encompass the governance of *how* work and practice should be organised (Nedlund, 2012). Policies such as legislations and guidelines are interpreted, made sense of and enacted by actors in e.g. welfare institutions such as care managers assessing the need of social services for people living with dementia. This is what commonly is referred to as policy work and policy practice. Professionals have to work with policies, e.g. legislations and guidelines, which guide their practice. First of all, policies are not always easy to directly apply to specific situations that occur in the workplace. Not least, since as shown in Sweden, referring to the study presented above, there are not many policies specifically targeting people living with dementia. Rather, care managers have to find guidance within policies concerning older people and people with disabilities and apply them to the target group of people living with dementia (Nordh and Nedlund, 2016a and 2016b). However, cases that concern people living with dementia in a specific situation may differ from that of older people or people with disabilities which might make it difficult to directly apply them to the target group of people living with dementia. Concerning policies, there can also be tensions between different policies; for example, local policies may not conform completely to national policies.

Second, policy documents can, in our view, never be directly implemented as such. Above all, the work is also within policies, since policy becomes a pattern of activity which encapsulates different meanings for different policy participants. Also, developing policies is not merely about 'making' policy, 'making' plans and 'making' decisions; it is also about interaction and meaning-forming activities (Nedlund, 2012). Hence, policy participants, such as care professionals and care managers, always need to interpret and make sense of what should be done and how it should be done in a specific situation. Therefore, it is of interest to study the policy work and the policy practice. By studying interviews with care managers we can shed light on how they work with, reflect upon, interpret and use policy documents in their work.

Even though the examples given in this chapter are from the context of social services and focus on care managers, the analysis of policies can be applied to other contexts such as nursing or home-care services and how professionals within these contexts are working with and practising their respective policies (in the study of occupational therapists, physiotherapists and senior managers, c.f. Nedlund, 2012).

Examples of how the method – or combination of social research methods – can be used

In the following sections, we will emphasise certain aspects that need to be addressed when critically analysing policies. We will introduce theoretical and methodological aspects of policy analysis as well as providing examples from our studies. The first example will be drawn from a textual analysis.

Constructions in texts

In studies of the constructions of text that we have made (see Nedlund and Nordh, 2015; also Nedlund and Nordh, 2017) consists of qualitative textual analysis of national level policy documents in Sweden, such as those from the Government and Parliament Offices, the National Board of Health and Welfare (NBHW), and the Swedish Association of Local Authorities and Regions (SALAR) over the period 1975 to 2013. In one study (Nedlund and Nordh, 2015) we were interested to study how policy narratives in national policy documents in Sweden had informed associated politics on people living with dementia. The focus was to know how people living with dementia were constructed as a policy target group and what the problems and imminent solutions have been constructed/presented as, and if and how these have differed over time. The search strategy and selection of policy documents was broad and covered differing policy areas, since people living with dementia, both explicitly but many times implicitly, are to be found in various policy areas. So, when selecting documents, the criterion was not that people living with dementia had to be an explicit target group, but that the policies could cover people who had dementia, particularly in the early documents. In total, 165 documents were identified comprising mainly investigations and reports, but also political proposals or changes to existing laws. The analysis was an iterative process, exploring both horizontally across texts and longitudinally through time. The documents were carefully read to find views and conceptualisations, including their constructed problems and suggested solutions related to people living with dementia, which revealed different narratives. By doing this we were making sense of the stories and non-stories, whereby we then identified various policy narratives (see Figure 10.1).

As Figure 10.1 shows, people living with dementia have been recognised as a differing political problem where various dominant narratives have been established at a national policy level. When this group emerged as a policy target it was discovered that a large number of people living with dementia were institutionalised at mental institutions. However, it was difficult to suddenly relocate them, so in the beginning they were still treated at mental hospitals but also in nursing homes and this was also emphasised as the better solution. Over time this has changed, with a greater emphasis on care, which has put people living with dementia in residential homes.

However, the residential homes had difficulties in accommodating large numbers of people living with dementia and the solution was then that people living with dementia should be taken care of in their own home. The motives for

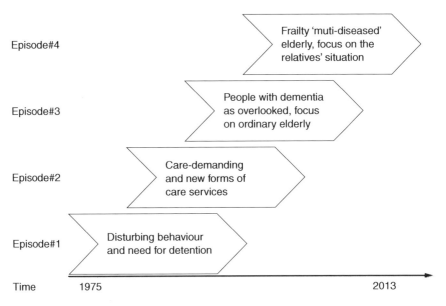

Figure 10.1 Identified episodes and policy narratives relating to people living with dementia in the studied documents.

Source: figure taken from Nedlund and Nordh (2015).

this change was in the policy narrative presented as people living with dementia were better off by being taken care of at home where the environment was familiar and by familiar people, e.g. relatives, thus giving a better quality of life for people living with dementia. However, another story was that the public sector was stressed by economic austerity in which the welfare state could not be responsible for care to the extent that it had been before and it was cheaper to take care of people in their own homes with relief from e.g. day care centres. This also caused a shift in the importance of relatives. There has been an increasing emphasis on relatives and their role concerning people living with dementia. However, this may also have shaped the policy area, and the construction of people living with dementia, since relatives' voices are commonly more heard than that of people living with dementia. Dominating stories are the ones that direct policies and institutional actions. However, there can also be competing stories struggling to influence the policy narrative. As such, policy narratives can be comprised of several competing accounts at different levels, but held together by a similar conception of the world. Even though narratives of people living with dementia have varied through the episodes, the consistent construction of people living with dementia has to a large extent followed the same line of reasoning; someone who is disturbing or a burden to relatives, to partners, to healthcare personnel and other actors, but also to society in general by being 'cost-demanding'. This politics of dependence seems to be framed as a failure in contrast to that of, for example, a child, or someone who is sick where this human condition is expected to end. In the case of elderly dependence, and particularly in the case of dementia, this dependence is framed as a failure and sometimes even unnatural where the only way forward is backwards, i.e. increased dependency until death.

The policies have shaped the construction of target groups, which informs us that some citizens are valued while others are not as important, which subsequently shapes the meaning of citizenship and its content. The relation between policies and narratives is dynamic and iterative, where the policy is also shaped by the dominant narrative. We can see that emerging narratives could challenge the specific dominant narrative, which implied a shift in how people living with dementia were constructed in national policy documents. This implies that the process, in which problems and their imminent solutions become recognised and thereby legitimatised, is not only a struggle over ideas and interests but also, very interestingly, a struggle over policy narratives where various actors compete.

An important aspect of studying policies is to discern the actors that have the power to be involved in the process. The construction and re-construction of problems is dependent on the participants in the process and who is claimed to have, or who claims to have, knowledge. It is commonly the actors that claim to have knowledge, or are claimed to have knowledge, that are able to influence the policy narrative. The narrative that has been the driving force concerning people living with dementia in Sweden, and which has informed policies, has been from a medical perspective. Focus has been on presenting people living with dementia in relation to their physical and psychological attributes, such as people living with dementia as being 'disturbing' as well as being 'a burden' (see e.g. Episode 1 in Figure 10.1). Thus, they therefore present a problem since their deviant behaviour does not neatly fit the expectations of the conception of an 'ordinary' older person. As such, the medical perspective can be considered as a dominant story in the discourse of people living with dementia. Furthermore, policy narratives do not only make simplified conceptualisations of problems and solutions but also of the target group. What is shown is that people living with dementia have been presented as a homogenous group. What is *not* shown in the policy documents, at least the earlier ones, is the heterogeneity of the group in relation to e.g. type of dementia, stage of dementia, identities, backgrounds and preferences etc. Also, by looking at the actors that are involved we can also see, very importantly, actors that are not involved and by that disentangle the power relations involved in the making of policies.

Our study shows that the medical model has been dominant in this policy area. Dominant actor's stories commonly become the only possible way of defining and solving problems while other stories get silenced. Other models, such as a citizenship model, rather than the medical one have to a large extent been absent. The personhood model has been visible, hence the shift from 'demented' to 'people living with dementia' but has not been able to influence policies as much as the medical one. The reason could be that these stories have been silenced due to the power of the medical model. Representatives of these models may not be considered as experts and thus not as legitimised as the representatives of the medical model. The emergence of a new perspective is only possible if the policy process becomes more inclusive and democratic. However, powerful actors are commonly not willing to easily give up the power to influence the policy process, which is why policy resistance is more common than policy change. Revealing these power relations in policy areas is central in having a critical approach to policy analysis. The narrative often stabilises a certain meaning and is commonly drawing on similar and previous narratives which help to undermine certain narratives and actors as influential. Accordingly, narratives are not univocal but rather polyphonic. It is thus important to discern not only what the narrative is but also 'how' and 'why' it is like that.

This study sheds light on the temporal character of political problems. The shift in who does or does not become a policy target is often related to the practical work. In the next section we will draw from an interview study to illustrate how policies can be critically and interpretively analysed by focusing on the policy work and the policy practice of actors working in welfare institutions.

Constructions in policy work and policy practice

In a study (partly reported in Nordh and Nedlund, 2016a and 2016b; Nordh, 2016) we analysed care-managed work with people living with dementia. The study focused on how people living with dementia, as well as policies targeting them, are understood by care managers; this includes the practice and meetings in which people living with dementia are involved. We were interested to study how people living with dementia are understood and addressed in the practices and meetings between the representatives from local authorities, responsible for the welfare services targeting people living with dementia. Interviews were generated with 19 care managers in four organisations at three different municipalities in Sweden. One of the municipalities is divided into several different districts and separate organisations, from which we selected two organisations to study.

A semi-structured open-ended topic guide was designed with key themes, such as important policies and guidelines, possibility of influencing local policies, and handling various situations when encountering people living with dementia and their relatives. The interviews followed the 'Expert interviews' format (Bogner *et al.*, 2009), implying that interviewees were considered experts. The interviewer thus allowed interviewees to converse about what they found relevant on the topics. Accordingly, the topic guide had an intentional flexibility, implying that it was open to alteration depending on what the interviewees found interesting or if/when they introduced new topics (cf. Alvesson, 2011). Follow-up questions were used as a way to get the conversation started or to explain questions that were not understood by the interviewees.

A thematic content analysis of the interviews was carried out which allowed analyses from an abductive perspective, meaning that there was an interaction with previous knowledge (e.g. the interview guide and the empirical findings that were obtained during the interviews). The whole analytical process followed a critical and interpretive approach (Yanow, 2000) where we were interested in the underlying accounts of the interviewees' stories: What did they do, how did they do it, and what was the meaning behind it? A conceptual framework was created that covered both recurring themes from the care managers and topics from the topic guide. The aim was to retain the expressions that originated from the interviewees. Even if coding is an important part of the analysis, the interviews should not be seen as a building block for knowledge production, and the ambition of finding specific categories should not stand in the way of creative and critical thinking (Alvesson, 2011). We did not count the occurrences of the identified topics. Our understanding is that an event is an experience independent of the number of interviewees who have had it. However, by sorting the data into themes, we could identify overlapping experiences of the interviewees. The interview texts were read again to reflect and ensure that they corresponded to the analysis.

So, by analysing the policy work and policy practice we discovered that care managers encounter situations where they cannot find guidance on how to solve them. There can be several reasons for this, such as there being a lack of guidelines or no guidelines that neatly fit the specific situation. Care managers thus have to find their own ways to solve these problematic situations (Nordh and Nedlund, 2016a and 2016b; Nordh, 2016). This means that policies such as legislation and guidelines may not capture what actually happens in the activities within the organisations in which they are enacted. As such, policies operate within macro, meso as well as micro levels. Accordingly, professionals that work within these organisations add value to existing policies or create their own routines and procedures. As such, policy processes are dynamic and what happens in the activities of the organisation are the policies that citizens see – e.g. concerning people living with dementia encountering social services – and also as seen as the outcome of policies. Policy analysis should thus also concern itself by making visible, and interpreting, the activities that are ongoing within organisations. By conducting and analysing interviews with the professionals that work within these organisations it can become visible what the actual policies really are and also 'why' and 'how' they are. By using a critical and interpretive policy analysis approach we could see in our study that care managers find routines and procedures in order to handle dilemmas that occur in their work. This concerns both how they should handle existing legislation and guidelines as well as handle situations that arise in which that they cannot find guidance in legislation and guidelines. They do this by reflecting upon dilemmas, interpreting them and discuss amongst themselves. As such they add values to existing policies, work contradictory to them as well as creating new ones. Policies do not merely exist as written documents but as ongoing activities and practices within organisations.

Studying the practices of public officials may shed light on how norms and values in policy documents are transferred, changed and added into practice. But also that norms and values of professionals, sometimes contradictory to those in policies, are shown by studying their activities.

Insights gained from the method

Utilising critical discourse analysis and critical interpretive policy analysis we can shed light on how political and social problems become formulated and how power relations constitute and reinforce social structures. Rather than only asking what the problem is, a critical discourse analysis and policy analysis makes it possible to also ask 'how' and 'why', in order to understand underlying meanings of policies, and reflect on 'what is not', as well as 'who' are involved in the policy process. Policies also have to be studied within the environment or the socio-historical and political context in which it occurs and is developed. Hence, a critical policy analysis also involves reflecting upon 'how' policy works in practice by those implementing the policies and to ask if there are other societal movements affecting the policy field. There are several possible approaches and steps to critically analyse policies. What approach to eventually use must, for that reason, be guided by the research questions in focus. By studying policy narratives in policy documents, we can shed light on the power of stories that in the end create the content of citizenship for people living with dementia. By studying interviews with care managers, we can shed light on the practices that add value to policies in what, in the end, become the policy that citizens experience. However, the different levels should not be considered as detached from each other since they are constantly influencing one another.

By using these methods, we can see that there is still a lot of work to be done for people living with dementia for them to fully participate in their community. Even in cases of health and social care, the self-determination of people living with dementia is questioned concerning their own everyday situation (c.f. Nedlund and Taghizadeh Larsson, 2016). People living with dementia are given social rights but do not have the possibility, as yet, to influence the policy areas that influence social rights and further social citizenship. Sometimes they are considered as not even having the possibility to influence their own everyday situation. Accordingly, people living with dementia have been covered by policies and legislation concerning older people and people with disabilities, showing that they are overlooked from the point of view of having their own specific situations which society needs to acknowledge. It can thus be questioned whether people living with dementia can be considered full citizens.

We can also see that people living with dementia, as a policy target group, have been, and to a large extent still are, negatively constructed. Negative construction thus tends to be reproduced. People living with dementia and their advocates thus need to be able to be a part of this process in order to influence their construction and further to be able to influence their social citizenship. Using people living with dementia as a label, which in policies, i.e. legislation, are categorised as either older people or people with disabilities, sheds light on the discrepancies between policy target groups and individual heterogeneity within these target groups. This becomes apparent by studying the experience of care managers who encounter citizens such as people living with dementia, but also how they experience the legislation, policies and guidelines that guide their work. There is also a tension between the legislation and policies, and the practices of the care managers enacting these legislations and policies. As legislation and policies from high-level officials and politicians tend to consider citizens as abstract target groups, they also tend to homogenise these target groups. However, street-level bureaucrats encounter 'real' citizens with different situations and different needs. Accordingly, there is heterogeneity within these abstract and homogenous target groups which surfaces when citizens meet the welfare system. This means that the care managers experience different 'realities' than those which are presented in legislation and policies.

It is vital to keep in mind that policy narratives are co-constructed. Thus, it is important to reflect on the selection of policy documents along with the time frame i.e. where to begin and where to end. Studying policy narratives is also interpretative and thus the researchers own role must come into consideration.

Ethical issues encountered in the use of the social method

Throughout the course of the study, it is of importance to consider and reflect upon ethical issues. In our case, established research ethics practice and ethical guidelines concerning informed consent, assurances of confidentiality and the consequences of how the collected information would be used were followed. Informed consent was obtained from participants. Throughout the course of the work with the data analyses, consideration was given to how the statements and quotes were displayed to minimise the risk of identification. The informants were assured that their statements would be treated confidentially in all presentations. The informants not only have the right to withdraw from the study at any time, but also have the right to anonymisation, implying that possible identification through their comments should be eliminated.

The design of the study (including choosing empirical examples) is highly interrelated with the theoretical considerations and the research questions, but also with the perspective that we, as researchers, represent when we grasp the phenomenon concerned. The process behind a study can rarely be described as a linear progression. Rather, it is a puzzle-solving process, starting with a rough idea, reading relevant (and irrelevant) literature, going back and forth to construct potential research questions and thinking about how this fascinating idea could be developed into a study, continuing by generating data, analysing reading and thinking of the theoretical implications (also in an iterative dynamic way). This could be described as a fluidity of shifts and changes, which take their form as the research process progresses. Nonetheless, through the whole research process there needs to be solid focus on the core that is studied. Another solid part in the process of puzzling and making-sense of a fascinating phenomenon has, of course, been our ontological and epistemological stance. This is critical in understanding and evaluating the value and appropriateness of this type of research. The choice of methods will be affected by a researcher's epistemological orientation and her/his views on different methods for investigating the central phenomena under study. Also, the researcher's background and position will affect what she/he chooses to research.

This research is based on a constructivist approach. We adhered to the view that social reality is a construction created by acts of interpretation. This implies that all sorts of social influences shape how people understand, experience and feel about any given social phenomenon. The meaning people attach to a social phenomenon influences the structure and functioning of e.g. institutions, social practices and public policies – that is, bring them into meaning. Following that, we do not regard analysing policies – either policy documents or policy work and practices – as an event of transferring 'pure' information but instead a process of interpreting. By that, we are telling our story and interpretation of how we have read the policy documents and how we have understood the interviewees' stories. Furthermore, the interview is an example of joint activity in the sense that we – the researcher and the interviewee – are together telling a story. The interview is a process of co-production, a process where the telling of a story is dependent on both the interviewee and the researcher, and their interaction and communication.

Highlighted learning points from the method

- Doing research by a discourse and critical policy approach is an iterative process going back and forth during the whole process.
- 'Knowledge' is always co-constructed between researcher and data, this is apparent both in interview studies as well as in policy documents. By that narratives are affected by the researcher.
- Policies – both in documents as well as the work and practice – need to be critically analysed in order to find power relations, underlying accounts, influential actors, etc.
- Policies influence the content of citizenship, e.g. citizenship rights. Policy analysis is a way of understanding the processes that influence citizenship and thus makes a useful tool in understanding living with dementia, citizenship for people living with dementia, how welfare institutions and its professionals are organised and working with dementia.

Key references

- Nedlund, A.-C. and Nordh, J. (2017). Constructing citizens: a matter of labelling, imaging and underlying rationales in the case of people living with dementia. *Critical Policy Studies.* Published online: 13 March 2017.
- Nedlund, A.-C. and Nordh, J. (2015). Crafting citizen(ship) for people living with dementia: how policy narratives at national level in Sweden informed politics of time from 1975 to 2013. *Journal of Aging Studies,* 34: 123–133.
- Nordh, J. and Nedlund, A-C. (2016). To co-ordinate information in practice: dilemmas and strategies in care management for citizens with dementia. *Journal of Social Services Research.* Published online: 8 September 2016.
- Nedlund, A-C. and Taghizadeh Larsson, A. (2016). To protect and to support: how citizenship and self-determination are legally constructed and managed in practice for people living with dementia in Sweden. *Dementia: The International Journal of Social Research and Practice,* 15: 343–357.
- Nordh, J. (2016). *Social citizenship and people living with dementia: designing social care policies in Sweden.* Linköping: LiU-Tryck.

Recommended future reading

- Boréus, K. and Bergström, G. (2017). *Analyzing text and discourse: eight approaches for the social sciences.* London: Sage Publications.
- Roe, E.M. (1994). *Narrative policy analysis: theory and practice.* Durham: Duke University Press.
- Schwartz-Shea, P. and Yanow, D. (2012). *Interpretive research design: concepts and processes.* New York: Routledge.
- Yanow, D. and Schwartz-Shea, P. (eds) (2013). *Interpretation and method: empirical research methods and the interpretive turn* (2nd edition). Armonk, NY: M.E. Sharp, Inc.

References

Alvesson, M. (2011). *Interpreting interviews*. London: Sage Publications.

Baldwin, C. (2013). *Narrative social work: theory and application*. Bristol: Policy Press.

Bogner, A., Littig, B. and Menz, W. (2009). *Interviewing experts*. London: Palgrave Macmillan.

Colebatch, H.K. (2009). *Policy* (2nd edition). Buckingham: Open University Press.

Nedlund, A-C. (2012). *Designing for legitimacy – policy work and the art of juggling when setting limits in health care*. Linköping: LiU-Tryck.

Nedlund, A.-C. and Nordh, J. (2015). Crafting citizen(ship) for people living with dementia: how policy narratives at national level in Sweden informed politics of time from 1975 to 2013. *Journal of Aging Studies*, 34: 123–133.

Nedlund, A-C. and Taghizadeh Larsson, A. (2016). To protect and to support: how citizenship and self-determination are legally constructed and managed in practice for people living with dementia in Sweden. *Dementia: The International Journal of Social Research and Practice*, 15: 343–357.

Nedlund, A.-C. and Nordh, J. (2017). Constructing citizens: a matter of labelling, imaging and underlying rationales in the case of people living with dementia. *Critical Policy Studies*. Published online: 13 March 2017.

Nordh, J. (2016). *Social citizenship and people living with dementia: designing social care policies in Sweden*. Linköping: LiU-Tryck.

Nordh, J. and Nedlund, A-C. (2016a). To co-ordinate information in practice: dilemmas and strategies in care management for citizens with dementia. *Journal of Social Services Research*. Published online: 8 September 2016.

Nordh, J. and Nedlund. A-C (2016b). Care managers as street–level bureaucrats implementing legislation and policies concerning people living with dementia: a qualitative study. Submitted to *Journal of Social Work*.

Yanow, D. (2000). *Conducting interpretive policy analysis*. London: Sage Publications.

11 Privileging the play

Creating theatre with people living with dementia

Hannah Zeilig and Lucy Burke

Outline

This chapter outlines some of the ways that theatrical techniques may be used with people living with dementia in both care home and community settings. The role of theatre as a powerful method for communicating and collaborating with people living with dementia is highlighted with reference to two recent artist-led projects that emphasise the importance of aesthetics rather than instrumental outcomes. The case studies demonstrate that theatre can be effective in encouraging people living with dementia to improvise, create and co-produce and may thus prompt new learning and experiences.

Introduction

The use of theatrical techniques for engaging alternative audiences (including people in prisons, hospitals, and residential care settings) is well established. Known by the umbrella term 'applied theatre', this field is characterised by the development of a set of theatrical practices and creative activities that move beyond the spaces of traditional theatre and its cultures of performance and spectatorship in order to respond to the experiences and needs of particular communities and their distinctive localities (Prentki and Preston, 2009, p. 9). Underpinned by the 'belief that theatre experienced both as a participant and as audience might make some difference to the way in which people interact with each other and with the wider world' (ibid.) and can therefore help to develop new possibilities for everyday life (Nicholson, 2014), this form of arts practice draws upon the political and conceptual lineages of avant-garde theatre and particularly Brechtian Epic Theatre with its distinguished history of challenging traditional theatrical hierarchies such as those between audience, performers and the performance. This emphasises the political dimensions of applied theatre and its origins in the activities of groups such as the Workers' Theatre Movements of the 1920s which set out to use theatre practices to empower socially marginalised and subordinate groups.

The very different uses and conceptions of theatre encompassed under the term 'applied theatre' demonstrate the flexibility and openness of theatre as an art form; one that can encompass diverse audiences and performers, that does not need to take place in formal 'theatrical' spaces and that does not intrinsically require participants to possess particular levels of cultural or symbolic capital. As noted by Quinlan (2009, p. 119):

> Theatre in particular, has the capacity to convey meanings that pertain to the flux of social relationships because these meanings are so inherently embodied in gestures and actions. Symbols, emotion and performance are constitutive of human communication; by explicitly incorporating these expressive forms, theatre expands our communicative capacities.

Quinlan's emphasis upon the expressive and embodied aspects of theatre which privilege affect and the importance of non-verbal communication has particular relevance for the ability of theatre to engage people living with dementia.

Although a number of scholars and practitioners have explored the role of theatre and theatrical techniques in the reshaping of perceptions of dementia amongst carers, healthcare professionals and the wider public (Gjengedal *et al.*, 2014; Mitchell *et al.*, 2006) it is only recently being explored *with* people living with dementia as co-producers (Basting, 2001; Basting *et al.* 2016). As eloquently noted by commentators, the dramatic ambience itself conveys feelings and ideas and thus drama provides a powerful mode of communication for those living with dementia. The ability of drama to operate on a visual and sensory and therefore physical basis rather than solely relying on building linear narrative is another important feature for people living with dementia who, it is increasingly recognised have embodied selves (Kontos, 2003; Kontos and Naglie, 2007; Sabat, 2001, 2014).

In the USA, Anne Basting has pioneered participatory theatre activities for people living with dementia in her innovative *Time Slips* (2001) and *Penelope* (2012) projects. Basting's work in this area has been important for demonstrating that people living with dementia can actively participate and co-direct a theatrical production. Others have explored the notion of embodied learning in dementia using theatre as a pedagogical tool; however, the importance of creating an aesthetic experience that increases confidence and supports the identity of participants with dementia has received less attention. Equally, the tendency to view creative interventions with people living with dementia in instrumental terms as forms of 'therapy' (Stevens, 2012), the efficacy of which is solely evaluated in relation to measurable outcomes, arguably misses what makes an aesthetic experience valuable and enriching. This chapter will discuss two different projects in which theatre is a central and collaborative endeavour with people living with dementia in both the community and a residential care setting. Our first case study focusses on *The Island*, a unique performance created with people living with dementia by the UK based group Small Things Creative Projects. Locating this project in the broader context of the theory, practice and challenges presented by the introduction of applied theatre into residential care settings, it will investigate the extent to which the novel theatrical methods that were used in *The Island* project may provide insights: both into ways of working with people living with dementia and also into the condition dementia. The insights gained from working on *The Island* and the ethical dilemmas that were confronted will also be addressed. Our second case study is derived from interviews with the Enrichment Director of Punchdrunk (a company who have innovated immersive theatre in the UK) and recently (2016) created a form of immersive theatre in a single care home.

Applied theatre in residential care

It is widely appreciated that the arts have an important role in fostering well-being and quality of life particularly in the absence of pharmacological interventions for the complex syndrome encompassed by the term dementia (Killick and Craig, 2012; Basting, 2014; Zeilig *et al.*, 2014; Young *et al.*, 2015). The proliferation of participative arts based initiatives for people living with dementia is well documented (Camic *et al.*, 2013a and b) within this context, the role of theatre is burgeoning, the majority of this can be described as applied theatre.

Helen Nicholson describes applied theatre as that which takes place in different and sometimes unglamorous places – on the streets, in city farms, in gardens and bombsites or, for example, in care homes for the elderly (Nicholson, 2014, p. 4) It is thus an innately socially engaged theatre that is designed to benefit individuals, communities and societies. 'In practice, applied theatre is often multi agency, bringing together theatre makers with, for example … health professionals' (Nicholson, 2014, p. 6). In terms of applied theatre for people living with dementia the necessity of including a number of different stakeholders (including care home providers, health care professionals and carers for instance) is particularly relevant and may influence the aims, intentions and outputs of the theatrical offering. This should alert us to the diverse expectations and evaluative frameworks that different stakeholders may bring to the performances. As Hatton notes:

> Historically, the value of arts practices in care homes has largely been attributed to health outcomes, particularly in the context of dementia care. While these outcomes are undoubtedly important there has been little research that considers the aesthetic value of the work.
>
> (2014, p. 364)

The role of the professional artist who works with people living with dementia (rather than, say, an arts therapist or activities coordinator) is gaining prominence in accounts of the role of the arts for people living with dementia. Commentators have noted that professional artists have the ability to retain the aesthetic integrity of their art form as opposed to focusing on the metrics of healthcare and wellbeing (Coaten *et al.*, 2013; Gjengedal *et al.*, 2014). Currently much of the theatrical work is aimed at those aged over 65 years and those who reside within a care home, as evidenced in the work of Ladder to the Moon (UK) and TimeSlips (USA).

The importance of considering the peculiar properties of the spatial dynamics of the care home as a setting for artistic interventions, including theatrical performances has been noted by Hatton (2014). Care homes tend to be measured by their success with completing functional tasks including the bathing and feeding of residents within certain time periods, they are spaces characterised by the reiteration of particular routines (Hatton, 2014, p. 358). As Hatton goes on to point out care homes have a historical legacy as being places of discipline and order and this continues to dominate modern conceptions of how they should function. However, she also notes that 'care home spaces are unique in that they enable different activities to coexist simultaneously' (p. 359) and therefore have potential for being creative places. The recent interest in relational aspects of care and attention to the wider network of other spaces that constitute a care home open up exciting possibilities for theatre artists who can engage with a care home as a creative place: 'which is constructed through a multitude of different environments' (p. 364). The potential for the arts and theatre to alter the care home environment, to help shift organisational structure from a rigid hierarchy to one that is more 'horizontal' and team based is also noted by Basting (2014).

In contrast to the case studies outlined below, theatrical interventions often focus on the carer as a staff member and tailor the work towards developing improved staff carer and person living with dementia relationships. This tends to view the creative process as a means to an instrumental end in which attitudes can be shifted in a readily quantifiable manner. This emphasis upon measuring change is often underpinned by the requirements of funding bodies to support projects that have measurable outcomes. Thus, in the Netherlands the Veder Method was developed by a theatre group whose artistic director had a nursing background. The technique used theatrical stimuli (songs and poetry) in combination with person centred communication techniques to improve the interactions of care staff with residents with a dementia (van Haeften-van Dijk *et al.*, 2014). The technique can either be applied by professional actors or by trained care home staff and, in the last decade, has been implemented widely in Dutch care homes:

> A living room theatre activity has a central theme, and every caregiver/actor plays a role that refers to this theme. Costumes, props and recognizable characters are used to create a stage set. Songs and poems are used as well as objects, smells and flavours that refer to the central theme.
>
> (van Haeften-van Dijk *et al.*, 2014, p. 537)

Despite challenges regarding the practical implementation of an innovative theatrical technique (including, for instance, staff turn-over) that threatened the continuity of the project and ethical objections regarding the use of living room theatre activities for people with early stage dementia (van Haeften-van Dijk *et al.*, 2014, p. 545), most staff respondents stressed the added value of using this method for communicating with residents. In contrast, there has been an increased use of improvised drama to connect with people living with dementia and to arouse a sense of playfulness, indeed this is a burgeoning field (Killick, 2013). For instance, the use of clowns (all professionally trained actors) to evoke responses from people living with dementia in hospitals has been pioneered in the UK by Elderflowers, based in Edinburgh. This group use a finely tuned humour to connect and communicate with those who are often living with quite severe dementia. In addition, Magic Me (2016) are taking circus skills into a number of dementia care homes across London.

A primary benefit of drama based projects (as with music and dance) is the emphasis on non-verbal communication (Harries *et al.*, 2013). As eloquently noted by Zeisel (2009, p. 106) the dramatic ambience itself conveys feelings and ideas and thus drama provides a powerful mode of communication for people living with dementia. The Storybox Project is a UK theatre based project (run by the company Small Things whose project *The Island* is discussed in detail below) that emphasises creating rather than reminiscing with people living with dementia in care home settings and has an underlying philosophy that co-creativity with people living with dementia can improve wellbeing. Improvisa-tion is often central to applied/participatory theatre and as noted by Basting (2001) allows people living with dementia to dare, to play and to create in a process that many find liberating. The UK group Ladder to the Moon have used a model of applied and interactive theatre that similarly encourages co-creation and experimentation in care home settings. As described by Killick:

> Their performances usually involve two actors, but they arrive armed with a plot and props. The story may come from Shakespeare or a film classic, but they invite residents to take some of the main roles. The potential leads are approached and addressed perhaps as 'my lord' or 'my gracious queen' with a bow and a proffering of a crown. The reaction soon tells if the offer is accepted.
>
> (2013, p. 36)

Commentators such as Benson (2009) HAVE remarked on how the playfulness inherent in this form of theatrical practice may be particularly effective for people living with dementia who are more disinhibited and also the positive effects on care home staff who see residents grow in confidence and stature as the play progresses.

It seems that there is a gradual diversification in the ways in which theatre is used with people living with dementia towards a more co-productive, improvisa-tory and collaborative approach that emphasises the value of process and parti-cipation, and that distinguishes between intention and outcome.

The Island: theatre and co-production with people living with dementia

Funded by Arts Council England, *The Island* brought together six artists (dir-ector, assistant, designer and three performers) and 10 older people living with dementia living at Shore Green extra care housing scheme in Wythenshawe in Manchester. Based around Shakespeare's *The Tempest*, the project set out to explore the story of Prospero's island in a series of 15 workshops between July and September 2014 culminating in a two-week residency at Shore Green starting on 22 September and a sharing of work on 3 October. Our discussion of the project is supported by the project director Liz Postlethwaite's generous agreement to share the project archive and her director's notes.

Drawing upon Liz Postlethwaite's previous work with people living with dementia (Story Box) and her decade long relationship with Shore Green, *The Island* was conceived as an opportunity for all participants – artists, carers and residents at Shore Green – to work together in the development of the imaginative and symbolic potential of Shakespeare's play. In the 15, one to one and a half hour workshops that took place over the summer of 2014, participants interacted with the play's characters and themes via an encounter with a range of objects, from evocative photographic images of islands and seascapes, extracts from the text, songs and sounds and material objects such as pieces of fabric and puppets.

These interactions enabled the transformation of the play text as inspiration into a range of new, co-created artworks and materials from sounds, songs and poems, to visual images and puppets all of which contributed to the final residency and sharing with which the project culminated. In keeping with Anne Basting's emphasis on the possibility of facilitating self-expression and the uniqueness of an individual history for a person living with dementia outside of the injunction to remember one's past (2009); the opportunity to interact and respond to elements from the play enabled the residents at Shore Green to express themselves in a creative way that encapsulated their personal values and unique experiences. For instance, elements from sessions were captured in co-written poems comprising the participants' responses to the shared visual, tactile and aural stimuli:

Ariel's poem
He looks like a spook,
A man in a tent,
Looks like a ghost.
He looks like a weird thing!
He's got no arms and legs.
He's going wild!
He's dancing...
All things floating about...
He can teach Prospero how to dance.
He can make your money disappear!
He might be an apparition –
He could appear out of nowhere!
He could swim.
He could fly!

The Forest – part 1

It looks like Wythenshawe park
Lovely and green
Peaceful and quiet
So many leaves, they don't blur the vision
It's a beautiful view
Big
It reminds me of paintings with golden frames around them that my husband used to paint

Foxes, squirrels and magpies on the branches
Little squirrels jumping from tree to tree
Rustic orange and brown
Fishes swimming in a lake
A path to a town or a haunted house

These poems were collated and illustrated with striking photographic images in a poem book for the residents as one part of the legacy of the project. Individual workshop sessions were also captured in short cartoon style booklets that comprised contributions by the resident participants which were left in the shared living room area of the residence in order to support recollection and connectivity with the project between the workshop sessions.

Unlike other notable arts-based interventions that follow a pre-determined and replicable methodology such as Anne Bastings' *TimeSlips* in which groups of people living with dementia sit in a semicircle with their care-givers and each person is given an image about which they are prompted to make observations and comments in the development of a prose poem, *The Island* was underpinned by a more flexible and reflexive approach on the part of the project team. The workshop sessions were designed in advance and informed by an initial creative planning day involving artists, actors, designers, directors and academic input. However, in the course of the delivery of these sessions, activities and approaches changed and developed in response to the needs and interests of the group. The project archive contains notes and reflections from each of the workshop sessions that indicate a willingness to try new approaches and actively to develop the work in a way that was responsive to the particular perspectives about the play that emerged within the group. For instance, Sarah Hunter, a member of the project team who facilitated a number of the sessions, reflects on the introduction of play's major female character Miranda during session six:

> The introduction of Miranda was well received and I thought some interesting things came out in the writing of her story. I liked that everyone seemed to agree that there was conflict in her relationship with Prospero (scenes between them – a father and a daughter–would be nice to enact in future weeks once we start to animate the puppets with the sticks). I thought it was interesting that a few people felt she was quite a lonely character, as this

echoed conversations in earlier weeks about the best islands being the ones that are easily accessible and therefore easy to leave. I enjoyed the idea of Miranda as a feisty female character (who gets in trouble for always fiddling, having messy hair and messy clothes etc.) and with so many women in the group this strong female role might be interesting to explore further or to bring out in the final piece.

As this indicates, whilst the project team determined the theme, shape and broad direction of the workshop sessions, the contributions and reflections of the Shore Green residents played an important role in developing the materials and emphases of the final piece through their interactions with the artists and comments on the characters and themes of the play. The dialogue between participants (the artists, facilitators and the residents) and the attentiveness and reflexivity of the workshop facilitators is arguably central to the ethos of the project and its aim to capture and express the individuality of its participants. The flexibility of this approach is linked and certainly facilitated by the integral role of artists in the development of the project from its initial planning phases through to the final sharing of the work at the end of the period of residency. Some illustrative photographs from the Storybox project are shared below:

Photograph 11.1 Togetherness.

Photograph 11.2 Puppeteers.

Photograph 11.3 Making memories.

Source: reproduced with kind permission of The Storybox Project: Small Things Creative Projects CIC.

Greenhive Green: using immersive theatre with people living with dementia

One form of applied theatre is known as immersive theatre. Immersive theatre involves an aesthetic approach to detail and space, work tends to be site specific or responsive and is experiential in that it is multi-sensory (relying on new sound-scapes as well as smell) and involves creating contained new worlds that are meant to be explored by the audience as part of the theatrical practice. Integral to the practice is a sense that the space has been transformed and the audience is transported into a new world, this is described by the Enrichment Director of the company Punchdrunk as a 'Narnia' experience. Visceral responses are provoked and promoted. Immersive theatre is innately innovative (including the use of new technologies) in that theatrical experiences take place in non-traditional spaces and invites new forms of engagement with the audience. The potentially emancipatory and liberating nature of this style of performance, in which there is an intimate closeness between the audience and performer has been theorised by Bourriaud (2002) and is of interest when the audience is primarily composed of people living with a dementia, a group who may be less able or concerned to distinguish the boundaries between performer and audience. Others have argued that the lack of distance between performer and audience is 'stultifying' (Rancière, 2007). This may also be worth considering, for immersive theatre in relation to people living with dementia may heighten confusion and evoke unexpected (and possibly negative) emotional responses. Participation within an immersive theatre environment also depends on the agency of the individual, something that can be problematic for many reasons for people living with dementia – especially those within care home settings.

The particular immersive approach of the company Punchdrunk is explained by the Enrichment Director Pete Higgin:

> We want to impact our audiences emotionally, that is where the practice comes from. We fully adapt that practice for where we are working and who we are working with, whatever space we create is appropriate for those participants. We are completely responsive to site. That could be a care home, what does it tell us? How do we work with them in their space?

Thus (and in line with Hatton's (2014) work on the spatial dynamics of care homes) the practice of Punchdrunk is to respond flexibly to the space in which they are working but also to focus on the present (Mendes, 2016), again in contrast with the hitherto persistent emphasis on reminiscence work with people living with dementia. Although Punchdrunk has been creating immersive theatre experiences for people since 2000 (Mendes, 2016, p. 326) their work in Greenhive Care Home was the first occasion they had worked in a care home setting. The involvement of Magic Me was central, a company that has worked with older people and people living with dementia using the arts for over two decades. The following account of the Greenhive Green project, its methods and process has arisen from in-depth discussions with Punchdrunk's Enrichment Director, Pete Higgin.

Over a seven-week period of time during 2016, the company worked in a care home where they created a space called 'Greenhive Green' which was a village green with a pub and notice board, a flower shop and a post box. In addition to the transformation of the physical space, the village was brought alive through lighting, smell (the smell of freshly cut grass and flowers) and sound (the ringing from the telephone booth and clinking glasses from the pub). Each week there was a committee meeting – thus each week the journey of Greenhive Green was developed further (building on the sense that it was part of a bigger shire). A narrative was created concerning a neighbouring village, and the logic of the project was about the re-kindling of a relationship between two villages. In the first week, the focus was upon discovering who the residents of Greenhive Green were, then in week two a 'villages in bloom' competition was established. Residents made flower boxes and aimed to win the competition and in this sense participated in the fictional world. Each week the company produced a newsletter that detailed the activities that had taken place and relayed the narrative, including a *Dear Debbie* agony aunt column. Thus, Punchdrunk created a sense of village life which the residents contributed to – there was a theatrical waking up of the constrained care home space. For instance, the session would be 'kick started' by the receipt of post or a phone call from the Lady Mayor and this would initiate what was happening that week, often the logic of the event was about the two villages coming together. As in *The Island*, the residents were co-creators of the story and interactive participants although it was noted (in discussion with Pete Higgin) that residents were not able to lead the narrative as directly as was initially hoped by the company. Nevertheless, a system of engagement was established between the residents and the facilitator that was effective. At the culmination of the seven-week project there was a party/celebration about the villages coming together, including a visit from the local Mayor of Southwark and from Lady Mayor and she handed the reins of Mayorship over to Connie the manager of the care home. It was well received by staff. This was important because at the outset, the staff were unsure about the project – it represented a risk for them too.

Throughout the residency, the peculiar features of the care home environment were constantly assessed and a running log was used to keep track of the mood and responses of participants, so for example the questions that were asked included:

- Is Barry more engaged this week?
- Is Barry more comfortable?

In this way, and with the help of an experienced mentor (Julian West from Music for Life) the work was evaluated constantly, there was recognition that the project had to be responsive and adapt or evolve to the changing needs of the participants. Similarly, there was an understanding from the actors that they might need to alter their practice as they were working in an unfamiliar area:

> The most exciting thing about the project was that we had never worked in an environment like this before – we did not know what we would find out!
> We need a healthier understanding of the benefits of risk.

Although, as noted above, research has tended to focus on the benefits of theatre for care staff, there has been much less exploration of the ways in which artists may benefit from working with people living with dementia. However, as observed by Pete Higgin, it was precisely finding new ways of working within new spaces that excites and invigorates the practice of Punchdrunk. The creative benefit of taking risks by the artists was echoed by those working on another recent multi-arts project (Living Arts Report Project 2016 – www.spitalfieldsmusic.org.uk/livingarts) that was based in a care home. Here, the artists realised that they could not adhere to any predetermined structures and that ultimately this liberated their practice and allowed them to realise that they needed to see differently. Mendes (2016) comments briefly on the impact of working with people living with dementia on the actors. She observes that a different audience response can be evoked from people living with dementia who are often 'more open and frank' than traditional audiences and also that the artists who had never worked with people living with dementia before:

> were surprised by the element of getting to know the residents and the emotional effect it had on them.
>
> (Mendes, 2016, p. 327)

The influence of the care home setting formed an important feature of the residency, the artists realised that it is people's home and that whatever was created had to acknowledge that crucial and central feature of the space. In addition, the varying cognitive and physical abilities of the residents needed to be accommodated and yet without underestimating the innate creative abilities of the participants. There was a strong desire on the part of Punchdrunk to tell a story in which the residents were important protagonists but which incorporated the actors within the space and the story too. The notion of 'forum theatre' became relevant to the method used by Punchdrunk. This was established by the Brazilian Augusto Boal who developed Theatre of the Oppressed, in which the actors begin with a dramatic situation from everyday life and try to find solutions – parents trying to help a child on drugs, a neighbour who is being evicted from his home, and individual confronting racial or gender discrimination, or simply a student in a new community who is shy and has difficulty making friends. Audience members are urged to intervene by stopping the action, coming on stage to replace actors, and enacting their own ideas. Bridging the separation between actor (the one who acts) and spectator (the one who observes but is not permitted to intervene in the theatrical situation), the Theatre of the Oppressed is practiced by 'spect actors' who have the opportunity to act and observe (from https://brechtforum.org/abouttop).

According to Pete Higgin, an adapted version of forum theatre was used in their practice which was found to be a useful metaphor for the project; the overall structure was not as formal or rigid as traditional forum theatre. Rather, the flexible model that was developed was an effective means of allowing participants to take on character if they wanted to and to therefore facilitate a sliding level of engagement. The ethos of the theatrical experience of Greenhive Green was that people could engage at whatever level suited them best. There were difficult moments of revelation from one resident and participants often got very emotional. There is the potential for this form of immersive practice to unlock negative emotions with people living with dementia; however, this is not necessarily a bad thing: perhaps theatre can create a safe place in which participants feel able to express themselves.

Practice and care implications

- The need to manage group relationships is vital to using theatrical techniques with people living with dementia; there are potential tensions between the aims of the project and the way in which participants respond to prompts that mean a project has to be extremely flexible and responsive to the needs of the participants.
- The role of the facilitator is crucial; a theatrical production depends upon the experience and confidence of the professional artist who has to accommodate the competing demands of the artistic vision and the diverse needs of participants.
- People living with a dementia are an inherently heterogeneous group of people some of whom might happen to be living in a care home in which a theatrical production are taking place but may not want to engage creatively with the process.
- There are difficulties with evaluating the impact of theatre for and with people living with dementia. There is thus a necessity for more responsive and subtler forms of measurement, using qualitative methodologies.
- There is potential for theatrical interventions in care home settings to introduce collaborative working between care staff, actors and residents with a dementia and to alter the spatial dynamics of the care home.

Ethical issues

- The varying cognitive and physical abilities of people living with dementia need to be inclusively considered and taken into account. Although some participants can build a narrative on a weekly basis others may find this challenging, however gestures and in the moment contributions can be incorporated into the theatrical offering.
- Where there is a final production there may be difficulty about who the final work belongs to, who it is authored by and the ownership of the end result.
- Throughout the process of theatrical creation there may be a fluctuating ability for participants to consent to being part of the event, this must be acknowledged.
- There should be awareness that co-production does not necessarily negate the persistence of asymmetrical power relations between actors, directors and participants, this may include the process of interpretation and meaning making throughout the theatrical experience.

Concluding thoughts/overview

Theatrical practices are deployed in a range of ways for people living with dementia. We have focused on two artist-led projects that draw upon the traditions of applied and immersive theatre. The case studies both emphasise the ability to create with people living with dementia that which could not have existed before, to make new and to innovate through the process of creative collaboration. They are distinctive in adhering to aesthetic standards rather than using theatre primarily as a tool to effect measurable outcomes in relation to psycho-social makers (such as cognitive processes, behaviour, sustained attention or even wellbeing). There is a marked difference in this approach to that of 'tool-kit' approaches, such as the Veder technique in Holland or even the Time Slips approach that is applicable to a wide range of different settings. These are both methods that are replicable and more easily measurable through the collation and comparison of their particular outcomes. In contrast, the work of both Small Things and Punchdrunk outline the importance of careful listening, the need to be profoundly flexible and to emphasise the qualitative experience of the process rather than the product. The emphasis for both companies is on the creation of a unique work of art that cannot be predetermined and is reliant on the relationships between all of those who participate. As highlighted by De Medeiros and Basting (2014) there is no easy way to capture these processes, there needs to be a more reflexive framework to capture findings and the value of this work. Nonetheless, co-producing theatre can liberate people living with dementia from their singular identities as 'dementia sufferer' allowing them to play with new possibilities and explore the creativity that they may have few other opportunities to express.

Highlighted learning points from the method

- People with a dementia can collaborate with artists to co-create theatrical experiences.
- Care homes can be re-envisioned as creative spaces.
- There is an increasing emphasis on theatre with people living with dementia that is characterised by co-production and the use of improvisation.
- The expressive and embodied nature of theatre which privileges non-verbal communication can be especially effective for people with a dementia.
- Theatre can provide 'in the moment' experiences for people with a dementia, which does not rely on exclusively on reminiscence.
- Artists learn about taking creative risks when they work collaboratively with people living with dementia.
- A 'sliding level' of engagement may be the most inclusive way of ensuring participation.
- The use of a range of tactile and sensory objects can prompt engagement from people living with dementia in the process of creating a play.

Key references

- Basting, A.D (2014). The arts in dementia care, Chapter 10 in Downs, M. and Bowers, B. (eds), *Excellence in dementia care: research into practice* (2nd edition). Maidenhead: Open University Press. *This provides a concise overview of the unique role that the arts have to play in dementia care with a particular emphasis on practical issues including location and funding.*
- Killick, J (2013). *Playfulness and dementia.* London: Jessica Kingsley Press. *An important account of the nature of play and what it has to offer people living with dementia. Chapter 4 concentrates on the use of improvised drama to connect with people living with a dementia.*
- Hatton, N. (2014). Re-imagining the care home: a spatially responsive approach to arts practice with older people in residential care. *The Journal of Applied Theatre and Performance*, 19(4): 355–365. *An article that explores theatre with people with people living with dementia in terms of the spatial challenges presented by the care home environment and argues that care homes can be re-imagined as creative spaces.*

Recommended future reading

- Basting, A.D. and de Medeiros, K (2014). 'Shall I compare thee to a dose of donepezil?': Cultural arts interventions in dementia care research. *Gerontologist*, 54(3): 344–353.
- Kontos, P and Naglie, G. (2007). Expressions of personhood in Alzheimer's disease: an evaluation of research-based theatre as a pedagogical tool. *Qualitative Health Research*, 17(6): 799–811.
- Nicholson, H. (2014). *Applied drama: the gift of theatre.* London: Palgrave Macmillan.
- Schneider, J and Myers, T (2015). Transforming dementia care through theatre. *The Journal of Dementia Care*, 23(1): 28–31.
- White, G. (2012). On immersive theatre. *Theatre Research International*, 37(3): 221–235.

References

Basting, A.D. (2001). 'God is a talking horse': Dementia and the performance of self. *The Drama Review*, 45: 78–96.
Basting, A.D. (2014). The arts in dementia care. In Downs, M. and Bowers, B. (eds), *Excellence in dementia care: research into practice* (2nd edition). Maidenhead: Open University Press.
Basting, A.D., Rose, E. and Towey, M (eds) (2016). *The Penelope project: an arts-based odyssey to change elder-care.* Iowa: University of Iowa Press.
Bourriaud, N. (2002). *Relational aesthetics.* Dijon: Les presses du réel.
Benson, S. (2009). Ladder to the moon: interactive theatre in care setting. *Journal of Dementia Care*, 17(4): 20.

220   *H. Zeilig and L. Burke*

Camic, P.M., Tischler, V. and Pearman, C.H. (2013a). Viewing and making art together: s multi-session art-gallery-based intervention for people living with dementia and their carers. *Aging and Mental Health*, 18(2): 161–168.

Camic, P.M., Williams, C.M. and Meeten, F. (2013b). Does a 'Singing Together Group' improve the quality of life of people with a dementia and their carers? A pilot evaluation study. *Dementia: The International Journal of Social Research and Practice*, 12(2): 157 176.

Coaten, R., Heeley, T. and Spitzern N. (2013). Dancemind's 'Moving Memories'. evaluation and analysis a UK based dance and health project for people living with dementia and their care-staff. In White, M., Atkinson, S., and Meagher, M. (eds), *International perspectives on the development of research-guided practice in community based arts in health*. Australia: University of Melbourne.

De Medeiros, K. and Basting, A. (2014). 'Shall I compare thee to a dose of donepezil?': Cultural arts interventions in dementia care research. *The Gerontologist*, 54(3): 344–353.

Gjengedal, E., Lykkeslet, E., Sørbø, J.I. and Sæther, W.H. (2014). 'Brightness in dark places': theatre as an arena for communicating life with dementia. *Dementia: The International Journal of Social Research and Practice*, 13(5): 598–612.

Harries, B., Keady, J. and Swarbrick, C., (2013). *The Storybox project: examining the role of a theatre and arts based intervention for people living with dementia*. Manchester: University of Manchester.

Hatton, N. (2014). Re-imagining the care home: a spatially responsive approach to arts practice with older people in residential care. *The Journal of Applied Theatre and Performance*, 19(4): 355–365.

Killick, J (2013). *Playfulness and dementia*. London: Jessica Kingsley Press.

Killick, J. and Craig, C. (2012). *Creativity and communication in persons with dementia. A practical guide*. London: Jessica Kingsley Publishers.

Kontos, P.C. (2003). 'The painterly hand': embodied consciousness and Alzheimer's disease. *Journal of Aging Studies*, 17(2): 151–170.

Kontos, P.C. and Naglie, G. (2007). Expressions of personhood in Alzheimer's disease: an evaluation of research-based theatre as a pedagogical tool. *Qualitative Health Research*, 17(6): 799–811.

Mendes, A. (2016). Immersive theatre for the person living with dementia. *Nursing and Residential Care*, 18(6): 325–327.

Mitchell, G.J., Jonas-Simpson, C. and Ivonoffski, V. (2006). Research-based theatre: the making of *I'm Still Here! Nursing Science Quarterly*, 19(3): 198–206.

Nicholson, H. (2014). *Applied drama: the gift of theatre*. London: Palgrave Macmillan.

Prentki, T and Preston, S. (eds) (2009). *The applied theatre reader*. Oxford: Routledge.

Quinlan, E. (2009). Using participatory theatre with health care workers. *Action Research*, 8(2): 117–133.

Rancière, J. (2007). The emancipated spectator. *Artforum*, 45(7): 271–291.

Sabat, S.R. (2001). *The experience of Alzheimer's disease. Life through a tangled veil*. Oxford: Blackwell Publishers.

Sabat, S.R. (2014). *A bio-psycho-social approach to dementia*. In Downs, M. and Bowers, B. (eds), *Excellence in dementia care: research into practice* (2nd edition). Maidenhead: Open University Press.

Stevens, J. (2012). Stand up for dementia: performance, improvisation and stand up comedy as therapy for people living with dementia; a qualitative study. *Dementia: The International Journal of Social Research and Practice*, 11(1): 61–73.

van Haeften-van Dijk, A.M., van Weert, J.C. and Droes, R-M. (2014). Implementing living room theatre activities for people living with dementia on nursing home wards: a process evaluation study. *Aging and Mental Health*, 19(6): 536–547.

Young, R., Camic, P.M. and Tischler, V. (2015). The impact of community based arts and health interventions on cognition in people living with dementia: a systematic Literature Review. *Aging and Mental Health*, 20(4): 337–351.

Zeilig, H., Killick, J. and Fox, C. (2014). The participative arts for people living with a dementia: a critical review. *International Journal of Aging and Later Life*, 9(1): 7–34.

Zeisel, J. (2009). *I'm still here, a breakthrough approach to understanding someone living with Alzheimer's*. New York: Penguin Group (USA).

12 Conclusion

Messages and futures in social research methods in dementia studies

Lars-Christer Hydén, Caroline Swarbrick,
Ann Johnson and John Keady

As we argued in the introduction, the field of dementia studies has grown over recent years and, as a consequence, several new methods have both started to be used and been developed for exploring, describing, explaining and reporting the lived experience as well as the everyday lives of people living with dementia and their significant others. Further, many researchers have discovered that quite a few of the traditional methods cannot be used in dementia studies because people living with dementia are often challenged in their use of language as well as some cognitive functions, especially memory. This has resulted in attempts from researchers to either adapt already well-established methods or to develop new methodological approaches. This book must be seen as a first attempt to collect and present at least some of the innovative methodological development in the area.

Behind the methods and methodological development, it is possible to identify an interest in describing and understanding the varieties of human existence, and, in particular, the various ways it is possible for humans to experience and act in the world. Living with dementia most often implies that the taken-for-granted ways of encountering and acting in the world no longer work. Sometimes this can result in the everyday world becoming opaque, alien and frightening; it can also lead to quite new ways to approach and act so the world again becomes possible to inhabit. The effort and aim to understand and describe how the fundamental being-in-the-world change for people living with dementia will result in a re-thinking of traditional research methods, as these often are designed for the inhabitants of the ordinary world.

Developing and designing methods that can capture a wide variety of being-in-the-world, implies an effort to include both the person and their experiences as belonging to what is possible for human beings. It is an effort that therefore enlarges and widens our notions of what it is to be a human being. At the same time, it involves social inclusion by engaging with people that otherwise would have been left out and positioned outside the circle of understanding. Indeed, in this book, and to take one example, this was seen in Chapter 8 when May Yeok Koo and Helen Pusey reported that people living with dementia were unable to be included in their study because of the (referring) organisation's fear about what such a decision may evoke for the person who lives with the dementia.

Such negative positioning of people living with dementia requires a response by people living with dementia to ensure that their views and rights are not undermined. The majority can be quick to 'other' when faced with perceived fear and risk in people who are somehow 'different' or who will act 'differently' to the mainstream. As we have seen in this book, and viewed through another lens, participatory methods are another way to challenge such fears and stigmatising attitudes and promote the values of inclusion and innovation that were so important to us as we put this collected volume together.

Perhaps one of the most important issues in undertaking research which involves people living with dementia is the need to create a 'conversational space' and for this space to be shared/owned by people with lived experience. One central problem in research involving people living with dementia is for that voice to be expressed. For a number of reasons, their voice is often not requested, or wanted, or it is not even noticed. This may be because people living with dementia often express their voices and experiences in ways that is not in accordance with given social expectations and communicative and narrative norms. Therefore, creating a space for voicing and embodied communication, such as through British Sign Language in Chapter 9 of this book, implies a setting that reassures that there is request and wish to listen to these voices, as well as a possibility for these voices to find a form to communicate. This might imply the creation of tools and settings that are facilitating and supportive, but also researchers that are active co-communicators who will aim at actively understanding the voices and co-produce outcomes that have inherent meaning to those taking part in the work – in other words, authentic participation with authentic outcomes.

As several of the chapters in this book make clear, many of the invoked methods aim at creating a new kind of space. As it turns out, many of these spaces tend to put more stress on the visual rather than on the auditory; on showing and enacting, rather than on telling and reporting in retrospect. The reason for this is that traditional research methods often draw on an implicit preference for verbal and textual communication, as these forms of communication come close to our cultural preference for unambiguous statements that are well-expressed as well as logically and verbally coherent. Most people living with dementia are severely challenged in living up to these verbal and textual norms and expectations. For people living with dementia it is rather other kinds of expression that are important. It is primarily forms that favour other aspects of communication and experience: the whole rather than the analytical deconstruction of events and images that language use presupposes; the immediate rather than the sequential organisation that language imposes on the world; the tactile rather than the disembodied engagement of language; and the concrete in contrast to the analytical categorisation implied in language use. Seeing, touching, reaching, pointing and showing; enacting/doing and walking rather than sitting – these are the important characteristics of the spaces created through the development of traditional research methods, taking the challenges people living with dementia encounter into account.

Creating a space and an opportunity to express voices also implies that people can be and are *included* in an ongoing conversation and dialogue about their life. People living with dementia can contribute their specific experiences and perspectives on their lives and their worlds; others can listen – and learn to listen – and thus start to understand what people living with dementia understand and experience. We have come a long way from the not so far away discussions in the 1990s about whether it was possible and advisable for researchers and clinicians to listen to what people living with dementia said – let alone engage in talk *with* rather than *to* people living with dementia.

With attempts to include people living with dementia in the ongoing conversation that constitutes research, we will also follow discussions not only about *empowerment* but also about *power* over the research process, material, interpretations and reports. By tradition, researchers have designed and conducted studies, and then written reports and articles. Conducting research not only about people living with dementia, but *together*, will shift the power axis: people living with dementia might voice opinions and objections, questioning the taken-for-granted ways, and suggest other way of designing, understanding and interpreting, as well as writing up and reporting research. As Caroline shared in the first chapter of the book, the COINED model presents a notable challenge – not to people living with dementia, but to the (academic) research community as it is 'we' who have to change and accommodate these new times and new directions. The status quo is not an option.

Finally, the *ethical* stance. As a researcher, it is a fundamental virtue to not hurt or affect people that take part in studies. This means that, for instance, interviewees are always supposed to be anonymous – no one is supposed to be able to identify and recognise someone taking part in a research study. Facilitating the expression of voices is partly detrimental to this ethical standard. Some people taking part in studies will argue that they want to be identified and recognised because they are not ashamed of their lives and of who they are; rather, they want to be presented as activists challenging the conventional notions of what a person living with dementia is. Although this is not something that is easily made part of the traditional thinking around research ethics, it is an important issue for future discussions.

By collecting these chapters that report and discuss a wide variety of methods/methodological approaches, developments and suggestions, it is our hope that we will contribute to inspiring and moving forward the discussion about the social inclusion of people living with dementia. There can be no more worthwhile cause.

Index

Page numbers in *italics* denote tables, those in **bold** denote figures.

Printed in Great Britain
by Amazon